Behind the Bill of Rights

TIMELESS PRINCIPLES THAT MAKE IT TICK

BY BILL NORTON AND JEREMY NELSON

Credits:
Portions of this book have been taken from Speaking the Language of Liberty by Bill Norton and Mark Herr.

A Brief History section in Part One was written by Dan Sheridan

Cover design by Bill Norton

ISBN
979-8-88680-493-5

Contents

Introduction

Behind the Bill of Rights was written to present the principles upon which the Bill of Rights was created. Principles are set forth to give guidance. Understanding the fundamental principles behind the Bill of Rights will give the reader a profound appreciation for the first ten amendments to the Constitution and a greater ability to protect their own rights.

During the founding era, Americans sought to evolve a better society based on the principles of natural law and thereby establish good government. Natural law is the natural consequence of action—e.g., what goes up must come down, for every action there is an equal and opposite reaction, etc. There are natural laws for science, mathematics, good government, human relations, and more. The Founders sought to discover natural law principles for an advanced society. Their attempts were declared in the Declaration of Independence and codified in the national and state constitutions.

Before we get into what natural law is in relation to the Bill of Rights, we will clarify what it is not. There is a relatively modern alternate definition that natural law is a moral or religious code. Based on that definition, natural law is subject to opinion, not reason, and may or may not be observable and measurable. This modern definition is not the definition used by the Founders and is therefore not relevant to this discussion of the Bill of Rights.

Natural law and morality may overlap from time to time because many ideas of morality are based on natural law, but natural law is not based on morality. Natural law is based on reason. It applies to everything and is unchanging.

Natural law can be cruel and brutal. It is natural for the lion to kill the lamb. It is natural for the strong to devour the weak. It is natural for the conqueror to enslave the conquered. It is natural for rulers to oppress the ruled. All these natural law principles make for a primitive society.

In 1776, Americans set out to establish a society in which the lamb could lie down with the lion. They wanted to discover and establish sophisticated rather than primitive natural laws. The Bill of Rights was a triumphant accomplishment in their endeavor.

Behind the Bill of Rights dives into the sophisticated natural law principles that are behind the first ten amendments to the U.S. Constitution. They are the principles that make each amendment tick. Natural law principles are what give the Bill of Rights authority above any ruler, government official, law, constitution, or even the Bill of Rights itself. They existed before human laws. These foundational laws of nature make writing our laws possible in the first place. The inherent authority of natural law principles provides the power to make, execute, and adjudicate laws, so long as they are in agreement with those natural law principles.

Primitive natural law is rarely good policy for human relations. The primitive natural law of survival of the fittest will always result in a bloody relationship between the lion and the lamb. It is because the law says the "fittest" is superior over all others. Once the ideas are introduced that all are created equal, all have equal rights, and all are protected by the law, the relationship changes. The lion and the lamb are equal. Enemies can find common ground in the law. In doing so, they can become friends and pursue a nobler course.

When a society is established based on sophisticated natural law, it is the right of that society to preserve itself. It is that people's right to defend themselves against those who would return them to primitive natural law. This is done through criminal codes to ward off the criminal; an army, including the militia, to ward off the conqueror; and a well-defined, limited government to ward off the tyrant.

As a citizen in a sophisticated natural-law society, self-preservation is not only a right, but a duty as well. If the citizen expects to retain their rights in that society, they have a duty to protect those same rights for others. They have a duty to prevent that society from devolving to primitive natural law.

The Bill of Rights is sophisticated natural law in written form. It provides a societal foundation that protects its citizens from those who would revert our society to primitive natural law—especially the tyrant. Government is a necessary evil to ward off the criminal and the conqueror, but if left unchecked, it too will revert a society to primitive natural law.

The doctrines of the divine right of kings, collectivism, anarchy, Plato's "ideal society," totalitarianism, aristocracy, democracy, socialism, communism, and many other forms of government are based on primitive natural law. They do little to protect the rights of individuals. In fact, they have a history of abusing unalienable rights far more than protecting them.

The Constitution of the United States established a mixed form of government. It mixes many of these primitive forms of government in an effort to keep the good and remove the bad. The Bill of Rights supports that effort by defining the foundation upon which the Constitution rests. *Behind the Bill of Rights* dissects that foundation to determine what principles give it its strength.

This book is not intended to provide legal advice in regard to your rights in the Bill of Rights. Many of our modern laws have strayed from the original intent and meaning behind the Bill of Rights. Some points made herein may not be applicable to current judicial interpretations of your rights.

The book is also not intended to be a comprehensive commentary on the modern application of the various provisions in the Bill of Rights. Like the wandering legal interpretations, modern opinions about individual rights vary dramatically. The Bill of Rights is all too often looked at through a modern lens. That lens sometimes presents the Bill of Rights as a nonsensical kaleidoscope of contrasting colorful opinions that prevent the viewer from seeing true principles beyond its hypnotic effects.

A few modern and legal examples are used from time to time to illustrate a point. For the most part, this book is intended to reveal the most fundamental underlying natural law principles upon which each provision in the Bill of Rights rests. As such, the ideas presented are the ideal application of each principle, which, unfortunately, is not always the reality of how each amendment is interpreted and applied in modern society—which is why this book is needed in the first place.

PART 1
HISTORY AND GENERAL PRINCIPLES

A Brief History

"For God's sake, fire!" cried Major Buttrick of Concord, and the Minutemen responded with "the shot heard 'round the world."[1] When the dust settled on that Massachusetts evening, 49 Americans and 73 British soldiers lay dead.

Gunfire, troop movements, and the actions of heroic soldiers thrill the soul. Ideas and principles, however, are not quite so thrilling. They do not level enemy troops, wear uniforms, engage in flanking movements, cross the Delaware River, charge down Little Roundtop with fixed bayonets, or parachute into Normandy. Principles do not make for exciting television or thrilling stories, nor do they inspire majestic soundtracks. Or do they? Major Buttrick would have never given his command at Lexington and Concord unless principles were at stake.

A proper study of history must look beyond gunfire and military strategy to ideas worth defending. Military actions are thrilling, loud, and decisive. However, ideas and principles are conceived through contemplation, matured through quiet discussion, perfected through experience, individually professed through conviction, and then implemented in society. We will be visiting this battlefield in the coming pages and pausing to admire its intellectual monuments.

The first ten amendments to the U.S. Constitution, commonly known as the Bill of Rights, are ideas and principles that matured through many centuries of struggle. Americans should take some time to understand related historical events to appreciate this compendium of liberty. We live in a fast-paced age of technology in which people have grown accustomed to receiving information and

---

[1] Ralph Waldo Emerson, "Concord Hymn," 1837

results immediately. However, the years leading up to the American Bill of Rights measured progress in months, years, lifetimes, and centuries. Political and religious philanthropists secured our freedoms at a slow and steady pace. They considered their work generationally, as if they were but stepping-stones for posterity. Many of these died having only planted seeds, not seeing the results of their work.

After centuries of religious and civil persecution, today we enjoy civil and religious liberty. That history of persecution underlies the Bill of Rights. "The blood of patriots is the price of civil, the blood of martyrs the price of religious liberty,"[2] Philip Schaff writes. "The conquest is dear, the progress slow and often interrupted, but steady and irresistible."[3]

The colonists, when facing oppression from King George III, appealed to their natural rights as Englishmen. They wanted those rights honored, but their pleadings fell on deaf ears. When they separated from Great Britain, Americans guaranteed these rights to themselves in their state constitutions. Later, the first ten amendments of the U.S. Constitution ensured these rights on a national level.

Therefore, to understand what these rights are, we need first to dig a little into English history. Let us, in reverent appreciation, quiet our minds for a while.

HERE COME THE NORMANS!

On September 28, 1066, Duke William of Normandy, a French-speaking Norman king, crossed the English Channel in small open boats with a force of 5,000 men and 2,500 horses. William the Conqueror, as the duke came to be known, defeated King Harold at the Battle of Hastings and crowned himself King William the First. This event is what we know today as the Norman Conquest.

---

[2] Philip Schaff, *History of the Christian Church* volume 1, p. 8, 1858
[3] Ibid.

William, a ruthless man, ruled his French duchy of Normandy with a rod of iron, and he continued the same practice in England. His main goal was to increase his own power, and he succeeded in making England one of the world's strongest nations. However, just because a country is independent and powerful does not mean that its people are empowered and free. William's subjects learned that lesson painfully.

William claimed ownership of everything. He took away the estates and lands of those he conquered and granted them to fiefs, his loyal Norman followers, under the condition that they recognize his authority and not fight with each other. In short, the Normans brought elements of feudalism to the island of Britain, which corrupted the Anglo-Saxon system of common law.

To further emphasize that everything belonged to him, in 1086, William compiled his famous *Domesday Book*, a census of people and property, down to the last pig and cow. Through his book, William was able to collect every tax dollar and feudal fee owed to him.

The Norman Conquest changed Britain forever, especially its language and culture. The most immediate change, however, was political. During the Norman rule, English farmers lost their freedom and became serfs. William's successors only enhanced royal authority until finally, in 1215, there was a reaction against the royal rule after a long train of abuses.

HERE COME THE BARONS!

June 15, 1215 marked the first significant step and the subsequent development of the system of representative government, constitutionalism, and the principles of individual liberty, all of which became more perfectly expressed in the U.S. Constitution and its Bill of Rights.

During the early Middle Ages, English kings ruled oppressively. Neither the nobles nor the people had any voice in the affairs of state. The nobles despised the absolute rule of the king, and the ordinary people resented the high taxes. The clergy, the nobles, and the middle class concluded that they could only fix the problem by banding together. When King John came to the throne, they decided to act.

John was dishonest, treacherous, and hated by all classes. He seemed to be at war with everyone: he overtaxed the common people, quarreled with his vassals, and fought with the Pope. John also engaged in a war with the king of France in which he lost many English possessions. The people, suffering from tyranny and oppressive taxes, refused to help obstinate John.

But John added one more transgression to this long list, probably his worst—he imprisoned, without trial, the liberty-loving subjects who objected to his arbitrary rule. Many of those poor souls rotted in filthy dungeons for years. Pause for a moment and think about what it cost to secure for us the right of trial by jury.

The nobles had had enough. They decided their only option was to compel John to restore their liberties. On June 15, 1215, armed barons gathered at Runnymede and forced King John to sign the Magna Carta, the Great Charter. It was a lengthy document setting forth limitations on arbitrary power, drafted by Stephen Langton, Archbishop of Canterbury, and a committee of noblemen. Let us look at the Great Charter in a nutshell.

- It assured the freedom of the church.

- It respected the feudal rights and privileges of the nobility.

- It forbade the king from extorting money from the people in the form of fines, taxes, or any other tricky measures without first consulting the barons.

- The king could not arbitrarily imprison his subjects.

- The accused could not be tried or punished more than once for the same offense.

- It prohibited the king from taking a freeman's property or banishing them without just cause.

- It forced the king to allow the nobles to appoint a committee to monitor him and punish him if he violated the charter.

- It guaranteed the right of trial by jury. This was a significant provision that Thomas Jefferson considered the only way to keep government within its prescribed bounds:

> *The only anchor, ever yet imagined by man, by which a government can be held to the principles of its constitution.* [4]

The provisions in the Magna Carta are a historic foreshadow of the American Bill of Rights that came almost six hundred years later. The Magna Carta laid down the law—not to govern the people, but to govern the government by law and not by men. This was an important distinction.

John Adams, in his famous treatise *A Defense of the Constitutions of Government of the United States of America*, wrote,

> *The interest of the people is one thing—it is the public interest; and where the public interest governs, it is a government of laws, and not of men: the interest of a king, or of a party, is another thing—it is a private interest; and where private interest governs, it is a government of men, and not of laws. If, in England, there has ever been any such thing as government of laws, was it not the Magna Carta?* [5]

Let the English historian Thomas Babington Macaulay paint the picture to appreciate better the importance of the Magna Carta, its place in English history, and its impact on English identity and English rights.

---

[4] Letter From Thomas Jefferson to Thomas Paine, 11 July 1789

[5] John Adams, *A Defense of the Constitutions of Government of the United States of America*, letter XXVI, 1786

From that moment her prospects brightened. John was driven from Normandy. The Norman nobles were compelled to make their election between the island and the continent. Shut up by the sea with the people whom they had hitherto oppressed and despised, they gradually came to regard England as their country, and the English as their countrymen. The two races, so long hostile, soon found that they had common interests and common enemies. Both were alike aggrieved by the tyranny of a bad king. . . The great-grandsons of those who had fought under William and the great-grandsons of those who had fought under Harold began to draw near to each other in friendship; and the first pledge of their reconciliation was the [Magna Carta], won by their united exertions, and framed for their common benefit. . . Here commences the history of the English nation.[6]

When the American colonists claimed their rights as Englishmen, they went to the very principles that made them English, removed animosities, and made brothers out of the worst of enemies—principles found in the Magna Carta.

Tyrants hate restraints. According to historian John Fiske, King John, after signing the charter, went to his room, rolled on the floor like an angry child, cursing at the top of his lungs, and chewed on sticks and straw because he could not get his way. And, as you can guess, John and his successor, Henry III, violated the charter, thus causing civil wars and a constitutional crisis. But these upheavals led to the creation of a system of representation by establishing Parliament in 1295.

The Magna Carta laid the foundation of constitutional liberty, and the rest of the structure would be slowly erected over the following centuries. The system would consist of representative government

---

[6] Thomas Babington Macaulay, *History of England*, 1849

and written charters, including declarations of rights, constitutions, and laws.

REPRESENTATIVE GOVERNMENT

On various occasions from the English kingdom's earliest days, councils or assemblies were called to assist the king. During the Anglo-Saxon era, the body was called the Witenagemot,[7] or assembly of wise men. The body consisted of leading officers in the kingdom, the king's lords, bishops, and abbots. After the Norman conquest, feudal lords made up this assembly, but the members looked very much like the Witenagemot. This Great Council aided and advised the king, but they had no control over him.

The Magna Carta changed the nature of this body. The king promised in the charter not to collect taxes without the consent of the people. As a result, those representing lower classes, like knights of the shire (who represented nobles), and borough representatives (who represented traders), were called to the assembly. These bodies met from time to time until 1265. In that year, when Simon de Montfort was in power, he called for representatives from each town to meet in the Parliament. In 1295, King Edward I established the rule that Parliament must have representatives from counties and towns. Historians call this the Model Parliament because it became the model for future ones.

Those in the lower peasant classes were not protected by the Magna Carta initially. In the late 1500s, Sir Edward Coke,[8] an English judge, declared that the rights outlined in the Magna Carta were not only for the upper and middle classes, but for all English people.

WRITTEN CHARTERS

The word *charter* originally meant paper or a written document. It applied to real estate transfer deeds, contracts, and other vital negotiations that required something in writing as proof of the

---

[7] An Anglo-Saxon parliament.
[8] Pronounced *cook*

transaction. People in English towns began to refer to their town charter as "title-deeds of their liberties."[9]

After the Magna Carta, the next liberty-based charter was the Petition of Right in 1626. Parliament passed this act during the reign of Charles I and forced him to accept it as law. It guaranteed that no man would be compelled to give any gift, loan, or tax to the government without common consent by an act of Parliament. It also ensured that no one should be imprisoned contrary to the laws of the land, even if the king ordered it. It also forbade the quartering of soldiers or mariners in private homes. Furthermore, the act outlawed the issuing of military or martial law.

Next came the Habeas Corpus Act of 1679. One of the most significant victories of liberty took place during the reign of Charles II with this act's passage. Habeas corpus is Latin for "show me the body," or "present the body," as in, let the body come before the court to receive due process rather than rot in a jail cell. By it, Englishmen were protected from arbitrary and illegal imprisonment.

Finally, the English Bill of Rights, 1689. Formally known as *An Act Declaring the Rights and Liberties of the Subject and Settling the Succession of the Crown*, the English Bill of Rights was "a declaration of the true, ancient, and indubitable rights of the people of this realm."[10] It settled constitutional questions of that day. It declared that the people have the right to petition the king, that it is illegal to keep standing armies in times of peace without the consent of Parliament, and that excessive bail should not be required, excessive fines imposed, or cruel and unusual punishments inflicted.

These liberty charters completed the structure of the English constitutional monarchy. English common law expounded on the general principles of these liberty documents. Thomas Cooley wrote:

---

[9] John Fiske, *Civil Government in the United States Considered with Some Reference to its Origins*, 1890
[10] English Bill of Rights, 1689

> *That law was the growth of many centuries; its maxims were those of a sturdy and independent race of men, who were accustomed in an unusual degree to freedom of thought and action, and to a share in the administration of public affairs. So far as they declared individual rights, they were a part of the constitution of the realm, and of that "law of the land" the benefit of which was promised by the charter of King John to every freeman. They were modified and improved from age to age, by changes in the habits of thought and action among the people, by modifications in the civil and political state, by the vicissitudes of public affairs, by judicial decisions, and by statutes.[11]*

The colonists brought this proud heritage with them to the New World, and they claimed them as their natural rights and appealed to them when King George violated them.

> *The colonists claimed that this code of law accompanied them, as a standard of right and of protection in their emigration, and that it remained their law. . . . Relying upon it, they had well known and well-defined rules of protection; without it, they were at the mercy of those who ruled, and, whether actually oppressed or not, were without freedom.[12]*

RECURRENCE TO FUNDAMENTAL PRINCIPLES

Fast forward to 1776. King George III refuses to honor the long-cherished rights of the American colonists. As a result, the colonists declare their independence. That fateful year was also one of constitution-making. The new states were busily drafting constitutions that embraced proven governing ideas and experimented with new innovations. Americans were answering history's unanswered question: Who has the right to declare the law?

---

[11] Thomas McIntyre Cooley, *The General Principles of Constitutional Law in The United States of America*, 1880

[12] Ibid.

A constitution written by representatives of the people, and ultimately ratified by the people, was a novel idea, especially its actual implementation. It was only to be outdone by framing unalienable rights into a bill that formed the foundation of government.

Virginians would be the first to draw up such a list of principles. Knowing independence was imminent, Virginia statesmen met in convention in June of 1776 to decide what form of government they would establish. Most importantly, they wanted it in writing, which was a relatively new thing in the annals of world history. Great Britain conducted government affairs under an unwritten constitution, which proved to be an insufficient check on arbitrary power. Ancient nations had written codes of laws, like those created by the ancient Babylonian ruler Hammurabi and the Sumerian king Ur-Nammu. These monarchs made, interpreted, and enforced the laws, which the Founders considered the very definition of tyranny. The people had no voice, and many of the laws were inherently unjust. Americans were on the verge of altering the course of humanity.

The Virginia convention, in the light of human history, was embarking on a new experiment. Their goal was to determine the powers and branches of their state government, check that power with restraints, ensure that it emanated from the people's will, and have stability and permanence by putting it in writing.

However, what was needed most was a Bill of Rights enumerating the people's unalienable rights as the foundation of their new government. George Mason came forth with a list of principles. Mason was a humble man, a "reluctant statesman."[13] While some sought to use this crisis as an opportunity for self-glorification, Mason won the day in the wisdom of humility. Edmund Randolph said:

> *Many projects of a bill of rights and Constitution, discovered the ardor for political notice, rather than a*

---

[13] As described by historian Robert Rutland.

ripeness in political wisdom. That proposed by George Mason swallowed up all the rest by fixing the grounds and plan which after great discussion and correction were finally ratified.[14]

On June 12, 1776, the Virginia Declaration of Rights was approved by the Virginia Constitutional Convention, and it became the preamble to the Virginia Constitution.

The Magna Carta granted or secured certain liberties and privileges to the English clergy, barons, and freemen. However, to the majority of the population, it only guaranteed that they should not be deprived of their carts, plows, and implements of husbandry without due process. The English Bill of Rights of 1689 was built upon the 1628 Petition of Right. Both improved upon the Magna Carta. William Wirt Henry wrote that the Virginia Declaration of Rights:

contained all that was of value in these celebrated papers, and much more, and as a summary of the rights of man, and of the principles of free government, stands, and is destined to stand, without a rival in the annals of governments.[15]

THE BILL OF RIGHTS: AMERICA'S GREATEST EXPORT

When drafting their constitutions, other states followed Virginia's example. They used Mason's work as a prototype while making revisions of their own. Yet each of them with one voice proclaimed their shared beliefs about the role of government, the need for restraints, and the securing of natural rights. For instance, they guaranteed the freedom of speech, the press, and religious worship. Individual liberty was the fundamental law. "A freeman's remedy against a restraint of his liberty ought not to be denied or delayed,"[16] declared the North Carolina Constitution. They recognized other

---

[14] Edmund Randolph, "Essay," *Virginia Magazine of History and Biography, 1893,* 1936
[15] William Wirt Henry, *Patrick Henry; Life, Correspondence and Speeches,* 1891
[16] North Carolina Constitution, 18 December 1776

freedom principles too: representative government, trial by jury, the protection against unreasonable searches of people and papers, the forbidding of cruel and unusual punishment, and more. The Declaration of Independence and the first ten amendments of the U.S. Constitution echo Mason's work.

Furthermore, the Northwest Ordinance of 1787 followed Mason's lead—liberty was catchy! That ordinance promoted freedom, enlightenment, and religious free exercise more than any previous legislative body ever had. Article 1 guaranteed religious liberty. Article 2 guaranteed the benefits of the writ of habeas corpus, trial by jury, proportionate representation, and other natural rights.

The Virginia Declaration of Rights contains sixteen declarations. George Mason wrote the first fifteenth; Patrick Henry wrote the sixteenth, concerning religious liberty.

Declaration 15:

> *That no free government, or the blessings of liberty, can be preserved to any people, but by a firm adherence to justice, moderation, temperance, frugality and virtue, and by frequent recurrence to fundamental principles.*[17]

The word *recurrence* means "to return to." Mason is declaring to the world that a government based on principles of freedom will not survive unless the people are continually returning to and applying correct principles to every area of life. Principles guide us in making the right decisions personally and politically, and are essential for good character. When Mason wrote the Virginia Declaration of Rights, these principles were well known, believed, and applied. The culture of that day was in harmony with universal principles of justice.

Americans studied these principles, publicly acknowledged them, and dared to proclaim them as the foundation of our country. Unfortunately, we as Americans have not always lived up to our beliefs, especially in the case of slavery. Part of the American

---

[17] George Mason, Virginia Declaration of Rights, 1776

experience is the challenge of living up to our principles. Americans did make amends for previous errors through amendments to the Constitution.

The lesson from George Mason is clear—Americans will not retain their freedom unless "We the People" return to fundamental principles frequently. This book aims to unearth the underlying fundamental principles found in the Bill of Rights.

William Cabel Rives writes,

> *When we look at the Declaration of Rights prepared by him [Mason], and which, with few alterations, was adopted by the Convention, we shall find it a condensed, logical, and luminous summary of the great principles of freedom inherited by us from our British ancestors, the extracted essence of the Magna Charta [sic], the Petition of Rights, the acts of the Long Parliament, and the doctrines of the Revolution of 1688 as expounded by Locke—distilled and concentrated through the alembic of his own powerful and discriminating mind. There is nothing more remarkable in the political annals of America than this paper.[18]*

For the first time in human history, individuals' natural and unalienable rights—not just for Americans, but all human beings— were written down and acknowledged as the law of a commonwealth. Dumas Malone wrote:

> *Universal in its appeal, it directly affected the French Declaration of the Rights of Man and the Citizen of 1789. In our own time it is echoed in the Declaration of Human Rights of the United Nations. Writing in his old age, Lafayette said: "The era of the American Revolution, which one can regard as the beginning of a new social order for the entire world, is, properly speaking, the era of declarations of rights." More than any other single*

---

[18] William Cabell Rives, *History of the life and times of James Madison*, p. 137, 1882

> *American, except possibly Thomas Jefferson, whom in some sense he anticipated, George Mason may be regarded as the herald of this new era; and in our own age, when the rights of individual human beings are being challenged by totalitarianism around the world, men can still find inspiration in his noble words.*[19]

RELIGIOUS LIBERTY

Most of the ideas and principles in the Bill of Rights are a refinement of the ideas from those previously discussed English events and documents, except for one essential idea—the freedom of religious exercise. The freedom of religion was implemented in America more thoroughly than at any previous time in history. This was a relatively new idea.

> *Freedom of religion must be recognized as one of the inalienable rights of man, which lies in the sacred domain of conscience, beyond the restraint and control of politics, and which the government is bound to protect as much as any other fundamental right.*[20]

Mason's work in the Virginia Declaration of Rights emphasized the role of religion. It is important to pause a moment and consider the context of that reference. Religious freedom is the natural and unalienable right of each person to worship God as they see fit, as long as they are not infringing on others' rights. Religious beliefs and practices are voluntary. No civil or ecclesiastical power has the authority to compel people to worship a certain way, believe a specific creed, or be taxed to support a particular religious institution. Today, this is a principle we take for granted.

---

[19] Dumas Malone, from the foreword in Robert A. Rutland's *George Mason Reluctant Statesman*, 1961 (The quote attributed to Lafayette was taken from *Memoirs, Correspondence and Manuscripts of General Lafayette, Published by His Family*, Volume 2, p. 289, 1837. It is not a direct Lafayette quote, but his paraphrased sentiments as expressed by his family.)
[20] Philip Scaff, *History of the Christian Church*, p. 9, 1858

However, from the Magna Carta days until 1776, most thought the world would fall apart if the government did not force faith to some degree. Many believed that we ought to give Caesar the things that are Caesar's, but they thought that Caesar was entitled to the things that were God's, too. Very few dared dream of religious liberty.

That changed with Mason's immortal pen. Not a single government in the Old World recognized the principle of religious liberty, and the New World did not advance very far during the colonial era. One sect squared off against another, and the sect with the power of the law, and sometimes the sword, on its side emerged victorious. If the minority sect gained control, it would commit the same religious persecution upon those who persecuted them.

This pattern of religious persecution happened over and over again. In the American colonies, the pattern began to break, albeit slowly. The people treated Catholics so poorly that they were not accepted anywhere. Finally, the people in Maryland welcomed them to their colony. Once those Catholics became the majority, they persecuted and expelled the very people who had given them shelter. Virginia allowed a few Protestant denominations, yet Baptists had to meet in secret lest their ministers be imprisoned. Finally, in Article 16 of Virginia's Bill of Rights, Virginia fully and unequivocally recognized religious liberty in its governing document.

Later, in 1786, Virginia passed the Virginia Statute for Religious Freedom. Written by Thomas Jefferson and carefully led through the legislature by James Madison, the statute was the most advanced law establishing religious liberty in history. It paved the road for the freedom of religious exercise in the Constitution and the Bill of Rights.

THE NECESSITY OF THE BILL OF RIGHTS

> *Show me that age and country where the rights and liberties of the people were placed on the sole chance of their rulers being good men without a consequent loss of liberty! I say that the loss of that dearest privilege has*

ever followed, with absolute certainty, every such mad attempt.[21]

The Founding Fathers met during the hot summer of 1787 to create a new form of government. Four months of debate produced the most unique form of government the world had ever seen. After stating that he did not agree with every provision of the new Constitution, Benjamin Franklin confessed, "I am not sure that it is not the best."[22] George Washington and James Madison called the convention a miracle.

However, as the convention was coming to a close, George Mason rose to his feet and said, "I would rather cut off my right hand than put it to that document."

"But Colonel Mason," James Madison pleaded, "Why at this late hour would you not sign it?"

"Because it does not have a Bill of Rights," Mason replied.

"But Colonel Mason, we have not given the Federal Government enough power to trample our rights."

Mason's answer was classic: "But they will, they always do."[23]

Edmond Randolph, the governor of Virginia, agreed with Mason. The Constitution was sent, despite those objections, to the states for ratification. Heated debates followed, especially in New York and Virginia.

The lack of a bill of rights came up at the state ratifying conventions. Patrick Henry argued that unless specific restraints are in place, a government will always abuse its power.

---

[21] Patrick Henry, speech before the Virginia ratifying convention, 5 June 1788

[22] Benjamin Franklin's final speech in the Constitutional Convention of 1787 as recorded by James Madison.

[23] The exchange between Mason and Madison is not taken word for word from actual events. It is meant to dramatize the sentiments of the two. The dramatization is taken from *The Miracle of America* by William Norton and Brian Trotter, 2010. Madison documented Mason's actual words as, "he would sooner chop off his right hand than put it to the Constitution as it now stands," in his *Notes of Debates in the Federal Convention of 1787.*

> *It is so in Great Britain, for every possible right, which is not reserved to the people by some express provision or compact, is within the king's prerogative. . . It is so in Spain, Germany, and other parts of the world.*[24]

While some argued in favor of a bill of rights, Alexander Hamilton argued against one. He reasoned that such bills were traditionally written to restrain monarchs, and since America was to be a republic, a bill of rights was unnecessary. He laid out his argument in *Federalist* No. 84. First, he argued about the nature of bills of rights.

> *It has been several times truly remarked that bills of rights are, in their origin, stipulations between kings and their subjects, abridgements of prerogative in favor of privilege, reservations of rights not surrendered to the prince. Such was MAGNA CHARTA [sic], obtained by the barons, sword in hand, from King John. Such were the subsequent confirmations of that charter by succeeding princes. Such was the PETITION OF RIGHT assented to by Charles I in the beginning of his reign. Such, also, was the Declaration of Right presented by the Lords and Commons to the Prince of Orange in 1688, and afterwards thrown into the form of an act of parliament called the Bill of Rights.*[25]

Next, Hamilton brought his warning home.

> *I go further, and affirm that bills of rights, in the sense and to the extent in which they are contended for, are not only unnecessary in the proposed Constitution, but would even be dangerous. They would contain various exceptions to powers not granted; and, on this very account, would afford a colorable pretext to claim more than were granted. For why declare that things shall not be done which there is no power to do? Why, for instance, should it be said that the liberty of the press*

---

[24] Patrick Henry, speech before the Virginia ratifying convention, 16 June 1788
[25] Alexander Hamilton, *Federalist* No. 84, 1788

shall not be restrained, when no power is given by which restrictions may be imposed?[26]

Among others, Alexander Hamilton gave three reasons why a bill of rights was not necessary:

1. The Constitution is a declaration of rights. Hundreds of rights are directly and indirectly codified in the document itself.

2. Under the constitutionally limited form of government, with specific enumerated powers granted to the national government, there is no authority to regulate or invade a citizen's freedom of religion, freedom of press, freedom to assemble, or freedom to petition. There is no national authority granted to regulate firearms, invade the privacy, quarter troops, deprive a citizen of due process, impose cruel or unusual punishment, or deprive citizens of any powers not specifically delegated to the government. The constitution delegates authority to the national government. If it does not delegate an authority, the national government cannot usurp that authority.

3. There is danger in making a list of individual rights because any rights left off the list might be presumed to be forfeited on purpose.

THE PEOPLE WANTED A BILL OF RIGHTS

Despite arguments against a bill of rights, the people still insisted upon one. They knew from experience that limiting government to specifically delegated powers was not enough to keep government within its bounds. As Thomas Jefferson wrote, "the natural progress of things is for liberty to yield, and government to gain ground."[27]

Without the promise of a bill of rights, several of the large states would have remained outside the Union. When George Washington

---

[26] Ibid.
[27] Letter from Jefferson to Edward Carrington, 27 May 1788

and others invited the states to accept the Constitution and make suggestions for additional improvements, including a bill of rights, several states withdrew their opposition and ratified the Constitution.

With the promise that a bill of rights would be added, James Madison got the ball rolling at the very first Congress, and the "Father of the Constitution" now became the assembler of the Bill of Rights.

The states gave nearly two hundred suggested amendments to Congress. After weeding out duplicate proposals, James Madison boiled these down to seventeen, but Congress approved only twelve. When Congress sent them to the states, they ratified ten, effective December 15, 1791.

An interesting historical note:

> *Unlike recent amendments, with set time limits for ratification, the first 12 amendments were open-ended. So in 1992, the states ratified one more of those originally proposed amendments, 203 years after Congress submitted it to the states. The Twenty-Seventh Amendment requires that no congressional pay raise go into effect until after the next election, allowing the voters to register their approval or disapproval.*[28]

TWO UNIQUE FEATURES OF THE BILL OF RIGHTS

Today portions of the Bill of Rights would be unrecognizable to the Founders because of several reframing decisions of the Supreme Court. A few examples include the reinterpretations of "general welfare" and "necessary and proper," misconstruing the Ninth Amendment, and making the national government the overseer of rights using the Fourteenth Amendment. The Founders' original intent needs to be examined and emphasized to understand the Bill of Rights in terms of their original design.

---

[28] "Congress Submits the First Constitutional Amendments to the States," www.senate.gov

The first interesting feature of the Bill of Rights is the fact that it is not a declaration of rights at all. It is a declaration of prohibitions against the national government. In the minds of the Founders, usurpation and intervention by the national government in the affairs of the states and the people were the most ominous threats to the happiness and welfare of American society. Therefore, the Bill of Rights opens with a bold prohibition against national intervention in specific areas by stating, *"Congress shall make no law. . ."*

The second unique feature is the repeated declaration that the Founders did not want to have the national government serve as the watchdog over the states' responsibility to protect the rights of the people. If a state failed to protect the rights of some of its citizens, the Founders wanted the pressure to build up to force a correction within the confines of the state, without any interference from the national government whatsoever.

James Madison learned this when he tried to include a provision in the Bill of Rights which stated: *"No state shall violate the equal rights of conscience, or the freedom of the press, or the trial by jury in criminal cases."*[29] His proposal was designed to authorize the national government to intervene if a state failed to perform its duty. The Congress turned it down flat. They wanted the national government to stay out of the business of the states. If the people found their state derelict, they were to correct it on the state level and not come running to Washington or the federal courts to have it corrected.

PURPOSE OF THE BILL OF RIGHTS

The purpose of the Bill of Rights was set forth in a preamble that is seldom included in texts of the Constitution anymore. The preamble reads:

> *The Conventions of a number of states, having at the time of their adopting the Constitution, expressed a desire, in order to prevent misconstruction or abuse of its powers,*

---

[29] James Madison, House of Representatives, 1789

that further declaratory and restrictive clauses be added; and as extending the ground of public confidence in the government, will best insure the beneficent ends of its institution...[30]

The primary purpose of the desired bill of rights was to prevent "misconstruction or abuse of... powers." The states did not want the Constitution to be interpreted contrary to its original intent as they understood it at the time of ratification.

Some states included statements made to express their understanding of what the Constitution is, and what it is not, with their notice of ratification. New York, for example, asserted:

... every Power, Jurisdiction and right, which is not by the said Constitution clearly delegated to the Congress of the United States, or the departments of the Government thereof, remains to the People of the several States... And that those Clauses in the said Constitution, which declare, that Congress shall not have or exercise certain Powers, do not imply that Congress is entitled to any Powers not given by the said Constitution...[31]

To satisfy the concerns of New York and other states, the preamble makes it clear that the national government is not to interpret the powers delegated in the Constitution in a way as to expand its powers or diminish those retained by the people—a directive reiterated specifically in the Ninth and Tenth Amendments. The entire proposed Bill of Rights was designed to prevent "misconstruction or abuse of... powers."

There are other remedies for unconstitutional actions by the national government that some thought sufficient for preventing abuse. Some felt the very act of misconstruction would nullify that act because no authority had been granted in the first place. At the Massachusetts state ratifying convention, Theophilus Parsons said:

---

[30] Preamble to the Bill of Rights, 1789
[31] Ratification of the Constitution by the State of New York, 26 July 1788

> *. . . no power was given to Congress to infringe on anyone of the natural rights of the people by this Constitution—and should they attempt it, without constitutional authority the act would be a nullity and could not be enforced.*[32]

In the New York ratifying convention, Thomas Tredwell did not agree that the Constitution itself, as a delegatory document, was sufficient to protect liberty:

> *The first and grand leading, or rather misleading, principle in this debate, and on which the advocates for this system of unrestricted powers must chiefly depend for its support, is that, in forming a constitution, whatever powers are not expressly granted or given the government, are reserved to the people, or that rulers cannot exercise any powers but those expressly given to them by the Constitution. . . . the absurdity of this principle will evidently appear, when we consider the great variety of objects to which the powers of the government must necessarily extend, and that an express enumeration of them all would . . . fill . . . many volumes*
>
> *. . .*
>
> *In this Constitution, sir, we have departed widely from the principles and political faith of '76, when the spirit of liberty ran high, and danger put a curb on ambition. Here we find no security for the rights of individuals, no security for the existence of our state governments; here is no bill of rights, no proper restriction of power; our lives, our property, and our consciences, are left wholly at the mercy of the legislature, and the powers of the judiciary may be extended to any degree short of almighty. Sir, in this Constitution we have not only*

---

[32] Theophilus Parsons, Massachusetts ratifying convention, 1788

neglected—we have done worse—we have openly violated, our faith—that is our public faith.[33]

After much back-and-forth debate on the subject, the final consensus by the majority of Americans was that it would be safer to have a bill of rights to avoid misinterpretation, expansion, and abuse of the Constitution than it would be not to have one. While there may have been several reasons why various Founders wanted a bill of rights, "to prevent misconstruction or abuse of...powers" was the collective purpose.

AN EMPIRE OF REASON

We have traveled through time in our imaginations, from medieval Runnymede to revolutionary Lexington, and from Concord to the 1776 Virginia State House, to Independence Hall in 1787, to the state ratifying conventions. We have traced the movement of ideas which Americans enshrined in their highest form in written constitutions. Americans are meant to be readers, for readers alone can maintain freedom.

We learned that the word *charter* originally meant paper or a written document. Writing implies ideas, thinking, wisdom, and reading. Our written Constitution and Bill of Rights are the "title-deeds of their liberties." These rights are our rights, and we can read them in our founding documents. Our forefathers brought us our liberties by both pen and sword, but the pen will produce lasting results. America is an Empire of Reason, which requires that Americans use their minds.

George Mason declared:

> *That no free government, or the blessings of liberty, can be preserved to any people, but by a firm adherence to justice, moderation, temperance, frugality and virtue, and by frequent recurrence to fundamental principles.*[34]

---

[33] Thomas Tredwell, New York ratifying convention, July 2, 1788
[34] George Mason, Virginia Declaration of Rights, 1776

Let us think about, resort to, and return to fundamental principles, and in that spirit, look at the accumulated wisdom of the ages in our Bill of Rights.

General Principles

To put the Bill of Rights into context, it is necessary to understand some essential principles. Knowing the Founders' perspective and underlying principles will help the serious student understand the Bill of Rights more fully. The general principles covered in this section are those important concepts related to the Bill of Rights as a whole. Additional principles are covered in each amendment in the Bill of Rights as they specifically relate to their respective amendment.

OUR ESTABLISHED FEDERALIST FORM OF GOVERNMENT

Throughout this book, we frequently refer to the three branches of government in Washington, D.C. as the *national government* instead of the more commonly used term of *federal government*. We do this for two reasons. First, the words *national* and *general* are more commonly seen in the Founders' writings than *federal* when referring to the new governmental structure they created.

Second, this new system was designed to unite the separate independent states into a confederation while preserving the sovereignty of each state. The term *federal* or *federalism* was derived from the word *confederation*, and, prior to the Constitutional Convention, had never been used to describe a type of government. The Founders developed a system that constitutionally divided power among the national and state governments, calling it federalism. This term distinguishes our governmental system from any other in existence and is regarded as one of America's most valuable contributions to the science of government.

Thus, to emphasize this concept and clarify the part of the federal system we are referring to, we use the term *national* when speaking of the United States government in Washington, D.C. In doing so, we make no intent to put extra emphasis or importance on that part of the system, but rather as Thomas Jefferson stated, "they are coordinate departments of one simple and integral whole."[1]

The use of the term *national* does not imply that we have a national system of government. A national system is a form of government in which all authority is centralized in a national government and all other governments are subordinate to it. Ours is a dual sovereignty system in which the national and state governments are each sovereign and are connected only by an agreement that delegates specific responsibilities to each in a balanced federation.

Since government tends to overstep its delegated bounds, the Founders knew it would be challenging to maintain a balanced federalism. In fact, that was one of the central issues raised by the state ratifying conventions as they met to decide whether to approve the new constitution. Responding to this concern, Alexander Hamilton expressed his hope that "the people will always take care to preserve the constitutional equilibrium between the general and the state governments."[2] He believed that:

> *. . . this balance between the national and state governments forms a double security to the people. If one [government] encroaches on their rights, they will find a powerful protection in the other. Indeed, they will both be prevented from overpassing their constitutional limits by [the] certain rivalship which will ever subsist between them.[3]*

The concept of federalism is covered in greater detail in our discussion on the Tenth Amendment.

---

[1] Letter from Thomas Jefferson to John Cartwright, 5 June 1824

[2] Alexander Hamilton, *Federalist* No. 31, 1 January 1788

[3] Alexander Hamilton, New York ratifying convention (Francis Childs' version), 21 June 1788

HISTORY'S PHILOSOPHERS OF FREEDOM

The best way to understand the Founders' philosophy of government is to get acquainted with the books they read, who influenced them, and the concepts they advocated for.

In 1984, a detailed study was made of thousands of political documents and speeches written and given in the founding period between 1760 and 1805. The purpose was to identify the sources of the Founders' ideas and who influenced their thinking.

The study showed that, by far, the most quoted source was the Bible, particularly the book of Deuteronomy. The next most quoted sources were Montesquieu, William Blackstone, and John Locke.

The study identified 33 other philosophers and thinkers from ancient times to the Founders' day, including Cicero, Edward Coke, Polybius, and others.[4]

In our study of the Bill of Rights, we will show how some of these writers influenced the Founders' thinking to understand why they outlined specific rights in the Bill of Rights. Let us acquaint ourselves briefly with some of these philosophers (in chronological order):

Polybius (205–125 B.C.)

Polybius was Greek but spent most of his life in Rome and compiled forty volumes on the rise of the Roman Republic. He addressed the oft-asked question of which type of government was the best and concluded that each of the three— monarchy, aristocracy, and democracy—had its advantages. Therefore, a mixed government containing elements of all three

---

[4] Donald S. Lutz, "The Relative Influence of European Writers on Late Eighteenth Century American Political Thought," *American Political Science Review*, p. 189; cited by John Eidsmoe in *Restoration of the Constitution*, H. Wayne House, ed. p. 78, 1987

would be the best. His writings laid dormant for 1,700 years until revived by Montesquieu in his separation of powers doctrine.

Marcus Tullius Cicero (106–43 B.C.)

Dr. William Ebenstein of Princeton writes: *The only Roman political writer who has exercised enduring influence throughout the ages is Cicero. . . Cicero studied law in Rome, and philosophy in Athens. . . He became the leading lawyer of his time and also rose to the highest office of state.*[5] Cicero was admired for his valiant but unsuccessful defense of the Roman Republic against the coming Empire. He encouraged the people to stay with natural law as the basis for government.

Sir Edward Coke (1552–1634)

Coke was an English judge who consistently held that the king lacked constitutional authority to add to or change the common law. He was eventually removed from the bench and wrote his famous *Institutes of the Laws of England.* He was an untiring advocate for the belief that human rights belong to all people, not just an elite class.

---

[5] William Ebenstein, *Great Political Thinkers*, 1963

John Locke (1632–1704)

John Locke, born to a Puritan family, lived about one hundred years before the Founders. The value he placed on the characteristics of human reason was enshrined in his book, *Essays on Human Understanding*. His thoughts on independence and individual rights influenced the generation of Americans that forged a free nation.

Baron Charles de Montesquieu (1689–1755)

Montesquieu was left a fortune by a wealthy uncle, which he used to undertake twenty years of study on law and government. He traveled extensively and wrote his famous book, *The Spirit of Laws*, described as one of the most outstanding books of the French 18th century. In it, he picked up some ideas of the Greek writer Polybius concerning a "mixed constitution" and advocated a system of government with a separation of powers. The Founders of America provided an opportunity to put Montesquieu's ideas into practice, and they referred to him as "the celebrated Montesquieu."

William Blackstone (1723–1780)

The author of the most famous treatise on the common law of England was William Blackstone. In early America, no authority on the subject of the law was more widely read than Blackstone. He established the classes for the first law school at Oxford in 1753. His lectures on English law were as popular in America as they were in England.

PRIMARY FOUNDERS WHO INFLUENCED THE BILL OF RIGHTS

In addition to the philosophers of freedom, three Founders should be highlighted. Many people contributed to the evolution and development of the ideas that make up the Bill of Rights. But three key figures from the founding era had a direct hand in refining those ideas and putting them in written documents that stand strong today. They are:

George Mason (1725–1792)

From Virginia, Mason was a farmer, politician, and delegate to the Constitutional Convention of 1787. He was the primary author of the Fairfax Resolves and the Virginia Declaration of Rights, precursors to the Declaration of Independence and the Bill of Rights. He felt a bill of rights was so crucial that he refused to sign the Constitution because it did not include such a bill.

Thomas Jefferson (1743–1826)

A Virginian farmer and statesman, Jefferson is most known for authoring the draft of the Declaration of Independence. He is known around the world as one of history's most outstanding scholars on individual rights. He also served as governor of Virginia and the third president of the United States.

James Madison (1751–1836)

Madison spent many of his early years in bed as a sickly child, where he found ample time to read and enlarge his knowledge and understanding. Many considered him the ablest and most prepared delegate to the Constitutional Convention of 1787, earning him the title "Father of the Constitution." He was the primary author of the Bill of Rights. As a congressman and fourth president, arguably, he applied the principles of liberty to policy better than any other Founder.

PRINCIPLES OF NATURAL LAW

The Founding Fathers relied upon reason and logic above all else. Most of them believed that reason should be applied to everything, including religion, social behavior, and self-government. Many of their natural law discoveries about good government are embodied in the Bill of Rights. A basic understanding of a few of these discoveries is invaluable in understanding many concepts in the Bill of Rights. These natural laws form the basis upon which the Bill of Rights was written. Many of these natural law principles will be covered in each amendment section; however, a few general, overarching principles should be explored to complete our understanding of the Bill of Rights. Natural law itself is the first natural law principle that forms the basis of the other principles.

Before we get into what natural law is in relation to the Bill of Rights, we will clarify what it is not. There is a relatively modern, alternate definition, that natural law is a moral or religious code. Based on that definition, natural law is subject to opinion, not reason, and may or may not be observable and measurable. This modern definition is not the definition used by the Founders and, therefore, is not relevant to this discussion of the Bill of Rights.

Natural law and morality may overlap from time to time because many ideas of morality are based on natural law, but natural law is not based on morality. Natural law is based on reason. It applies to everything and is unchanging.

The Founders knew that government must have a fixed basis so people could have confidence in it. It must have order and it must be reasonable. To the Founders, the only sensible approach to government, justice, and human relations lay in terms of the constant and unchanging laws of nature. The order in nature by which everything works properly is called natural law. Over two thousand years ago, Marcus Tullius Cicero attempted to save the Roman Republic from falling into an emperorship by pleading with his listeners to stay with natural law, as opposed to man-made ruler's law. He explained that natural laws are the only true laws:

> *True law is right reason in agreement with nature; it is of universal application, unchanging and everlasting; it summons to duty by its commands, and averts from wrongdoing by its prohibitions. . . It is a sin to try to alter this law, nor is it allowable to repeal any part of it, and it is impossible to abolish entirely. We cannot be freed from its obligations by senate or people, and we need not look outside ourselves for an expounder or interpreter of it. And there will not be different laws at Rome and Athens, or different laws now and in the future, but one eternal and unchangeable law will be valid for all nations and all times, and there will be one master and ruler, that is God, over us all, for he is the author of this law, its promulgator, and its enforcing judge. Whoever is disobedient is fleeing from himself and denying his human nature, and by reason of this very fact he will suffer the worst penalties, even if he escapes what is commonly considered punishment.*[6]

---

[6] Marcus Tullius Cicero, *The Republic*, 54 to 51 B.C.

Natural law "summons to duty by its commands." If we are hungry, we work to obtain food. Hunger is the command; work is the duty. Natural law "averts from wrongdoing by its prohibitions." We are averted from eating poisonous foods because they will kill us. Those simple absolutes are the same regardless of the year or century—irrespective of race or creed. And if we try to flee from it, we will suffer even more.

The Founders looked upon natural law as the governing force of the universe and everything within it. William Blackstone, the principal authority of English common law of that day, stated the generally accepted idea that when the universe came into existence, there were certain principles that controlled all matter. He went on to say that this orderly arrangement of the universe is called "the law of nature" and that there are laws for "human" nature just as surely as they exist for the rest of the universe. These are referred to as "the laws of nature" in the Declaration of Independence.

Blackstone further stated:

> *Man, considered as a creature, must necessarily be subject to the laws of his Creator. . . This will of his Maker is called the law of nature. . . This law of nature, being coeval with mankind, and dictated by God, Himself, is of course superior in obligation to any other. It is binding over all the globe in all countries, and at all times: no human laws are of any validity, if contrary to this. . .*[7]

In addition to Blackstone and Cicero's comments about natural law's consistency through all times and peoples, John Locke believed that humankind has an obligation to treat others equally according to natural law:

> *The state of Nature has a law of Nature to govern it, which. . . teaches all mankind who will but consult it, that being all equal and independent, no one ought to*

---

[7] Blackstone, *Commentaries on the Laws of England*, 1765

> *harm another in his life, health, liberty or possessions;*
> *. . . And, being furnished with like faculties; sharing all*
> *in one community of Nature, there cannot be supposed*
> *any such subordination among us that may authorise us*
> *to destroy one another. . .*[8]

Natural law treats all people equally and is important as the basis of sound government and just human relations. For example, gravity has the same effect on the old and the young, rich and the poor, etc. Just like gravity, if the laws of nature treat everyone equally, our laws should also treat everyone equally. However, it is important to note that natural law does not demand equality in outcome, only equality under the law. If written law produces equality in outcome, it is likely violating natural law. This concept of equality will be explained in the "All Humans are Created Equal" section below.

If we desire stability in government and good human relations, we should consider natural laws first. The conditions are clear; if the laws of nature treat everyone equally, our civil laws should also treat everyone equally. Simply put, all of the laws should be for all of the people all of the time.

When a law is written to favor one group of people over another, it violates natural law. The consequences are division, resentment, unfair competition, discrimination, and many other divisive factors. Laws are what we all have in common; they are what unite us as fellow citizens. They are what distinguish us as members of the same society. Laws that do not apply to everyone equally have the effect of dividing people rather than uniting them. Division is contrary to the purpose of society and will have devastating results.

Natural law, as Cicero wrote, "is right reason in agreement with nature." It is observable and measurable. There are natural law principles for science, i.e., what goes up must come down, equal and opposite reaction, etc. There are fixed natural law principles for mathematics, for human happiness, and even good government.

---

[8] John Locke, *Two Treatises of Government*, 1764

The principle that all of the laws need to be for all of the people all of the time includes those people who serve in government, whether they be elected, appointed, or hired. It is an unequal application of the law to pass a different law for your neighbor than yourself and will pit neighbor against neighbor. It is a gross violation of equality under the law for lawmakers to make different laws for themselves—that action is tyranny.

Like scientific natural laws, natural laws for good government are equally observable and measurable. It is these laws that are the basis for principles in the Bill of Rights.

PASSING NATURAL LAW PRINCIPLES TO FUTURE GENERATIONS

It is true, our society is different than it was in 1791 when the Bill of Rights came into existence—in many ways, very different. There are laws written then that are outdated today and should be altered to fit our modern society. There are provisions in the Constitution that may need some adjusting for the times. This is precisely why the Founders built an amending mechanism into the Constitution. After all, that is how we obtained the Bill of Rights—by amendment.

Some people argue that the Constitution, including the Bill of Rights, was written for an 18th century agrarian society and therefore does not apply today. Others argue that the Constitution is a living, breathing document that should be reinterpreted based on the needs and definitions of the day. Still, others argue that the Constitution is beyond reproach, and altering it is some kind of civil blasphemy. Each argument may have some valid points, but it is easily predicted that the extreme enforcement of any one of those three arguments would lead to either chaos or oppression—society's most evil cousins.

As humans, we do a pretty good job at passing down our discoveries in most sciences. Doing so has allowed humans to develop cures for diseases once thought incurable, explore the earth and space, catalog almost countless plant and animal species, solve complex math and physics problems, etc. Political science, however, we are not so good at passing down. We tend to focus more on the "political" than we do on the "science" of the subject. We seem to be more interested in expressing our opinions than we have in discovering observable and measurable natural laws of the science of government. John Adams expressed that for humans to advance in many fields, it is important to study and pass on scientific knowledge so future generations can develop new and better skills.

> *The Science of Government it is my Duty to study, more than all other Sciences: the Art of Legislation and Administration and Negotiation, ought to take Place, indeed to exclude in a manner all other Arts. —I must study Politicks and War that my sons may have liberty to study Mathematics and Philosophy. My sons ought to study Mathematics and Philosophy, Geography, natural History, Naval Architecture, navigation, Commerce and Agriculture, in order to give their Children a right to study Painting, Poetry, Music, Architecture, Statuary, Tapestry and Porcelain.[9]*

To George Washington, passing down the knowledge of the science of government was imperative to perpetuating a country's existence:

> *A primary object. . . should be the education of our youth in the science of government. In a republic what species of knowledge can be equally important and what duty more pressing. . . than. . . communicating it to those who are to be the future guardians of the liberties of the country?[10]*

How do we pass on what we have learned? Should we adhere firmly to the documents of the past, to the detriment of the future? Or should we scrap what has already been discovered and replace it with our own more "civilized" worldview? Perhaps we should first ask, do we want to listen to the wisdom of the past? Are we obligated

---

[9] Letter from John Adams to Abigail Adams, 12 May 1780
[10] George Washington, Eighth Annual Message of George Washington, 7 December 1796

to do so? Do the citizens of the past have a right to bind the citizens of the future to their governmental structures? In a letter to James Madison, Thomas Jefferson pondered some of these questions:

> *The question Whether one generation of men has a right to bind another, seems never to have been started either on this or our side of the water. Yet it is a question of such consequences as not only to merit decision, but place also, among the fundamental principles of every government. . . . that no such obligation can be so transmitted I think very capable of proof. I set out on this ground, which I suppose to be self-evident, "that the earth belongs in usufruct[11] to the living": that the dead have neither powers nor rights over it.[12]*

Jefferson contends that once a person is dead, his property cannot be passed onto any other and that it is left to whoever shall occupy it next. Those newest occupants are likely to be the person's spouse or children, since they already occupy the place. To guarantee who owns the property after the previous owner is deceased must be a matter of societal law. But that returns us to the original question: can the dead bind the living?

In further consideration of that question, Jefferson presents a reorganization of the course of life and death into fixed generations of whom all its members are born, reach maturity, and die at precisely the same moment. Then, upon their deaths, a new generation is born, and the cycle repeats. He simplifies the generations in this way to wrap his head around the question of one generation binding another. Can they bind them to property, debts, obligations, etc.?

> *But when a whole generation, that is, the whole society dies, as in the case we have supposed, and another generation or society succeeds, this forms a whole, and*

---

[11] The right to the use or advantages of property belonging to another, without destroying its further use by others.

[12] Letter from Thomas Jefferson to James Madison, 6 September 1789

there is no superior who can give their territory to a third society, who may have lent money to their predecessors beyond their faculties of paying.[13]

He concludes that a dead person's debt cannot pass to the living, even if that living person occupies the property that belonged to the dead. Such a system of obligating the living occupant to the debts of the former occupant, he said, is "municipal" only. Meaning, it is simply a rule of civil conduct, not a principle of natural law.

We seem not to have perceived that, by the law of nature, one generation is to another as one independent nation to another.[14]

Jefferson moves on from property and debt to laws and constitutions. He surmises that because persons and property are why we create laws and government, and if persons die and their property with them, so too, laws and governments die with them as well.

On similar ground it may be proved that no society can make a perpetual constitution, or even a perpetual law. The earth belongs always to the living generation. They may manage it then, & what proceeds from it, as they please, during their usufruct. They are masters too of their own persons, & consequently may govern them as they please. But persons & property make the sum of the objects of government. The constitution and the laws of their predecessors extinguished then in their natural course, with those who gave them being. This could preserve that being till it ceased to be itself, & no longer. Every constitution then, & every law, naturally expires at the end of 19 years.[15] If it be enforced longer, it is an

---

[13] Ibid.

[14] Ibid.

[15] Using a table of mortality in his day and writing in his September 6, 1789 letter to James Madison, Jefferson concluded that "19 years is the term beyond which neither the representatives of a nation, nor even the whole nation itself assembled, can validly extend a debt."

act of force, & not of right. It may be said that the succeeding generation exercising in fact the power of repeal, this leaves them as free as if the constitution or law had been expressly limited to 19 years only.[16]

He reduced society to the most basic natural degree and concluded that, like the principle of survival of the fittest, nature is bare and raw. It separates the generations and leaves them on their own to begin anew again and again. For Jefferson, this was not simply an exercise in logical reasoning. He was concerned about the seemingly immoral prospect of leaving debts to future generations without their consent, given that the future is unable to consent. He presented these ideas to James Madison because he wanted him to contemplate the concept as he performed his duties in the House of Representatives: making laws, establishing codes, and authorizing national debt. Jefferson asked Madison to:

Turn this subject in your mind, my dear Sir, & particularly as to the power of contracting debts; & develop it with that perspicuity & cogent logic so peculiarly yours. Your station in the councils of our country gives you an opportunity of producing it to public consideration, of forcing it into discussion.[17]

James Madison turned the subject in his mind and responded with a more mature conclusion than the "hand to mouth" picture painted by Jefferson. He acknowledged the importance of the subject in the act of law-making, but had some skepticism as it relates to human affairs. Jefferson reduced the generations to their basic existence, it is true, but Madison reaches beyond "hand to mouth" and considers principles of natural law for human relationships on both individual and societal levels. This includes principles for laws and good government.

The idea. . . is a great one, and suggests many interesting reflections to Legislators; particularly when contracting

---

[16] Letter from Thomas Jefferson to James Madison, 6 September 1789
[17] Ibid.

> *and providing for public debts. . . My first thoughts lead me to view the doctrine as not in all respects, compatible with the course of human affairs. I will endeavor to sketch the grounds of my skepticism.*[18]

Madison starts with the most obvious problem with Jefferson's thoughts, the chaos that would ensue if government would potentially change every nineteen years. Such a proposal would create additional factions in society.

> *Would not a Government so often revised become too mutable to retain those prejudices in its favor which antiquity inspires, and which are perhaps a salutary aid to the most rational Government in the most enlightened age? Would not such a periodical revision engender pernicious factions that might not otherwise come into existence? Would not, in fine, a Government depending for its existence beyond a fixed date, on some positive and authentic intervention of the Society itself, be too subject to the casualty and consequences of an actual interregnum?*[19]

He then tackles the deeper ramifications of the subject. Jefferson reduced the generations to one grand general law of nature, as if that law were independent of all other laws, as if to say that because of gravity, all things must fall to the ground, without exception. In perfect Madison character, he weaved through the maze of natural law and presented a complete picture. Yes, gravity forces things to the ground, but it can be combined with other laws, like high and low air pressure and aerodynamics. The combination of those laws can allow things to fly. On the subject of the living and the dead, Madison introduced similar combinations of laws by bringing together the raw nature of the earth and natural human advancement.

> *If the earth be the gift of nature to the living, their title can extend to the earth in its natural State only. The*

---

[18] Letter from James Madison to Thomas Jefferson, 4 February 1790
[19] Ibid.

> *improvements made by the dead form a debt against the living who take the benefit of them. This debt cannot be otherwise discharged than by a proportionate obedience to the will of the Authors of the improvements.*[20]

There is a relationship between one generation and another. Sure, the next generation could reject everything from the previous generation, but to be intellectually and morally consistent, they must reject also all the improvements made by the previous generation. They could reject the debt and refuse to pay, for instance, but in doing so they reject the property purchased with that debt as well. What we accept from those in the past should be in proportion to the obedience we give to their wishes.

> *Debts may be incurred with a direct view to the interest of the unborn as well as of the living: Such are debts for repelling a Conquest, the evils of which descend through many generations. Debts may even be incurred principally for the benefit of posterity. . .*
>
> *There seems then to be some foundation in the nature of things; in the relation which one generation bears to another, for the descent of obligations from one to another. Equity may require it. Mutual good may be promoted by it. And all that seems indispensable in stating the account between the dead and the living, is to see that the debits against the latter do not exceed the advances made by the former.*[21]

Madison covers all the bases. After establishing the natural law principle that obligates future generations to their predecessors, he does not let the obligation the past generation has to future generations slip by. They cannot require a higher price of the future than the value of the advances. We cannot charge the future more than what we are leaving them is worth.

---

[20] Ibid.
[21] Ibid.

Three years before this conversation with Jefferson, Madison summed it up beautifully. The Founders in 1776 and 1787 paid attention to generations past, but not blindly. They combined their own experiences and discoveries with those of the past and, in doing so, formed a more perfect society based on natural law principles discovered across the generations.

> *Is it not the glory of the people of America, that, whilst they have paid a decent regard to the opinions of former times and other nations, they have not suffered a blind veneration for antiquity, for custom, or for names, to overrule the suggestions of their own good sense, the knowledge of their own situation, and the lessons of their own experience? . . . posterity will be indebted for the possession, and the world for the example, of the numerous innovations displayed on the American theatre, in favor of private rights and public happiness.*[22]

Below and throughout our exploration of the Bill of Rights, we lay before you some of those natural law principles discovered and codified in law and constitutions by generations of the past. It is up to us as the present society to determine what we will keep, what we will reject, and what we will contribute to the discovery of natural law for the continued advancement of humankind and our social interactions with each other.

ALL HUMANS ARE CREATED EQUAL

The Founders wrote in the Declaration of Independence that some truths are self-evident. One of these is that all people are created equal. Yet, everyone knows that no two human beings are exactly alike in any respect. They are different when they are born. They plainly exhibit different natural skills. They acquire different tastes. They develop along different lines. They vary in physical strength, mental capacity, emotional stability, inherited social status, and in scores of other ways.

---

[22] James Madison, *Federalist* No. 14, 30 November 1787

If people are so different, how can they be equal? The answer is, they can't. They can only be treated as equals according to natural law and by extension, under our written laws. Assuming, of course, that our written laws agree with the laws of nature. It is in this way that all men are created equal. It is the task of society to accept people in all their vast array of individual differences but treat them as equals. As the constitutional writer Clarence Carson explained:

Two kinds of equality, so far as individuals are concerned, are treated in the Declaration of Independence.

First, there is equality before the law. This means that every man's case is tried by the same law governing any particular case. Practically, it means that there are no different laws for different classes and orders of men. The definition of premeditated murder is the same for the millionaire as for the tramp. A corollary of this is that no classes are created or recognized by law.

Second, the Declaration refers to an equality of life. Each man is equally entitled to his life with every other man; each man has an equal title to God-given liberties along with every other.[23]

John Adams was in France when Jean-Jacques Rousseau was teaching that all men were designed to be equal in every way. Adams wrote:

That all men are born to equal rights is true. Every being has a right to his own, as clear, as moral, as sacred, as any other being has. . . But to teach that all men are born with equal powers and faculties, to equal influence in society, to equal property and advantages through life, is as gross a fraud, as glaring an imposition on the credulity of the people, as ever was practiced by monks, by Druids, by Brahmins, by priests or the immortal

---

[23] Clarence Carson, *The American Tradition*, 1964

> *Lama, or by the self-styled philosophers of the French Revolution.*[24]

Nevertheless, there are some who insist that people do not have "equal rights" unless they have "equal things." The Founding Fathers were well acquainted with this proposition. We are only equal in two ways, in our rights and under the law. It is interesting that when we attempt to make ourselves equal in other ways, it violates one or more of the natural ways we are equal.

For example, if Steve has $10 and Rex has $20, and you wanted to make them equal in wealth, you would pass a law to force Rex to give $5 to Steve. Now they each have $15. Are they equal? Perhaps in money, but that law makes them unequal in their rights and under the law because Steve's property ($10) was protected more than Rex's property ($20). They are unequal under the law because the law favored Steve over Rex.

Steve was more than happy with this arrangement, to be sure; he just gained things. Did he lose his equality under the law and in his rights? Seemingly, no. What if Fred, who has $0, is introduced into the scenario, and the law requires that they be equal in things? In obedience to the law, Steve and Rex each give $5 to Fred. All three now have $10. They are equal in things, but Steve discovered that, although he temporarily gained things, because he was not equally protected in his rights and under the law, he lost his newly acquired property ($5). And how could he protest now when he did not protest from the beginning?

When we attempt to use force to make ourselves equal in ways nature did not intend for us to be equal, the penalty will be inequality in ways nature did intend for us to be equal. That disobedience to natural law is exactly what Cicero warned us of:

---

[24] Adrienne Koch, *The American Enlightenment*, 1965

Whoever is disobedient is fleeing from himself and denying his human nature, and by reason of this very fact he will suffer the worst. . . punishment.[25]

All of us are created equal in our rights and under the law, not in talents or things. It will serve all self-governing societies to remember that. Written laws that exclude certain groups of people, laws that grant privileges exclusively to one group, laws that protect the rights of some but not others, or laws that take from some to give to others are a violation of the natural law of equality under the law. Those laws may seek to level the playing field in outcomes, but the result is a society where citizens are not equal under the law.

The United States has its sins in relation to exclusionary and special laws that carve out certain groups of people to exclude them or grant special privileges to others. These laws carve out groups of all types, including those defined by race, gender, age, religion, types of businesses, professions, socioeconomics, family, and the list goes on and on. And for many groups that are excluded in one aspect, one can find laws where that same group is granted special privileges. It gets extremely muddled, as expected. However, because the United States was founded on the idea that all humans are created equal and the idea that laws should be based on natural law principles, Americans have trudged through the mud of inequality in continual search of a more perfect union. While we continue to argue and struggle, we have traveled much closer to equality under the law than we were in 1776 or 1787 when the Declaration and the Constitution were written.

EQUAL RIGHT TO VOTE

Because voting is a public activity, it is one of the best mechanisms to determine if law, in this case voting rights, is being applied equally in society. A review of the timeline of voting rights illustrates the struggles of our past, the victories we've won, and the future we hope to find. If the idea that all humans are created equal under fixed, scientific, natural law is true, one must conclude that no

---

[25] Marcus Tullius Cicero, *The Republic*, 54 to 51 B.C.

person should be denied the right to vote. This is reinforced by the ideas discussed in other sections below, that each individual has the right to consent to their own form of government, and that that government can only do that which the people delegate to it.

The purpose of reviewing the history of voting in America is to show how important it is to found a nation upon the idea that there are fixed natural laws. In this case, the natural law that every human is created equal under the law and, therefore, all laws should be for all of the people all of the time, will eventually bring equality to all—if we strive for it. It has taken America a few hundred years and many setbacks, but the overall trajectory has been toward securing voting rights for all. This is because we are founded on the idea of equal rights—so we strive for it.

Before the timeline of voting rights and laws are presented here, it is important to understand the historical context of voting in America. The timeline presented is based on the general status of voting in America. There are many details not included. For instance, there are a number of recorded instances of women, free black men, and Native Americans voting during the colonial period, even though they generally could not. Presenting the historical context of voting is in no way meant to excuse the practice of giving special preference under the law. It is included only to gain a more accurate view of the prevailing ideas of the time and remind us that overcoming "legal" prejudice involves much more than changing the law; it requires a change in thinking, traditions, culture, etc. The right to vote is delicate, as James Madison said:

> *The right of suffrage is a fundamental Article in Republican Constitutions. The regulation of it is, at the same time, a task of peculiar delicacy. Allow the right exclusively to property, and the rights of persons may be oppressed. The feudal polity alone sufficiently proves it. Extend it equally to all, and the rights of property or the claims of justice may be overruled by a majority without property, or interested in measures of injustice. Of this abundant proof is afforded by other popular Govts. and*

is not without examples in our own, particularly in the laws impairing the obligation of contracts.[26]

According to Madison, the right to vote is not so easy. The circumstances of society, history, systems of government, etc. matter greatly when it comes to voting. It is also complicated when considering the form of government a nation has established and which form adheres to natural law the best. A pure democracy, for example, may seem just when it comes to granting universal voting rights to everyone for every issue and every candidate, but historically, democracies devolve into either ochlocracy (mob rule) or tyrannical oligarchy. The Founders rejected a pure democracy. Madison and Adams were clear on this position. They said:

. . . Democracies have ever been spectacles of turbulence and contention; have ever been found incompatible with personal security or the rights of property; and have in general been as short in their lives as they have been violent in their deaths. . .[27] *—James Madison*

Democracy has never been and never can be so durable as Aristocracy or Monarchy. But while it lasts it is more bloody than either. . .

. . . Remember Democracy never lasts long. It soon wastes, exhausts and murders itself. There never was a Democracy yet, that did not commit suicide. It is in vain to say that Democracy is less vain, less proud, less selfish, less ambitious or less avaricious than Aristocracy or Monarchy. It is not true in fact and no where appears in history. Those Passions are the same in all Men under all forms of Simple Government, and when unchecked, produce the same Effects of Fraud, Violence and Cruelty.[28] *—John Adams*

---

[26] James Madison, Note to His Speech on the Right of Suffrage, 1821

[27] James Madison, *Federalist* No. 10, 22 November 1787

[28] Letter from John Adams to John Taylor, 17 December 1814

Our form of government is a republic, which is a representative form of government, but not just any republic. The United States was formed as a mixed form of government. It is made up of different forms of government all blended together, keeping the best of each and rejecting the worst. We have a monarchy in the executive branch, but only for executing the law, not writing or adjudicating the law. We have democracy in the House of Representatives and an oligarchy in the federal courts. Originally, the Senate acted as an oligarchy, with senators chosen by their state legislatures. This was changed with the passage of the Seventeenth Amendment. Senators are now chosen by popular vote, making it democratic in nature. Each form handles what they do best, with checks and balances designed to prevent them from doing what that form does worst.

An understanding of our mixed form of government is important so we can determine how and when voting rights should be universal and when they should be limited. The Founders wanted various groups of people represented at various times, not divided by race, sex, age, etc., but by societal interests. The people are represented in the House, the states were represented in the Senate (prior to the Seventeenth Amendment), and the law is represented in the courts. The executive represents the nation as a whole, both the people and the states—that explains the strange creature that is the electoral college. The electoral college is designed for both the people and the states to engage in the election of the president. Altering our system to have the people directly elect the president would have the same devastating effects as directly electing our U.S. Senators. It would eliminate the checks on the "mob rule" tendency of democracy.

Prior to 1913, United States senators were appointed by their state legislatures. The Seventeenth Amendment changed that by having them directly elected by the people of their state. Directly electing senators transformed the Senate from an oligarchy to a democracy, a role already fulfilled by the House of Representatives. This left the state governments without representation in the Senate—in fact, the states are left with no representation in the national government at all. The states are no longer a check on an overreaching national government.

As a further exacerbation of the problem, the makeup of the Senate and term of office was designed for an oligarchical house, not a democratic house. In a democracy, representatives answer to the people; as such, they should represent fewer people and be required to return to answer to the people through election often. Hence, U.S. Representatives represent an average of 700,000 people and are up for reelection every two years. Senators, on the other hand, represent from 581,000 in Wyoming to 39.6 million in California, and serve for a lengthy six years.

Ironically, in an attempt to bring senators closer to the people, the Seventeenth Amendment moved them further from the people they represent. The average person may not have been able to influence their senator directly, but they could influence them through a member of their state legislature, likely a person very close to home. Today, senators are difficult to influence by individual constituents or state legislators.

Detailing the devastating effects of the Seventeenth Amendment and its failure to fulfill the goal of its authors will be saved for another book. The point is, the United States was founded as a mixed form of government. It was designed to represent specific entities at specific times and with specific, limited powers. That meant that sometimes the people vote, sometimes the state legislatures appoint, sometimes the Senate and President appoint, and sometimes the House and Senate remove officials from office. The Seventeenth Amendment significantly altered that original design.

Our mixed form of government was not designed to include universal voting for all offices. However, the offices that the people vote for should be universal. Though it seems archaic today, in early America only the men voted. Not because women were incapable. In fact, a single woman could own property, enter into contracts, engage in business, and sometimes vote, but once she married, that all changed. A married woman became part of her husband's identity, and all property, voting, etc., were under his stewardship. In a representative republic, the head of the house, in this case, the husband and father, represented the family. As the family's representative, he voted and handled all other business dealings for the family.

It is also important to remember some facts about voting after the Constitution was established. First, the Constitution did not prohibit any person from voting or holding public office. The document is neutral. The word *person* is used for eligibility for office. No person was prohibited from voting. That detail was left to the states. Second, United States citizens only voted for one national office— their representative in the United States House of Representatives. Up until 1913, senators were appointed by each state legislature, and still to this day, individual citizens do not vote for president. The president is still chosen by electors from each state, who are chosen by the state legislature, under the direction of the people as indicated by ballot. It may seem like the people vote for the president, but they do not.

That reality meant that voting rights were more important on a state level than they were on a national level. Hence, it may be observed that much of the headway in expanding voting rights came from individual states, not national law. It is also important to note, while "granting voting rights" may be a term used to explain what a written law is doing, voting rights are a fundamental natural right in connection with the fundamental right to establish, alter, and abolish our own form of government. Therefore, voting rights are already "granted" by natural law.

With all that said, let's now examine the timeline of general events of voting rights in the United States:

VOTING RIGHTS TIMELINE

1607

A previously appointed council of six men, out of 105 people in Jamestown, elects their first president, Edward Maria Wingfield.

1619

In accordance with the new Great Charter, the first representative assembly in English America convenes in Jamestown's church on July 30. Twenty-two representatives are elected to the House of Burgesses by "all inhabitants" from each of eleven settlements, "that they might have a hand in the governing of themselves."[29] All inhabitants meant landowners and non-landowners alike. There was no restriction on race, religion, sex, property, or social status. Indentured servants could not vote until they had completed their indenture (three to seven years), after which they would become a freeman. A freeman was an inhabitant that was not bound to indentured (contractual) servitude.

1621

Virginia divides the House of Burgesses into two chambers, the General Assembly to be "respectfully chosen by the inhabitants" (Article IV) of each community. There was no restriction on race, religion, sex, property, or social status.

1646

The Virginia House of Burgesses passes a law punishing those who failed to vote.

> *Freemen soever, having lawful summons of the time and place for election of Burgesses, that shall not make repairs accordingly, Such person or persons unless there be lawful cause for the absenting himself shall forfeit 100 lb. of tobacco for his non appearance, freemen being*

---

[29] Governor George Yeardley, Proclamation, May 1619

covenant. Servants being exempted from the said fine, to be levied by distress. . .[30]

The act stipulates that servants were exempted from the fine, likely because they had no property to pay a fine, but would be punished by "distress." This implies that indentured servants could vote. There was no restriction on race, religion, sex, property, or social status.

1655

The Virginia House of Burgesses stipulates that only the head of a household, then referred to as "housekeepers," can vote.

That all housekeepers whether freeholders, lease holders, or otherwise tenants, shall only be capable to elect Burgesses. . .[31]

The act also specifies that the sheriff of each settlement must give notice "to all persons interested in elections" within a specific timeframe. This was done so people were not disenfranchised by being unaware of an election.

Again, there was no restriction on race, religion, sex, property, or social status to vote, in that the act did not specify any of those classifications as requirements to be the head of a household.

1656

Virginia repeals the head of household restriction and opens voting to all free people.

We conceive it something hard and unagreeable to reason that any persons shall pay equal taxes and yet have no votes in elections, Therefore it is enacted by this present Grand Assembly, That so much of the act for

---

[30] Virginia House of Burgesses, ACT XIX, 1646
[31] Virginia House of Burgesses, ACT VII, 1655

choosing Burgesses be repealed as excludes freemen from votes. . .[32]

1670

Virginia restricts the right to vote to property owners only. The reasoning was because they thought other voters caused too much "tumult" in elections. However, there was still no restriction on race, religion, sex, or social status.

WHEREAS the usual way of choosing burgesses by the votes of all persons who having served their time are freemen of this country who having little interest in the country do oftner make tumults at the election to the disturbance of his majesties peace, then by their discretions in their votes provide for the conservation thereof, by making choice of persons fitly qualified for the discharge of so great a trust, And whereas the lawes of England grant a voyce in such election only to such as by their estates real or personal have interest enough to tie them to the endeavour of the public good; It is hereby enacted, that none but freeholders and housekeepers who only are answerable to the publique for the levies shall hereafter have a voice in the election of any burgesses in this country. . .[33]

1699

Virginia restricts women and those under twenty-one from voting.

. . . no woman sole or covert [married], infants under the age of twenty one years, or recusant convict being freeholders shall be enabled to give a vote or have a voice in the election of burgesses. . .[34]

---

[32] Virginia House of Burgesses, ACT XVI, 1656

[33] Virginia House of Burgesses, ACT III, 1670

[34] Virginia House of Burgesses, ACT II; An Act for Prevention of Undue Election of Burgesses, 1699

1723

Virginia restricts all free blacks and Native Americans from voting.

> *. . . no free Negro, Mulatto or Indian whatsoever shall have any vote at the Election of Burgesses or any other Election whatsoever.*[35]

This officially marks the year in which voting in Virginia was restricted to white property-owning males only. Rights that were once open to all inhabitants in 1619 would now take more than one hundred years to restore to all people in Virginia.

1756

Lydia Chapin Taft is the first woman known to vote in Massachusetts legally.

1765

Sir William Blackstone publishes Commentaries on the Laws of England, reinforcing the tradition of coverture. A legal doctrine that said that once married, a woman's property belongs to her husband, and she has no legal rights. Coverture was brought to America as a remnant of English common law.

1776

Men twenty-one or older who owned property in the form of real estate could vote in most states. Some women who owned property could vote.

The New Jersey State Constitution is adopted with voting rights that are gender-neutral and do not include racial restrictions. This is an important milestone early in the nation. New Jersey did not restrict the voting rights of women or minorities any more than restrictions on white men.

---

[35] Virginia House of Burgesses, An Act Directing the Trial of Slaves, Committing Capital Crimes; and for the More Effectual Punishing Conspiracies and Insurrections of Them; and for the Better Government of Negros, Mulattos, and Indians, Bond or Free, 1723

1777

The New York Constitution defines voters as "male inhabitants."

The Vermont Constitution becomes the first state constitution to provide for universal male suffrage and outlaw slavery.

1780

Though the road is still long to citizenship and voting for slaves, Pennsylvania passes the Act for the Gradual Abolition of Slavery. Soon other states follow.

1789

The United States Constitution goes into effect. It does not prohibit anyone from holding office or voting based on property, race, sex, etc. However, voting qualifications are left to the states to decide for their respective states.

1790

The New Jersey State Legislature passes an Act revising election law to include "he or she."

1792

New Hampshire eliminates property requirements for voting.

1797

John Adams recalls Eleanor "Nelly" Parke Custis riding to the polls in Virginia to demand her right to vote as a freeholder:

> *Miss Eleanor Custis, granddaughter of Mrs. Washington. . . mounted her [horse] and galloped to the hustings & demanded her right to vote as a free holder & a free holder she was to a large amount.*[36]

---

[36] Letter from John Adams to John Adams, 26 November 1821

1800

Out of 217 voters, twenty-nine women vote in a congressional election in Upper Penns Neck Township, New Jersey. Some continued voting year after year.

1801

Forty-six women and at least four black male voters, of 343 voters, vote in a New Jersey state election.

1807

New Jersey, where some women and African Americans had been permitted to vote since 1776, alters its laws to permit only tax-paying male citizens the right to vote after accusations of voter fraud. The accusations are in relation to the location of a courthouse. Of the two cities voting, around 5,000 votes are cast, while only around 2,000 eligible voters existed.

1821

The state of New York's new constitution eliminates property qualifications for male voters but creates new requirements that "persons of colour" must have $250 worth of property, "over and above all debts,"[37] to vote, and all male voters must have paid taxes or served the community in some other manner.

1828

Maryland becomes the last state to remove religious restrictions when it passed legislation allowing Jews to vote.

1838

Women are allowed to vote in school elections in Kentucky.

---

[37] New York Constitution, Article II, Section 1, 1821

1843

Rhode Island drafts a new constitution in which all free males are allowed to vote.

1848

Citizenship and voting rights are granted to those living in recently conquered territories after the Mexican-American War.

1855

Connecticut adopts the nation's first literacy test for voting. Massachusetts follows in 1857. The tests were implemented to discriminate against Irish-Catholic immigrants.

1856

North Carolina becomes the last state to remove the property requirement for voting.

1868

The Fourteenth Amendment passes. It grants citizenship to former slaves but does not guarantee the right to vote. That remains left up to the states.

1869

The territory of Wyoming passes woman's suffrage, another major milestone in voting rights. Although women could vote in early New Jersey, that only lasted thirty years. Wyoming's passage lasts to the present day.

1870

The Fifteenth Amendment passes. It prevents the denial of voting rights based on race. However, some states enact poll taxes and literacy tests to discourage former slaves from voting. To prevent literacy laws from affecting other poor and illiterate people who were not former slaves, some states grandfathered in citizens who could vote previously, or if their ancestors could vote previously.

The laws are designed to prevent former slaves from voting and no one else.

1872

Susan B. Anthony and fifteen other women are arrested in Rochester, New York for attempting to vote in the presidential election. A point of historical interest: President Donald Trump pardoned Susan B. Anthony on August 18, 2020.

Former slave and activist Sojourner Truth is turned away when she demands a ballot at her polling place in Detroit.

1876

The Supreme Court determines American Indians are non-citizens and therefore cannot vote.

1882

The Chinese Exclusion Act prohibits Chinese immigrants from becoming citizens and voting.

1887

The Dawes Act allows Native Americans citizenship, and by default the right to vote, so long as they accept the breaking up of tribal lands and sever their tribal ties.

The national government passes the Edmunds-Tucker Act, which takes away the voting rights of women in Utah. The act is in response to polygamy in that state. It includes a requirement that any potential voter must make an anti-polygamy oath, marking a return of religious requirement for voting.

1890

When Wyoming becomes a state, it is the first state to grant women the right to vote. Women could vote in the territory of Wyoming since 1869. Other states soon followed: Colorado (1893), Utah (1896), Idaho (1896), Washington (1910), California (1911), Arizona (1912), Kansas (1912), Oregon (1912), Alaska (1913),

Illinois (1913), Montana (1914), Nevada (1914), Indiana (1917), Nebraska (1917), New York (1917), North Dakota (1917), Ohio (1917), Rhode Island (1917), Michigan (1918), Oklahoma (1918), South Dakota (1918), Iowa (1919), Maine (1919), Minnesota (1919), Missouri (1919), Tennessee (1919), Wisconsin (1919).

Notice, women could vote in twenty-eight states prior to the Nineteenth Amendment, in contrast to twenty-one states in which they could not. This illustrates the point that actions on the state level were affecting voting rights before sweeping national action took place. A majority of women could vote in the United States prior to the Nineteenth Amendment.

1913

State legislatures lose their representation in the United States Senate when the Seventeenth Amendment removes their authority to appoint senators and provides for the people to vote directly for their state's senators. This largely alters the republic from a mixed form of government to place more weight on democracy.

1915

Oklahoma is the last state to implement a grandfather clause to its literacy requirement in 1910. In *Guinn v. United States*, the Supreme Court rules that the clause conflicts with the Fifteenth Amendment, outlawing literacy tests for national elections.

1916

Jeannette Rankin of Montana becomes the first woman elected to the House of Representatives in Congress.

1919

Native Americans and other minority groups who served in World War I are granted citizenship and the right to vote.

1920

The Nineteenth Amendment passes. It grants suffrage to all women citizens (not all Native American and Asian women could become citizens).

1922

The Supreme Court determines that people of Japanese heritage cannot become citizens.

1924

Congress grants full citizenship to all Native Americans. This theoretically gives them the right to vote. Some states, however, still maintain policies that make it difficult to do so in some cases.

1925

Voting rights are granted to Filipino men who served three years in World War I.

1926

African American women are beaten in Birmingham, Alabama, for attempting to register to vote.

1947

Legal barriers preventing Native Americans from voting are removed when Miguel Trujillo, a Native American and former Marine, sues New Mexico for not allowing him to vote.

1952

Asians are granted the right to become citizens and vote.

1961

The Twenty-Third Amendment passes. It grants national voting rights to the citizens of Washington, D.C. However, this only applies to presidential elections, because the District of Columbia is not a state and thus has no senators or representatives. Washington, D.C. does have a limited voting delegate in the House of Representatives.

1964

The Twenty-Fourth Amendment passes. It guarantees that the right to vote in federal elections will not be denied for failure to pay any tax.

1965

The Voting Rights Act of 1965 eliminates restrictions, such as poll taxes and literacy tests. It expands voting accessibility by adding accommodations for voters with limited English, such as access to translators and ballots in multiple languages. It requires the Department of Justice to oversee election practices among states with a history of voting discrimination, a practice repealed by the Supreme Court in 2013.

1971

The Twenty-Sixth Amendment passes. It reduces the voting age from twenty-one to eighteen.

1993

The National Voter Registration Act makes it easier to register to vote at DMVs and public assistance centers.

2000

A federal court determines that citizens of US territories like Puerto Rico and Guam cannot vote in national elections because without statehood they have no senators, representatives, or electors.

Today, there are state and national election laws that determine when, where, and how elections are to take place. There continue to be debates about voter suppression and intimidation, or election integrity and confidence. There are still a few groups who cannot vote. Children under the age of eighteen cannot vote. Some felons and some people who are deemed mentally incapacitated cannot vote.

Aside from those listed above, there are no longer any large groups of people who cannot vote in the United States if they want to. There are no restrictions based on social class, race, sex, or any other prohibition that makes tyrants of some and oppresses others. As Americans, we have come far to make sure that citizenship and voting rights are protected equally for every citizen.

Humanity continues to wrestle with the application of the principle that "all men are created equal" and, therefore, that all people should be treated equally under the law. America has succeeded in many areas in that struggle, especially in voting rights. We went from universal voting in Virginia in 1619, in an attempt to eliminate errors of the past, to excessive disenfranchisement in 1723. The Founders codified the idea in 1776 that all people should be treated equally under the law and started our march back toward universal suffrage. We may not always be good, but we can always strive to be such, especially if we have guiding natural law principles to lead the way.

HUMANS ARE ENDOWED WITH CERTAIN UNALIENABLE RIGHTS

The Founders did not believe that the basic rights of humankind originated from any social compact, king, emperor, or governmental authority. The Virginia Declaration of Rights, adopted on June 12, 1776, states:

> *All men are by nature equally free and independent and have certain inherent rights, of which, when they enter into a state of society, they cannot, by any compact, deprive or divest their posterity; namely, the enjoyment of life and liberty, with the means of acquiring and possessing property, and pursuing and obtaining happiness and safety.*[38]

Notice that the words of the Declaration of Independence are very similar when it says:

---

[38] Virginia Declaration of Rights, 12 June 1776

> *We hold these truths to be self-evident, that all men are created equal, that they are endowed by their Creator with certain unalienable rights, that among these are life, liberty, and the pursuit of happiness.*[39]

Some scholars have wondered just what Jefferson meant by "the pursuit of happiness," but the meaning of this phrase was well understood when it was written. Perhaps John Adams said it even more clearly:

> *All men are born free and independent, and have certain natural, essential, and unalienable rights, among which may be reckoned with the right of enjoying and defending their lives and liberties; that of acquiring, possessing, and protecting property; in fine, that of seeking and obtaining their safety and happiness.*[40]

Of course, the concept of unalienable rights was by no means exclusive to the Founders. It was well understood by English defenders of the common law. Eleven years before the Declaration of Independence, Sir William Blackstone had written concerning the natural rights of man:

> *And these may be reduced to three principal or primary articles; the right of personal security; the right of personal liberty, and the right of private property; because as there is no other known method of compulsion, or of abridging man's natural free will, but by an infringement or diminution of one or other of these important rights, the preservation of these, inviolate, may justly be said to include the preservation of our civil immunities in their largest and most extensive sense.*[41]

Can one person's rights supersede another's? Thomas Jefferson answered this question with his definition of liberty:

---

[39] Declaration of Independence, 4 July 1776
[40] Massachusetts Constitution of 1780: Part the First. A Declaration of the Rights of the Inhabitants of the Commonwealth of Massachusetts, Article 1, 1780
[41] William Blackstone, *Commentaries on the Laws of England*, 1765

> *Liberty. . . is unobstructed action according to our will:*
> *but rightful liberty is unobstructed action according to*
> *our will, within the limits drawn around us by the equal*
> *rights of others.*[42]

Jefferson gives a broad definition of liberty as "unobstructed action," but with rightful liberty he paints a clear picture that our liberty only goes as far as another person's liberty. The moment our liberty begins to encroach upon another's, it ends there. He further clarifies that a civil law violates liberty if it allows one person to encroach upon another person's liberty.

For example, a person may have the right to move from point A to point B, but they do not have the right to take any path they want from point A to point B. To do so may violate the personal space or property of another.

Another example, as will be explained in the section on the First Amendment, ". . . all men are equally entitled to the free exercise of religion, according to the dictates of conscience. . ."[43] As such, one person's beliefs cannot encroach on another person's belief. A person operating a private business, therefore, cannot be forced to enter into a transaction with someone with whom they disagree; and vice versa, a person cannot be forced to buy a product from a company with different beliefs than theirs.

And a final example: every person has a right to keep the fruit of their labor and do with it what they wish. To take from one to give to another would violate the equal right of the former. This is true on the small scale of petty theft all the way to the extreme of slavery, in which all the fruits of one's labor are taken. Thomas Jefferson explained that if we take from one person because we think they have acquired too much and give their "excess" to others, it is a violation of our right to enjoy the fruits of our labors.

> *To take from one, because it is thought his own*
> *industry. . . has acquired too much, in order to spare to*

---

[42] Letter from Thomas Jefferson to Isaac H. Tiffany, 4 April 1819
[43] Virginia Declaration of Rights, 12 June 1776

> *others, who. . . have not exercised equal industry and*
> *skill, is to violate arbitrarily the first principle of*
> *association, the guarantee to everyone the free exercise*
> *of his industry and the fruits acquired by it.*[44]

The subject of keeping the fruits of your labors will be covered in depth in "Life, Liberty, and Property" and other sections below.

EYE FOR AN EYE

Is there ever a point at which a person can or should lose an unalienable right? Or, if rights are unalienable, what happens if we are alienated from them? These are important questions for any human being that chooses to have any contact with another human being, and the questions become more complex when multiple humans choose to interact.

On an individual level it is reasonably simple. When a person uses their liberty, the consequence is either more liberty or less liberty. Individually, the penalty of alienating oneself from a right is met with the consequence of losing all or some of that right. Within an individual's relationship with nature, natural consequences can alienate them from their rights.

The term *unalienable* only relates to human-to-human interaction. One human cannot alienate another human from their unalienable right. Or can they? Each person has the right of self-preservation. If one person seeks to take another's life, the victim has the right to defend their life with deadly force. The result of this could be the death of the aggressor. The victim is justified in alienating the aggressor from their unalienable right to life.

Justice is satisfied when the aggressor loses the very thing that they were willing to take from the victim: in this case, their life. The Old Testament refers to this as "an eye for an eye." The term does not literally mean that if someone pokes your eye out, they must have their eye poked out, too. It does no good for society to have two half-

---

[44] Letter from Thomas Jefferson to Joseph Milligan, 6 April 1816

blind people walking around. It does, however, mean that the perpetrator must lose the very thing, at least in value, that they were willing to take.

The application of "an eye for an eye" in the Old Testament in the case of a stolen sheep demanded that the thief give the stolen sheep back to the owner and give them an additional sheep.[45] The thief lost the very thing they took from their victim—a sheep. The same concept exists in our time too. If a person intentionally bounces a check in the state of Arizona, the law demands the perpetrator pay the victim two times the value of the check.[46]

Jefferson defined rightful liberty as freedom to do what you want with restrictions based on the liberty of those around us. With that in mind, and the "eye for an eye" principle, if a person is willing to step over the boundary of liberty and take the unalienable right of another, justice demands that they restore the alienated right back to the victim and that the perpetrator be alienated from the same right.

PROTECT EQUAL RIGHTS, NOT PROVIDE EQUAL THINGS

In Europe, during the days of the Founders, it was very popular to proclaim that the role of government was to take from the "haves" and give to the "have-nots" so that all might be "equal."

Benjamin Franklin commented on the destructive nature of government welfare in England and in America. He told a friend:

> *I have long been of your opinion, that your legal provision for the poor [in England] is a very great evil, operating as it does to the encouragement of idleness. We have followed your example, and begin now to see our error, and, I hope, shall reform it.[47]*

---

[45] King James Bible, Exodus 22:1, 4
[46] Arizona Revised Statues §13-1809
[47] Letter from Benjamin Franklin to Mr. Small, 5 November 1789

He further wrote:

> *To relieve the misfortunes of our fellow creatures is concurring with the Deity; it is godlike; but, if we provide encouragement for laziness, and supports for folly, may we not be found fighting against the order of God and Nature, which perhaps has appointed want and misery as the proper punishments for, and cautions against, as well as necessary consequences of, idleness and extravagance? Whenever we attempt to amend the scheme of Providence, and to interfere with the government of the world, we had need be very circumspect, lest we do more harm than good.*[48]

As Samuel Adams wrote:

> *The utopian schemes of leveling, and [providing] a community of goods, are as visionary and impracticable as those which vest all property in the Crown; they are arbitrary, despotic, and in our government, unconstitutional.*[49]

The American Founders perceived that this proposition contained a huge fallacy. They recognized that the people cannot delegate to their government control over anything except that which they have the lawful right to do themselves. For example, every person is entitled to the protection of their life and property. Therefore, it is perfectly legitimate to delegate to the government the task of setting up a police force to protect the life and property of all the people.

But suppose a kind-hearted man saw that one of his neighbors had two cars while another neighbor had none. What would happen if, in a spirit of benevolence, the kind man went over and took one of the cars from his prosperous neighbor and generously gave it to the neighbor in need? Obviously, he would be arrested for auto theft. No matter how kind his intentions, he would be guilty of flagrantly

---

[48] Letter from Benjamin Franklin to Peter Collinson, 9 May 1753

[49] Letter from Samuel Adams in the name of the Massachusetts House of Representatives to Dennys de Berdt, 12 January 1768

violating the natural rights of his prosperous neighbor who was entitled to be protected in his property. Of course, the two-car neighbor could donate a car to his poor neighbor if he liked, but that must be his decision, and not the prerogative of the kind-hearted neighbor.

Now suppose the entire neighborhood got together and voted on whether the prosperous neighbor should give a car to the poor neighbor. Suppose the results were a landslide, and 99% voted to take the car and give it to the neighbor. What would happen? Ninety-nine percent of the neighborhood would go to jail.

Instead of holding a neighborhood election, you bring the issue to the legislature and convince a majority to pass a law requiring the prosperous neighbor to give his car to the poor neighbor. One day, soon after the law passes, the sheriff knocks on the prosperous neighbor's door to collect the car to give it to the poor neighbor. The sheriff, the very individual that at one time had authority to protect property, is now using that authority to take it.

What is wrong with these scenarios? Do we have the authority as an individual to take from one neighbor and give to another? No.

Do we somehow acquire the authority to take from one to give to another when we get together collectively as a neighborhood? No.

Do we have the authority to ask government to take from one neighbor and give to another? No.

Frederic Bastiat called this concept "legal plunder."

If we are to operate under the premise that government gets its authority from the people, then government cannot have authority that we do not already have ourselves. If we do not have the authority to take from one neighbor and give to another, as individuals or collectively, we do not have the ability to delegate that to the government. We can only delegate that which is ours—like the preservation of our life, liberty, and property.

What is the only way we can get the car from one neighbor over to the other? Take it? No. Buy it? No. Even if a neighbor offered the other one million dollars, would they be required to sell it? No. What is the only way? If the owner of the car consents to it—giving it away, selling it; no matter the method, the owner must consent.

What is it that binds the car owner so closely to their property that only they can consent to it leaving their possession? Because it is their property? How does the fact that it is their property bind it to them? What binds our property to us?

THE UNALIENABLE RIGHT TO PROPERTY

Suppose a person is in the wilderness. They are not on anyone's property. They come across a wild apple tree. Nobody owns this apple tree; it is a product of nature. The philosopher John Locke questioned how a person could take possession of an apple. He thought that because a wild tree is in a state of nature, everyone in the world owns it. Therefore, would the person need to ask everyone in the world permission to take an apple? No, John Locke concluded. He would starve if that were the case:

> *. . . will any one say he had no right to those acorns or apples he thus appropriated because he had not the consent of all mankind to make them his?. . . If such a consent as that was necessary, [the] man [would have] starved, notwithstanding the plenty God had given him. . .*[50]

The person decides to begin gathering some apples off the wild apple tree. They gather a bushel and carry them home. They begin to prepare the apples. Apple pie, applesauce, apple strudel, and whatever else you make out of apples. They get a bit hungry and decide to eat an apple.

They then chew the apple, or predigest it. Next, they swallow it and the stomach continues to break it down to allow it to move on into

---

[50] John Locke, *Second Treatise of Government*, Chapter 5: "Of Property," 1689

the intestines. Once in the intestines, their body extracts the nutrients from it.

Now, whose nutrients are those? The person's, of course.

At what point did it become theirs? Locke said:

> *Though the earth and all inferior creatures be common [as the gift from God] to all men, yet every man has a "property" in his own "person." This, nobody has any right to but himself. The "labor" of his body and the "work" of his hands, we may say, are properly his. Whatsoever, then, he removes out of the state that Nature hath provided and left it in, he hath mixed his labor with it, and joined to it something that is his own, and thereby makes it his property. . .*
>
> *He that is nourished by the acorns he picked up under an oak, or the apples he gathered from the trees in the wood, has certainly appropriated them to himself. Nobody can deny but the nourishment is his. I ask, then, when did they begin to be his? When he digested? or when he ate? or when he boiled? or when he brought them home? or when he picked them up? And it is plain, if the first gathering made them not his, nothing else could.*[51]

The person put something of themselves into it. They traded their labor; they traded their life and liberty for the apple, and it became theirs. Remember, the apple tree Locke is talking about is a wild apple tree. It is not owned by anyone.

LIFE, LIBERTY, AND PROPERTY

Consider the following equation:

LIFE + LIBERTY = PROPERTY

Your property is the sum of, or fruit of, your life and liberty. You purchase your property not with money, but with your life and

---

[51] Ibid.

liberty. Say you make $60,000 per year, you purchase a car for $30,000, and someone steals that car. If you never get the car back, what will you also never get back? If you recall, in algebra your teacher taught that if you take something from one side of the equal sign, you must take an equal part from the other side. If you remove property. . .

LIFE + LIBERTY =~~PROPERTY~~

. . . then you must remove life and liberty as well.

~~LIFE~~ + ~~LIBERTY~~ = ~~PROPERTY~~

The thief has not only stolen your car, but has stolen six months of your life and liberty.

Using the equation LIFE + LIBERTY = PROPERTY, in addition to our money and other physical property, there are many other things that can be considered property.

Education—we spend our life and liberty acquiring knowledge.

Intellectual property—we spend our life and liberty to invent.

Relationships—we spend our life and liberty cultivating relationships. Relationships often fail when one party is not willing to sacrifice life and liberty for the other.

Reputation—we spend our life and liberty contributing to society and building our reputation.

Good works—we sacrifice our life and liberty for others. This is what makes charity so sacred and why it is not charity if we do not freely give our life and liberty, but it is taken from us.

Bad works—ever heard of "owning your sins?" We own them because we purchase our bad works with our life and liberty.

This property equation does more than explain the value of property. It allows us to evaluate our lives—we know the value that we place on our life and liberty by the property we are purchasing with that life and liberty. Many people believe that the purpose of life is to obtain things of value, real value, things that bring true happiness. In other words, we are free to spend our life and liberty in the pursuit of happiness. Thomas Jefferson said:

> *Happiness. . . does not depend on the condition of life in which chance has placed [us], but is always the result of a good conscience, good health, occupation, and freedom in all just pursuits.*

Property is inseparably connected to life and liberty because we use our life and liberty to purchase our property. It is important to recognize that property itself is not sacred, but only the right which someone has to acquire that property. Justice George Sutherland of the U.S. Supreme Court once told the New York State Bar Association:

> *. . . the individual. . . has three great rights, equally sacred from arbitrary interference: the right to his LIFE, the right to his LIBERTY, the right to his PROPERTY. . . The three rights are so bound together as to be essentially one right. To give a man his life but deny him his liberty, is to take from him all that makes his life worth living. To give him his liberty but take from him the property which is the fruit and badge of his liberty, is to still leave him a slave.*[52]

Taking property "is still to leave him a slave." The seizure of property without consent is bondage because in the taking, that individual is losing the fruit of their life and liberty. In this same spirit Abraham Lincoln once said:

> *Property is the fruit of labor. Property is desirable, is a positive good in the world. That some should be rich shows that others may become rich and hence is just encouragement to industry and enterprise. Let not him who is houseless pull down the house of another, but let him work diligently to build one for himself, thus by*

---

[52] George Sutherland, Annual Address, New York Bar Association Annual Meeting, 21 January 1921

example assuring that his own shall be safe from violence. . . I take it that it is best for all to leave each man free to acquire property as fast as he can. Some will get wealthy. I don't believe in a law to prevent a man from getting rich; it would do more harm than good.[53]

We cannot take a person's car and give it to their neighbor without the owner's consent, because that car is connected to their life and liberty. If we take their car without their consent, it is theft and would deprive them of their life and liberty.

The protection of property, therefore, becomes the purpose of government. If we pass laws that protect our property, those laws are also protecting our life and liberty. Property becomes that great measuring device to determine where our liberty lies.

If we do not have the total right and control of our property because of theft, fraud, etc., we know we are too far toward anarchy or chaos. When we do not have the total right and control of our property because of excessive taxation, oppressive regulation, etc., we know we are too far toward tyranny. When we have the total right and control of our property, we know that we have found the balanced center between tyranny and anarchy—we have found liberty.

Where an excess of power prevails, property of no sort is duly respected. No man is safe in his opinions, his person, his faculties, or his possessions. Where there is an excess of [freedom], the effect is the same, tho' from an opposite cause.[54]

THE ORIGIN OF WEALTH

There are two schools of thought about wealth: either there is an almost infinite ability to create it or there is only a finite amount of wealth that must be shared. If there is only a finite amount, then if one person obtains wealth, someone else misses out on the ability to

---

[53] Abraham Lincoln, speech to the New York Workingmen's Democratic Republican Association, 21 March 1864

[54] James Madison, "Property," *National Gazette*, 29 March 1792

obtain it. The finite rule of thought can be likened to a pie. There are only so many slices of the pie. If other people get to the pie before you, you may not get a slice, or your slice may be much smaller than someone else's. It is the finite concept that leads society to the tendency to promote the redistribution of wealth rather than promote the creation of wealth. It's a "hard-knock life" mentality.

But what if wealth was infinite? Society could flourish. Neighbor would be less inclined to wrestle with neighbor in an effort to secure their slice of the pie. Forget the slice; instead, they could make their own pie—or two pies, or more.

If the LIFE + LIBERTY = PROPERTY equation is a true principle of natural law, then wealth can be created by trading life and liberty for it. Wealth can be obtained in many ways: inherited, gifted, stolen, etc. But it can only be created by exchanging it for life and liberty. The good news is the ability to create wealth exists as long as there is life and liberty to create it—for humankind's sake, we hope that is infinite. The bad news is you must work for it.

For example, the ingredients for a single loaf of bread cost approximately one dollar. If you take that dollar's worth of ingredients and make a loaf of bread, you could sell it for three dollars—five or six dollars if you're really good. How did a dollar's worth of ingredients suddenly multiply three to six times its value? The addition of your life and liberty. Let us return to an excerpt from the John Locke quote above:

> *. . . Whatsoever, then, he removes out of the state that Nature hath provided and left it in, he hath mixed his labor with it, and joined to it something that is his own, and thereby makes it his property. . .*[55]

The baker mixed their life and liberty (labor) into the dollar's worth of ingredients and made a loaf of bread worth more than the ingredients it includes. You could illustrate this created wealth with the following equation:

---

[55] John Locke, *Second Treatise of Government*, Chapter 5: "Of Property," 1689

(LIFE + LIBERTY) × PROPERTY = WEALTH

Life and liberty only exist within an individual, therefore wealth can only be created by an individual. Businesses and governments cannot create wealth. They can only do so by utilizing the life and liberty of individuals. However, it is fascinating to realize that individuals can combine their life and liberty to create wealth exponentially, which is exactly what businesses do. Their jointly-created wealth is greater than the sum of their individually-created wealth. That equation may look something like this:

[(LIFE + LIBERTY) + (LIFE + LIBERTY) + (LIFE + LIBERTY)] × PROPERTY = WEALTH[3]

The life and liberty contributed to the equation could be manual labor, skilled labor, managerial labor, and includes intellectual property, educational knowledge, etc. Each contribution may vary in value depending on skill level, talent, etc. Henry Ford's intellectual property of assembly line production, added to the skill of engineers, labor of line workers, and black paint, resulted in more pieces of automobile pie for the rich and middle class alike.

Adam Smith referred to this distribution of skills as the "division of labor." In his famous book, *The Wealth of Nations*, he explained the effectiveness of the concept by giving an example of it in the real world.

To take an example, therefore, from a very trifling manufacture; but one in which the division of labour has been very often taken notice of, the trade of the pin-maker; a workman not educated to this business (which the division of labour has rendered a distinct trade), nor acquainted with the use of the machinery employed in it (to the invention of which the same division of labour has probably given occasion), could scarce, perhaps, with his utmost industry, make one pin in a day, and certainly could not make twenty. But in the way in which this business is now carried on, not only the whole work is a peculiar trade, but it is divided into a number of branches, of which the greater part are likewise peculiar trades. One man draws out the wire, another straights it, a third cuts it, a fourth points it, a fifth grinds it at the top for receiving, the head; to make the head requires two or three distinct operations; to put it on is a peculiar business, to whiten the pins is another; it is even a trade by itself to put them into the paper; and the important business of making a pin is, in this manner, divided into about eighteen distinct operations, which, in some manufactories, are all performed by distinct hands, though in others the same man will sometimes perform two or three of them. I have seen a small manufactory of this kind where ten men only were employed, and where some of them consequently performed two or three distinct operations. But though they were very poor, and therefore but indifferently accommodated with the necessary machinery, they could, when they exerted themselves, make among them about twelve pounds of pins in a day. There are in a pound upwards of four thousand pins of a middling size. Those ten persons, therefore, could make among them upwards of forty-eight thousand pins in a day. Each person, therefore, making a tenth part of forty-eight thousand pins, might be considered as making four thousand eight hundred pins in a day. But if they had all wrought separately and independently, and without any of them having been educated to this peculiar business, they certainly could not each of them have made twenty, perhaps not one pin in a day; that is, certainly, not the two hundred and fortieth, perhaps not the four thousand eight hundredth part of what they are at present capable of performing, in consequence of a proper division and combination of their different operations.[56]

---

[56] Adam Smith, *The Wealth of Nations*, 1776

Adam Smith's example illustrates the multiplying effects of wealth creation when a number of people combine their life and liberty, and perhaps some already created wealth. Together they create more wealth than they could have created on their own, even if they added all their separately created wealth together.

The natural law principle of wealth creation, rather than wealth distribution, presents a society with infinite potential so long as the property and wealth purchased with life and liberty is protected with the same fervor as the protection of life and liberty itself. Before the importance of protecting property is explored, it should be established what is not property, but captivity.

PRIMITIVE NATURAL LAW OF PROPERTY RESULTS IN CAPTIVITY

There are two natural laws regarding property, one primitive and the other sophisticated. The primitive law says that property is obtained by the strong taking it from the weak, in whatever manner the strong wishes. The sophisticated is based on the idea that each individual is born with the right and control of their own person, what they obtain with their person is their property, and only the individual has the right to control that property—regardless of whether they are weak or strong.

Primitive natural law of property is a kind of "survival of the fittest" mentality, where however someone acquires something, it must be theirs because they had the strength to acquire it. Survival of the fittest is a natural law. Proof of this can be seen in the animal kingdom and primeval human history, but it is not a natural law for human relations because it disregards human reason, intellect, and relationships. Humans could choose to ignore human reason and base their society on this primitive natural law. Unfortunately, humans often do choose primitive natural law. It looks something like this:

- Anyone who is stronger or superior could take the life, liberty, or property of another (monarchy or oligarchy);

- A mob of people who are stronger, superior, or larger in numbers could take the life, liberty, or property of another group of people (ochlocracy or democracy);

- People, as individuals, a small group, or a large group, can delegate to others the taking of life, liberty, or property from other individuals or groups and redistribute it back to themselves (democracy or socialism).

However, if people choose to live under primitive natural law, they must be willing to lose their life, liberty, or property if a stronger person or group chooses to take it from them. Under the primitive natural law of property, bringing others into captivity by stealing property, taking life, and slavery would all be acceptable, be it blatant or subtle.

Primitive natural law of property is the condition most humans have found themselves in throughout history. The Founders sought to change the fate of humanity by liberating them from captivity by establishing a nation built on the more sophisticated natural law of property. Reason and intellect give humans the ability to rise above a hand-to-mouth, survival of the fittest, primitive natural law existence. Most humans desire a more peaceful, humane existence in which the weak and the strong can thrive in harmony. This is achieved by recognizing that only an individual has a right to their life, liberty, and property, and that laws should be established to protect those rights for the weak and the strong from encroachments by the weak or the strong.

We have explored what sophisticated natural law of property is in the sections above. Now, we'll explore what primitive natural law of property looks like and how it results in captivity—the loss of life, liberty, or property. But before moving forward, primitive natural law of property disregards human intellect and reason. It may be natural law in the animal kingdom, but it can be argued that it is not natural law in human relations. Therefore, primitive natural law of property is not natural law because it is contrary to human progress. From this point forward in this book, actions that prevent an individual's right and control of property, allowing one to bring another into captivity, will not be considered natural law for human relations. Conversely, actions that protect an individual's right of life, liberty, and property shall rightfully be considered natural law.

If the rightful acquiring of, and the complete right and control of property can be used as an indication of liberty, then the inability to acquire and control your own property must be an indication of captivity. If someone claims the automatic right to govern another, they are claiming the right and control of another's "person." This is captivity. If someone takes the fruit of what you have acquired with your "person," that too is captivity—that is slavery.

Remember John Locke's point before he theorized how the apple became the picker's:

> *every man has a "property" in his own "person." This, nobody has any right to but himself.*[57]

First and foremost, we are born with a property in our own person. Nobody is born with the inherent right to govern or take possession of another. It thus follows that no one is born with the inherent right to govern the property obtained by another without their consent.

We have property in our person and, as James Madison said, property in our rights, and property in what we have spent our life and liberty to obtain. However, the latter is only true if it has been obtained legally and morally. Possession alone does not make property yours. Locke indicated that your labor must be mixed with something that is in a state of nature—which all humans own in common—for it to become yours. The natural resource must be on land that is not owned by anyone.

A modern application of this principle can be found in mineral claims on public lands. Many states and the national government allow an individual to file a mining claim on public land for the purposes of surveying and prospecting for minerals. Most states require that the person holding the claim report what labor they have

---

[57] John Locke, *Second Treatise of Government*, Chapter 5: "Of Property," 1689

performed on the claim. If a claim is left dormant, meaning no labor has occurred, the claim may be forfeited. The claim holder who adds his labor to the minerals they extract from the public lands becomes the rightful owner of those recovered minerals. They do not pay money for the minerals, with the exception of a few fees. They pay for it with their labor—their life and liberty. The minerals are their property.

Conversely, if a person takes something that is already owned by another person, they have stolen that property and it is not theirs, even if they used their life and liberty to obtain it. This is so because the rightful owner already purchased the property with their life and liberty. The actions of stealing, robbing, or thievery are a violation of natural law because, first, the thief is knowingly depriving another of their life and liberty, and second, because they are stealing their own life and liberty in the process. If they are caught, they will have wasted their life and liberty used in the robbery and will lose more as they labor to pay restitution to their victim. If they end up in jail, they have undoubtedly brought themselves into captivity.

Most, if not all, people would agree that to take something that is not theirs without consent is wrong and a clear violation of the victim's natural rights. It is not just the taking that violates another's rights, it is doing so without their consent. If they consent, there is no foul. If they do not consent, it is theft, it is captivity.

Taxation without representation is taxation without consent—it is captivity. The confiscation of property through eminent domain laws without just compensation is captivity. The loss of property by theft or fraud is captivity. To labor without agreed-upon compensation is captivity. In a nutshell, anything a person obtains while bringing captivity upon another is not rightfully their property. This is most obvious if someone takes one hundred percent of the fruits of your labor. That is the most abhorrent form of captivity—it is slavery.

PARENTS HAVE AN INHERENT RIGHT TO GOVERN THEIR CHILDREN

But what about children and parents? Parents have a temporary right over their children, only because they have agreed to be responsible for the child in nourishing their body, mind, and heart until they reach maturity. John Locke explained it like this:

> *The power, then, that parents have over their children arises from that duty which is incumbent on them, to take care of their offspring during the imperfect state of childhood. To inform the mind, and govern the actions of their yet ignorant nonage, till reason shall take its place. . .*[58]

Locke explains that we are born with the liberty to act for ourselves, but while a child is in a state unable to act for themselves, they must be guided by their parents who have that obligation.

> *But when he comes to the estate that made his father a free man, the son is a free man too.*[59]

The question parents often ask themselves is, how do we know when our child is ready to make their own decisions? When are they ready to embark on their own? Locke covered that too:

> *Is a man under the law of Nature? What made him free of that law? What gave him a free disposing of his property, according to his own will, within the compass of that law? I answer, an estate wherein he might be supposed capable to know that law, that so he might keep his actions within the bounds of it.*[60]

A person must first understand a law of nature and keep his actions within the boundaries of that law. Knowing that a vehicle moving at fast speed can kill, and understanding that walking in the street is

---

[58] John Locke, *An Essay Concerning the True Original, Extent and End of Civil Government*, 1690
[59] Ibid.
[60] Ibid.

dangerous, are the first steps to knowing a child is ready to cross a busy road.

> *When he has acquired that state, he is presumed to know how far that law is to be his guide, and how far he may make use of his freedom, and so comes to have it; till then, somebody else must guide him, who is presumed to know how far the law allows a liberty. If such a state of reason, such an age of discretion made him free, the same shall make his son free too.*[61]

Reaching back to Jefferson's definition of liberty and mingling it with Locke's thoughts, a child is ready to embark on their own when they understand that their actions must stay within certain boundaries, and in a free society, those boundaries are drawn around them by the liberty of others. This explains why children are not granted the right to vote; they have not reached the level of maturity to exercise that right with a reasonable understanding of just human relations.

Children are never their parents' property, but the parents do have a duty to guide them to maturity in liberty and provide food and shelter while they progress toward that maturity. Children are not property even though their parents spend their life and liberty in raising them. Children are their own property, just like everyone else.

SLAVERY IS CONTRARY TO NATURAL LAW

The title of this section, "Slavery is Contrary to Natural Law," seems like an obvious, self-evident truth. History has proven that that truth is not so self-evident. There is no continent, no country, and no race that has not had slavery at some point in history. There has been no century and no decade that has not seen the practice somewhere in the world, even to this day.[62] This may sound like hyperbole—sadly, it is not. This is not said to condone, excuse, or diminish slavery. On

---

[61] Ibid.
[62] *Slavery: A World History*, by Milton Meltzer, 1993

the contrary, that history is a condemnation of all humankind. Slavery seems to be a natural condition of humankind, which makes it remarkable and encouraging that so many nations have rid themselves of the practice today.

It is important to point out the universal condemnation of humankind as participants in slavery, because a practice so widespread must have many advocates who claim that slavery is a natural law. Yes, there are many.

The purpose of this section is not to give a comprehensive history of slavery, or point fingers, as if to draw attention away from the guilt every nation bears over the practice. "Everyone is doing it" is not a valid excuse for slavery. The purpose of this section is to examine those arguments made by people who claim slavery is a right, a natural law, a gift from heaven, and property over which they have claim. We will then debunk those claims using natural law.

There is a decades-old debate about whether Plato included slavery in the utopian society promoted in his *Republic*. He clearly states that Greeks should not enslave Greeks. From there, his language is a bit fuzzy, hence the debate. It appears as if he promotes the enslavement of non-Greeks, whom he called barbarians. He also mentions slaves among those who shall find peace in his perfect city.

Plato may or may not have agreed with individual slavery, but he did promote a form of collective slavery in *Republic*. He divided society into three classes: a working class, a manager class, and a ruling class. The working class had no private property—theirs was collective property. They worked to feed and sustain the upper classes. They did not enjoy the control of the fruits of their life and liberty; it was taken without their consent. They were slaves.

Plato's view of slavery may be blurred in *Republic*, but in his writing, *Gorgias*, his thoughts are revealed. He contends that a ruling class should have more property than an inferior class, not by ambition and hard work, but by nature.

> *. . . nature herself intimates that it is just for the better to have more than the worse, the more powerful than the weaker; and in many ways she shows, among men as well as among animals, and indeed among whole cities and races, that justice consists in the superior ruling over and having more than the inferior.*[63]

One point that seems elusive to Plato, and other defenders of natural slavery, is that there is always a bigger fish. Their arrogance is revealed by their failure to recognize or admit that there is always someone smarter and stronger than them. If their law of nature is correct, they must submit themselves as slaves to their natural superiors. History has yet to present a willing candidate for slavery. This tells us that people believe in the superior oppressing or enslaving the inferior so long as they themselves are in the superior class. Or they are in a neutral class that is not affected by the oppression.

In contrast, Plato's pupil, Aristotle, was very clear about his view of slavery. His writings in *Politics* argued against those who thought slavery was contrary to nature. In doing so, he revealed his belief that slavery is a law of nature.

> *But is there any one thus intended by nature to be a slave, and for whom such a condition is expedient and right, or rather is not all slavery a violation of nature?*
>
> *There is no difficulty in answering this question, on grounds both of reason and of fact. For that some should rule and others be ruled is a thing not only necessary, but expedient; from the hour of their birth, some are marked out for subjection, others for rule.*[64]

Aristotle disagreed with Plato's belief that community-owned property, or communism, would produce a better society than privately-owned property. Aristotle surmised that private property gave more opportunity for voluntary charity and would produce a

---

[63] Plato, *Gorgias*, 380 B.C.
[64] Aristotle, *Politics*, 350 B.C.

more virtuous society. He then falsely concluded that nature considers a slave as a master's property.

> *Property is a part of the household, and the art of acquiring property is a part of the art of managing the household. . . And so, in the arrangement of the family, a slave is a living possession. . . whereas the slave is not only the slave of his master, but wholly belongs to him. Hence we see what is the nature and office of a slave; he who is by nature not his own but another's man, is by nature a slave; and he may be said to be another's man who, being a human being, is also a possession.*[65]

We see that the conflicting ideas of Aristotle's private property and Plato's community property have little bearing on their view that slavery is a law of nature. The commonality between Plato and Aristotle was not property, but superiority. The belief that nature made some better than others is the basis for their justification of slavery. Proponents believe that because one group of people are superior, that fact alone justifies and allows the superior to rob the fruits of the inferior in the form of slavery.

One prevailing thought today is that private property, in a free market or capitalistic society, is sympathetic towards slavery because slaves were considered private property. "American slavery is necessarily imprinted on the DNA of American capitalism,"[66] wrote Sven Beckert and Seth Rockman. The theory is that the idea of property rights and its critical importance in a free-market system was established to protect and institutionalize slavery. Historically, that theory is placing the cart before the horse. Laws institutionalizing the protection of private property existed in America long before laws institutionalized slavery as property.

Property as a fundamental natural right was well established in English common law hundreds of years before 1607, when

---

[65] Ibid.

[66] Sven Beckert and Seth Rockman, *Slavery's Capitalism: A New History of American Economic Development*, 2016

Jamestown, the first permanent English settlement in America, was founded. Jamestown began as a sort of martial law aristocracy. By the end of the first decade in Virginia, the settlers started to alter that system by applying private property rights that were ever so familiar in English common law. This led to the Great Charter. Written in 1618 and instituted in the spring of 1619, the Great Charter sought to protect property rights in an effort to encourage investors and settlers to participate in the Virginia venture. Protecting private property lowered the risk that they might lose their property after investing life and limb.

In the fall of 1619, twenty or so African slaves arrived on a Dutch ship, the *White Lion*, and were exchanged for food. They sailed to Virginia as slaves but disembarked the *White Lion* as indentured servants. The recently enacted Great Charter and acts passed by the new House of Burgesses had no provisions for slavery. Slavery was a practice long since abandoned in England, in approximately 1200 A.D.,[67] and was somewhat foreign to the Jamestown settlers in 1619. However, their new laws in the Great Charter had detailed provisions for indentured servants. As such, each African disembarked, not as a slave, but as an indentured servant. They worked for an indentured term, likely three to five years, for those who paid the captain for their passage. Upon completing their time, they were freed and given land of their own to work by the sweat of their brow and reap the fruits of their own labor. At that point, they would have been known as freemen.[68]

At the time, the indentured servant system was used to encourage people to come to Virginia. Someone had to pay for their passage if they could not do so themselves. Sometimes someone would pay for another's passage in advance, and other times someone would offer

---

[67] The history of slavery in England is much more complicated than indicated here. Slaves in England were from numerous European countries, including the English themselves. First, it was made law that a Brit could not enslave a Brit. Eventually slavery was outlawed, with the exception of a few single instances here and there throughout English history after 1200 A.D.

[68] Freeman: A person who enjoys their liberty, one who is not an indentured servant. They need not own property. It seems, for a time in the early years after the Great Charter in 1619 Virginia, any free person, black or white, male or female, was considered a freeman.

to pay once they arrived. On a few occasions, someone would not offer to pay until months or even years after their arrival. The point was, someone eventually had to pay. Whoever paid the passage was paid back by having the person they paid for work for them under contract for three to five years.

In 1619, those arriving Africans' passage required payment. Governor George Yeardly and his Cape Merchant Abraham Piersey provided food and supplies as a form of payment. In return, the new arrivals worked off the debt in the form of indentured servitude. Once the term of service was over, as per the law, they would have been given fifty acres of land, several bushels of corn, and other necessary supplies. Some eventually sponsored and employed their own indentured servants as the cycle repeated itself.[69]

To be sure, the English were not saints. Although they had eliminated slavery in England some four hundred years prior, in 1619, they were dabbling in the African slave trade between other countries and British territories. By 1800, the British were a leading slave-trading nation, bringing and selling more slaves to Americans than anyone else. But in 1619 British Virginia, there was no institution of slavery, only the institution of indentured servitude.

About thirty years into the settlement of Virginia, African indentured servitude began to morph. Within about fifty years, laws related to slavery began to appear, and in 1705, 1724, and 1725 the institution of slavery was officially codified into law. Private property and free market laws had been in existence for more than one hundred years in Virginia before slavery became an institution.

Understanding history in context is necessary to disconnect the idea of private property rights as a natural law principle from the claim that private property rights were declared to protect the institution of slavery. Protecting private property rights came first. The claim that slaves were property and therefore should be protected by

---

[69] This description is not meant to paint the picture that the twenty or so Africans that came to Virginia in 1619 did so willfully. To the contrary, they were stolen from their homeland in Africa by the Spanish ship *San Juan Bautista*. They were destined for the Spanish silver mines in Mexico.

private property rights was a bastardization of the natural law principle of private property. Pro-slavery advocates use superiority to justify slavery and private property rights to secure a false perception of it. Slavery is not about property—it is about superiority. Proponents are taking advantage of a natural law as important, unalienable, and sacred as life and liberty. This was why slavery proponents attempted to mold slavery into natural law; if they could convince the law that slavery was about property, they would tap into a right that was protected by English common law and was almost sacramental in America.

The type of pro-slavery property that Aristotle philosophized about, and the private property that Jefferson declared to the tribunals of the world, are not the same. Pro-slavery societies believe people are property because they think, like Plato, that property is obtained because of superiority. The Founders believed that property was acquired by exercising our equal rights of life and liberty without infringing on the life and liberty of others. The Founders' view of the natural law of property and the pro-slavery view of the natural law of property are polar opposites. The former is about equality of all and the latter about the inequality of all, divisible by superiority and inferiority.

Slavery promotes primitive natural law. Aristotle's message of "some are marked out for subjection, others for rule"[70] is very different from Jefferson's "all men are created equal."[71] Aristotle said many more unbelievable things in his attempt to justify slavery. He compared the slave to the evil part of human nature and eventually degraded the slave to an animal incapable of reasoning for themselves. But enough of Aristotle.

The elimination and permanent extinction of slavery will not occur if society demonizes private property. It will only be extinct in perpetuity if society continues to reject its true origin—superiority. One need not look far to find that almost all tyrannical oppression exists because one group deems themselves superior to another—

---

[70] Aristotle, "On Slavery," *The Politics*, c. 330 B.C.
[71] Declaration of Independence, 4 July 1776

bullying to the worst degree. If we want to prevent slavery, any form of it, from returning, we must root out the superiority complex in ourselves and others—and do so without developing a superiority complex.

The superiority slavery mindset gets much worse in the South. There are numerous nineteenth-century quotes from the people of South Carolina and Georgia that illustrate just how deeply rooted the slave culture had become in the South. Slavery was agreed to be an unnatural practice by most (if not all) delegates to the Constitutional Convention of 1787. By the 1830s, though, politicians from the South were declaring slavery a natural law. John C. Calhoun, senator from South Carolina, said:

> *The defense of human liberty against the aggressions of despotic power have been always the most efficient in States where domestic slavery was to prevail.*[72]

James H. Hammond, representative from South Carolina, said:

> *To such a country [slavery] is as natural as the climate itself, as the birds and beasts to which that climate is congenial. . . It is equally the order of Providence that slavery should exist among a planting people, beneath a southern sun. . .*

> *. . . it is no evil. On the contrary, I believe it to be the greatest of all the great blessings which a kind Providence has bestowed upon our glorious region. For without it, our fertile soil and our fructifying climate would have been given to us in vain. And as to its impoverishing and demoralizing influence, the simple and irresistible answer to that is, that the history of the short period during which we have enjoyed it has rendered our southern country proverbial for its wealth, its genius, and its manners. . .*

---

[72] John C. Calhoun, Congressional Debates, 24th Congress, 2nd Session, 1836–37

> *. . . Sir, I do firmly believe that domestic slavery, regulated as ours is, produces the highest toned, the purest, best organization of society that has ever existed on the face of the earth. . .*[73]

Notice some freedom-centric words in the quotes above: "defense of human liberty," "highest toned, the purest, best organization of society," etc. Some words may sound like freedom, but they are woven into the filthy tapestry of slavery—captivity of the most evil kind.

Jefferson may have written "all men are created equal"[74] in contradiction to his practice of owning slaves, but he never connected those words with a justification of slavery. "All men are created equal" was his hope. It was his goal. It was an idea he aspired to, even if he was not living that idea in its entirety. As Abraham Lincoln said, America "was conceived in liberty and dedicated to the <u>proposition</u> that all men are created equal."[75]

By February 4, 1860, seven states[76] had seceded from the United States. On that date, delegates from those states met in Alabama to form a new government. The Constitution of the Confederate States of America was completed on March 11, 1861, and ratified on March 29. It mirrored the U.S. Constitution in many ways. However, it differed significantly by establishing slavery as foundational. It included provisions such as, "no. . . law denying or impairing the right of property in negro slaves shall be passed."[77]

On February 18, 1861, Alexander Stephens, from Georgia, was chosen as vice president of the Confederacy. Only a few weeks before the South fired upon Fort Sumter, thereby starting the Civil War, he gave his famous Cornerstone Speech, where he declared the

---

[73] James, H. Hammond, *Register of Debates in Congress*, Vol. XII, 1 Feb 1836
[74] Declaration of Independence, 4 July 1776
[75] Abraham Lincoln, Gettysburg Address, 19 November 1863, emphasis added
[76] South Carolina, Mississippi, Florida, Alabama, Georgia, Louisiana, and Texas
[77] Constitution of the Confederate States of America, 29 March 1860

new Confederate Constitution superior to the "old" U.S. Constitution.

> *The new [Confederate] Constitution has put at rest forever all the agitating questions relating to. . . African slavery as it exists among us—the proper status of the negro in our form of civilization. This was the immediate cause of the late rupture and present revolution. Jefferson, in his forecast, had anticipated this, as the "rock upon which the old Union would split." He was right. What was conjecture with him, is now a realized fact. But whether he fully comprehended the great truth upon which that rock stood and stands, may be doubted. The prevailing ideas entertained by him and most of the leading statesmen at the time of the formation of the old Constitution were, that the enslavement of the African was in violation of the laws of nature; that it was wrong in principle, socially, morally and politically. It was an evil they knew not well how to deal with; but the general opinion of the men of that day was, that, somehow or other, in the order of Providence, the institution would be evanescent and pass away. . . Those ideas, however, were fundamentally wrong. They rested upon the assumption of the equality of races. This was an error. It was a sandy foundation, and the idea of a Government built upon it—when the "storm came and the wind blew, it fell."*

> *Our new [Confederate] government is founded upon exactly the opposite ideas; its foundations are laid, its cornerstone rests, upon the great truth that the negro is not equal to the white man; that slavery, subordination to the superior race, is his natural and normal condition. This, our new government, is the first, in the history of the world, based upon this great physical, philosophical, and moral truth. This truth has been slow in the process of its development, like all other truths in the various departments of science.*

> *... look with confidence to the ultimate universal acknowledgement of the truths upon which our system rests? [The Confederate States of America] is the first government ever instituted upon the principles in strict conformity to nature, and the ordination of Providence, in furnishing the materials of human society. Many governments have been founded upon the principle of the subordination and serfdom of certain classes of the same race; such were and are in violation of the laws of nature. Our system commits no such violation of nature's laws.*[78]

It seems incomprehensible, but Alexander Stephens and others in his day believed they were following divinely written natural law principles. They believed that the physical characteristics of Africans, i.e., darker skin, stronger bone and muscle structure, etc., were proof that nature intended for them to be laborers, and the "white race," having "intellectual superiority," was intended to be their masters. That "superiority" idea rears its ugly head again. They believed that those physical traits were well suited for the subtropical regions of North America. The thought was that the South was foreordained to host the practice of slavery. They also believed that because the practice was growing in the South, not diminishing, it was evident that God ordained their use of slavery.

Simply because something is happening does not mean it is natural law. Some say survival of the fittest is a natural law for humans. This belief would mean that a stronger person could kill a weaker person and justify their actions as natural law. That may be the case for primeval human behavior, but as advanced, logical creatures, accepting survival of the fittest thought in human relations is a gross simplification that discredits human complexity and potential. Jefferson concluded that because nature made humans social creatures, nature must have also created us with the skills to manage society.

---

[78] Alexander Stephens, Augusta, Georgia, *Daily Constitutionalist*, 30 March 1861

> *. . . it would have been inconsistent in creation to have formed man for the social state, and not to have provided virtue and wisdom enough to manage the concerns of the society.*[79]

The idea of slavery based on superiority is a stain upon humanity and a disgusting perversion of natural law. Like Plato and Aristotle, these southern politicians attributed "natural slavery" to one proof and one proof only, believing that some are born superior to others, and that "fact" justifies the self-appointed superior class in enslaving the other. A doctrine that is not dissimilar to the divine right of kings: that God (or nature) appoints a ruling class who has the right to rule without the consent of the governed.[80]

Perhaps the reason why the South was so efficient against despotism, as John C. Calhoun claimed, was because they were efficient tyrannical despots themselves and therefore could easily relate to the evil they saw in other despots. Or is it likely that James H. Hammond would agree to blacks owning white slaves in the North because the climate is suited for that reversal of circumstances? That is just as unlikely as Alexander Stephens willingly submitting to another race who thinks themselves superior to his. Like tyrants of the past, they failed to recognize or accept that there is always a bigger fish.

The primitive natural law slavery espoused by these historical characters is contrary to the correct natural law principles laid before humanity and were, as Alexander Stephens unwittingly said so clearly:

> *The prevailing ideas entertained by [Jefferson] and most of the leading statesmen at the time of the formation of the old Constitution were, that the enslavement of the African was in violation of the laws of nature; that it was wrong in principle, socially, morally and*

---

[79] Letter from Thomas Jefferson to John Adams, 28 October 1813
[80] King James, *On the Divine Right of Kings*, 1609

> *politically. . . They rested upon the assumption of the equality of races.*[81]

The Founders of the U.S. Constitution created the document on the "assumption of the equality of races," to the dismay of Stephens, Calhoun, and company.

Admittedly, the Founders failed to eliminate the institution of slavery in their day. Many of them were slaveholders themselves, even while they made numerous attempts to outlaw the practice. They made policy mistakes they thought would lead to abolition but that only made things worse, like the compromise to wait twenty years before regulating the importation of slaves. President Jefferson took immediate action when 1808 came. He petitioned Congress to outlaw the slave trade. He succeeded.[82] That well-intended success led to the terrible outcome of a higher demand for the breeding of slaves, ushering in an abhorrently intensified chattel slavery. Eventually, the slave economy in some states was more significant than the agricultural economy it supported. It increased the disgusting conditions of chattel slavery that finally drove Americans to kill Americans.

THE OBSERVABLE OUTCOME OF SLAVERY ON SOCIETY

Morally speaking and from our modern perspective, there is little need to prove the reprehensible nature of slavery. But since the previous pages have explored slavery from a natural law context, the following pages will explore the natural law consequences. Those consequences prove that slavery is contrary to an advanced social society, the unalienable right of property, and free market principles.

In 1831 Alexis de Tocqueville came to the United States to study the penitentiary system. Out of that trip came the famous book *Democracy in America*. In it, he included a chapter on slavery in which he concluded that "in general, the colonies in which there

---

[81] Alexander Stephens, Augusta, Georgia, *Daily Constitutionalist*, 30 March 1861
[82] An Act Prohibiting the Importation of Slaves, 2 March 1807

were no slaves became more populous and more rich than those in which slavery flourished."[83]

Tocqueville's firsthand observations reveal a dramatic contrast between the free state of Ohio and the slave state of Kentucky. *But this truth,* he wrote,

> *. . . was most satisfactory demonstrated when civilization reached the banks of the Ohio. . . Undulating lands extend upon both shores of the Ohio, whose soil affords inexhaustible treasures to the laborer; on either bank the aire is wholesome and the climate mild;. . . upon the left is called Kentucky; that upon the right [Ohio]. These two states only differ in a single respect; Kentucky has admitted slavery, but the state of Ohio has prohibited the existence of slaves within its borders.*

> *Thus the traveler who floats down the current of the Ohio. . . may be said to sail between liberty and slavery; and a transient inspection of the surrounding objects will convince him which of the two is most favourable to mankind.*

> *Upon the left bank of the stream the population is rare; from time to time one descries a troop of slaves loitering in the half-desert fields; the primeval forest recurs at every turn; society seems to be asleep, man to be idle, and nature alone offers a scene of activity and of life.*

> *From the right bank, on the contrary, a confuse [sic] hum is heard, which proclaims the presence of industry; the fields are covered with abundant harvests; the elegance of the dwellings announces the taste and activity of the labourer; and man appears to be in the enjoyment of wealth and contentment which are the reward of labour.*

> *Upon the left bank of the Ohio labour is confounded with the idea of slavery, upon the right bank it is identified*

---

[83] Alexis de Tocqueville, *Democracy in America*, translated by Henry Reeve, 1848

with that of prosperity and improvement; on the one side it is degraded, on the other it is honoured; on the former territory no white labourers can be found, for they would be afraid of assimilating themselves to the negroes; on the latter no one is idle. . .[84]

Based on Tocqueville's observations, he asserts that slavery does not produce wealth or a handsome society. Then he touches on another consequence of slavery's assault on sophisticated natural law. On the Kentucky side of the river, "no white labourer can be found." His thesis as to why touches on a superior-versus-inferior condition. The white laborer "would be afraid of assimilating themselves to the negroes." To them, it would be shameful to place themselves at the same level as their inferior, the slave.

The white slave owners became idle. Living off the labor of another caused them to turn to pleasure and leisure. They placed little value on labor because they did not need to work for their own support. Slavery corrupts the whole of society. A society based on a superior-versus-inferior construct is destined to collapse.

Nothing can be more fictitious than a purely legal inferiority; nothing more contrary to the instinct of mankind than these permanent divisions. . .

The white inhabitant of Ohio, who is obliged to subsist by his own exertions, regards temporal prosperity as the principle aim of his existence. . . he boldly enters upon every path which fortune opens to him; he becomes a sailor, pioneer, an artisan, or a labourer, with the same indifference, and he supports, with equal constancy, the fatigues and the dangers incidental to those various professions; the resources of his intelligence are astounding, and his avidity in the pursuit of gain amounts to a species of heroism.

---

[84] Ibid.

> *But the Kentuckian scorns not only labour, but all the undertakings which labour promotes; as he lives in an idle independence, his tastes are those of an idle man; money loses a portion of its value in his eyes; he covets wealth much less than pleasure and excitement. . . Thus slavery not only prevents the whites from becoming opulent, but even from desiring to become so.*[85]

Today, some criticize the idea of private property because slave owners invoked property rights in the ownership of their slaves. As established in previous sections, slavery is a counterfeit of the unalienable right to property because property cannot be rightfully obtained by stealing the labor of another.

Similarly, some criticize free market capitalism because slavery was used as human capital to create wealth in a system that they attribute to capitalism. They equate slavery with capitalism.

The engine that drives free market capitalism is the individual's need to survive and desire to gain more—be it opulence, wealth, happiness, etc. Tocqueville's examination exposes slavery as the opposite of that engine. "Thus slavery not only prevents the whites from becoming opulent, but even from desiring to become so."[86] The white aristocracy became focused not on wealth but pleasure and leisure. In this culture they "maintained the honour of inactive life."[87]

The founding principles of the unalienable rights of life, liberty, property, and the pursuit of happiness are the foundation of free market capitalism. The results of these are more industry, invention, and progression in society. Those rights are the antithesis of the slave economy, whose engine is driven by the idea that one people is superior to another. The results are oppression, regression, and a stagnant society whose most productive actions are pleasure and leisure. Slave masters found honor in an inactive life—truly the

---

[85] Ibid.
[86] Ibid.
[87] Ibid.

opposite of free market capitalism. Tocqueville summed up the results in one observation:

> *As the same causes have been continually producing opposite effects for the last two centuries. . . they have established striking difference between the commercial capacity. . . At the present day, it is only the northern states which are in possession of shipping, manufactures, railroads, and canals.*[88]

Tocqueville does not stop at the industry versus idleness of the free and slave states. He gets into the economy of it. He points out that the institution of slavery is impractical and unprofitable strictly from a business point of view.

> *The white sells his services, but they are only purchased at the times at which they may be useful; the black can claim no remuneration for his toil, but the expense of his maintenance is perpetual; he must be supported in his old age as well as in the productive years of youth.*[89]

Then there is the argument that masters posed, that the climate of the tropical region of the South demands that blacks were made to serve whites. From a law of nature context, Tocqueville addresses that too.

> *I cannot believe that Nature has prohibited the Europeans in Georgia and the Floridas, under pain of death, from raising the means of subsistence from the soil.*[90]

The idea that the South was idle, unproductive, and was less industrious than the North is a different narrative than what was being said by the South in the 1800s and echoed today—cotton is king! But was it really, though? It doesn't appear that Alexis de

---

[88] Ibid.
[89] Ibid.
[90] Ibid.

Tocqueville believed that. Nor did Frederick Law Olmsted, as presented in his book *The Cotton Kingdom*.

THE COTTON KINGDOM

Olmstead traveled the slave states from 1853 to 1861 to see the macro and micro effects of slavery on society for himself.

Olmstead was a very accomplished man. He is known as the father of American landscape architecture. But for his book, *The Cotton Kingdom*, he took on the role of a journalist for the *New York Times*.

The pot was steaming in 1853 when his journey began. The southern institution of slavery was at its peak. By the end of his travels in 1861, the country had reached its boiling point, and shots were fired on Fort Sumter, South Carolina—the official start of the Civil War.

Olmstead covers the topic of the South thoroughly. He addresses slavery, economy, culture, mannerisms, relationships, the rich, the poor, and much more. His overarching discovery was that the South had progressed very little in infrastructure, wealth, and industry and that slavery was the root cause of that condition.

The Cotton Kingdom goes into tedious detail comparing the quality and cost of slave labor versus free labor.[91] From a business point of view, Olmstead makes a sound and logical argument that slavery is not an efficient or profitable means of production. He discovered products and services cost more in the South than in the North. Many products and services were not available in the South because they were not profitable due to bad free labor or the poor economics of slave labor.

Those detailed facts and figures will not be covered here. Getting lost in the bad business practice of slave labor perhaps diminishes the reality that slavery is, first and foremost, bad because it is immoral. The poor economics of it is a distant second among the reasons the practice is reprehensible. However, the bad business

---

[91] Meaning that the person employed is a free person and not a slave or indentured servant. It does not mean that the labor is free.

practice of slavery tells us one important thing—slavery was not about free market capitalism. It would have been eliminated long ago if it were about capitalism, because there was often no profit in it.

The typical narrative of the southern economy was, and is, that the South was rich—cotton was king. In the 1850s, that was the narrative dictated by the South, primarily by southern politicians who were pushing policies to benefit the southern economy and slavery. As he recites the common southern narrative of the day, Olmstead mocks:

> *The institution of African slavery is a means more effective than any other yet devised, for relieving a large body of men from the necessity of labour; consequently, states which possess it must be stronger in statesmanship and in war, than those which do not; especially must they be stronger than states in which there is absolutely no privileged class, but all men are held to be equal before the law.*

> *The civilized world is dependent upon the Slave States of America for a supply of cotton. The demand for this commodity has, during many years, increased faster than the supply. Sales are made of it, now, to the amount of two hundred millions of dollars in a year. . . The world must have cotton, and the world depends on them for it. Whatever they demand, that must be conceded them; whatever they want, they have but to stretch forth their hands and take it. . .*

> *No! you dare not make war upon cotton; no power on earth dares to make war upon it. Cotton is king. . .*[92]

---

[92] All quotations in the remainder of this section are from Frederick Law Olmstead, *The Cotton Kingdom*, 1861

After reciting that narrative, Olmstead declared the fallacy of it. He observed that many in the North and the South had believed cotton was king, even though there was ample evidence to prove otherwise.

Almost every important man of the South, has at one time or other, within a few years, been betrayed into the utterance of similar exultant anticipations. . . this conviction is also held. . . by multitudes who know perfectly well that the commonly assigned reasons for it are based on falsehoods.

Recently, a banker, who is and always has been a loyal union man, said, commenting upon certain experiences of mine narrated in this book: "The South cannot be poor. Why their last crop alone was worth two hundred million. They must be rich:" ergo, say the conspirators, adopting the same careless conclusion, they must be powerful, and the world must feel their power, and respect them and their institutions.

Olmstead had to change his own thinking. He, too, had been victim to the "King Cotton" narrative, but he discovered its falseness for himself.

My own observation of the real condition of the people of our Slave States, gave me, on the contrary, an impression that the cotton monopoly in some way did them more harm than good; and, although the written narration of what I saw was not intended to set this forth, upon reviewing it for the present publication. . .

Coming directly from my farm in New York to Eastern Virginia, I was satisfied, after a few weeks' observation, that most of the people lived very poorly; that the proportion of men improving their condition was much less than in any Northern community; and that the natural resources of the land were strangely unused, or were used with poor economy. . .

> *I went on my way into the so-called cotton States, within which I travelled over, first and last, at least three thousand miles of roads, from which not a cotton plant was to be seen, and the people living by the side of which certainly had not been made rich by cotton or anything else. And for every mile of roadside upon which I saw any evidence of cotton production, I am sure that I saw a hundred of forest or waste land, with only now and then an acre or two of poor corn half smothered in weeds.*

Debunking the "King Cotton" narrative was as important then as it is now. In 1850 the narrative was used to justify the need for slavery. Today it is used to discredit free market capitalism. This is done by echoing the "King Cotton" narrative from the past to establish that slavery was institutionalized purely for capitalist means. Therefore, capitalism must be wrong and American prosperity was built upon slavery. Olmstead discovered just the opposite. Capitalism was not based on slavery, nor was slavery based on capitalism—slavery produced little capital, and American prosperity was much more apparent in the North than in the South.

There was a vast cotton economy in the South. Some slave owners were very wealthy because of cotton and slave labor, but Olmstead discovered that was the exception, not the rule. Plantations located on prime cotton-producing land near a major river, the Mississippi, for example, were highly profitable. Those wealthy plantations drove the value of slaves up, making lesser plantations unprofitable due to high slave labor costs.

> *A majority of those who sell the cotton crop of the United States must be miserably poor—poorer than the majority of our day-labourers at the North.*

The poor economics of slavery is one proof that slavery violates sophisticated natural law. It violates the natural laws of free market economics. But there are other natural law violations Olmstead discovered that better prove slavery's offense to those laws: the condition of the people of the South. It is obvious that the condition of the slaves was terrible. Even the best-treated, best-educated, best-dressed slave was still a slave—a most debasing condition of humanity. But what of the rest of the South? What did slavery do to the white population? Like Tocqueville, Olmstead observes that:

for every rich man's house, I am sure that I passed a dozen shabby and half-furnished cottages, and at least a hundred cabin—-mere hovels, such as none but a poor farmer would house his cattle in at the North. . .

. . . the citizens of the cotton States, as a whole, are poor. They work little, and that little, badly; they earn little, they sell little; they buy little, and they have little—very little—of the common comforts and consolations of civilized life. Their destitution is not material only; it is intellectual and it is moral. . . They boast and lack self-restraint. . .

The living conditions of most in the South were very poor. They were terrible laborers. They felt that being poor was better than lowering themselves to do the same work that slaves would do.

To work industriously and steadily, especially under directions from another man, is, in the Southern tongue, to "work like a [slave];"

Both the slave and the slave owner were corrupted, one from living in servitude and the other from believing they were entitled to the fruits of another's labor. The fact that whites in the South were living in stagnation should not readily classify them as victims equal to their slaves. They were victims of their own making.

Frederick Olmstead visited a farm worked by free labor. He inquired why slave labor was not used there. The proprietor informed him that he had freed his inherited slaves to avoid the corruption of slavery on his family.

I have been visiting a farm, cultivated entirely by free labour. The proprietor told me that he was first led to disuse slave-labour, not from any economical considerations, but because he had become convinced that there was an essential wrong in holding men in forced servitude with any other purpose than to benefit them alone, and because he was not willing to allow his own children to be educated as slave-masters. His father had been a large slaveholder, and he felt very strongly the bad influence it had had on his own character. He wished me to be satisfied that Jefferson uttered a great truth when he asserted that slavery was more pernicious to the white race than the black. Although, therefore, a chief part of his inheritance had been in slaves, he had liberated them all.

It is to be hoped that today it is a self-evident truth that slavery is a horrific practice. It is difficult to imagine a time when it was considered a blessing. That twisted view comes from a place of superiority.

From childhood, the one thing in their condition which has made life valuable to the mass of whites has been that [blacks] are yet their inferiors. It is this habit of considering themselves of a privileged class, and of disdaining something which they think beneath them, that is deemed to be the chief blessing of slavery.

The South claimed states' rights, property rights, "King Cotton" capitalism, etc. to justify their lifestyle. They claimed those rights to preserve one thing—slavery. Their lifestyle relied upon their belief that they were superior and blacks were inferior. They wanted to protect their right to be served by a race they perceived as inferior. But as it turns out, according to sophisticated natural law, that right does not exist. Slavery is contrary to natural law.

It is often said that the condition of slavery was not as bad as some say. Living conditions for most slaves were the same or better than the average citizen of the time. Only a few slave owners were cruel—it was not the norm. And the apologies go on and on. Fact or fiction, those points matter little as the moral depravity towers over those meaningless excuses. Slavery is an evil practice, even while wearing its Sunday best.

At the end of volume one of Olmstead's *The Cotton Kingdom*, an interesting observation is presented. Olmstead engages in a conversation with a southern gentleman while traveling on a steamship down the Red River. The Southerner opined that cruelty in slavery was rare, to which Olmstead pointed out that regardless of its rarity, cruelty in slavery was not prohibited by law. A point that indicated that the practice was wrong because it needed the legality of brutality to stay in existence. The dialog went:

I was sitting alone on the gallery, reading a pamphlet, when a well-dressed middle-aged man accosted me.

"Is that the book they call Uncle Tom's Cabin, *you are reading, sir?"*

"No, sir."

"I did not know but it was; I see that there are two or three gentlemen on board that have got it. I suppose I might have got it in New Orleans: I wish I had. Have you ever seen it, sir?"

"Yes, sir."

"I'm told it shows up Slavery in very high colours."

"Yes, sir, it shows the evils of Slavery very strongly." He took a chair near me, and said that, if it represented extreme cases as if they were general, it was not fair.

Perceiving that he was disposed to discuss the matter, I said that I was a Northern man, and perhaps not well able to judge; but that I thought that a certain degree of cruelty was necessary to make slave-labour generally profitable, and that not many were disposed to be more severe than they thought necessary. I believed there was little wanton cruelty. He answered, that Northern men were much mistaken in supposing that slaves were *generally ill-treated. He was a merchant, but he owned a plantation, and he just wished I could see his negroes. "Why, sir," he continued, "my n*****s' children all go regularly to a Sunday-school, just the same as my own, and learn verses, and catechism, and hymns. Every one of my grown-up n*****s are pious, every one of them, and members of the church. I've got an old man that can pray—well, sir, I only wish I had as good a gift at praying! I wish you could just hear him pray. There are cases in which n*****s are badly used; but they are not common. There are brutes everywhere. You have men, at the North, who whip their wives—and they kill them sometimes."*

"Certainly, we have, sir; there are plenty of brutes at the North; but our law, you must remember, does not compel women to submit themselves to their power. A wife, cruelly treated, can escape from her husband, and can compel him to give her subsistence, and to cease from doing her harm. A woman could defend herself against her husband's cruelty, and the law would sustain her."

"It would not be safe to receive negroes' testimony against white people; they would be always plotting against their masters, if you did."

"Wives are not always plotting against their husbands."

"Husband and wife is a very different thing from master and slave."

"Your remark, that a bad man might whip his wife, suggested an analogy, sir."

"If the law was to forbid whipping altogether, the authority of the master would be at an end."

"And if you allow bad men to own slaves, and allow them to whip them, and deny the slave the privilege of resisting cruelty, do you not show that you think it is necessary to

permit cruelty, in order to sustain the authority of masters, in general, over their slaves? That is, you establish cruelty as a necessity of Slavery—do you not?"

"No more than of marriage, because men may whip their wives cruelly."

"Excuse me, sir; the law does all it can, to prevent such cruelty between husband and wife; between master and slave it does not, because it cannot, without weakening the necessary authority of the master—that is, without destroying Slavery. It is, therefore, a fair argument against Slavery, to show how cruelly this necessity, of sustaining the authority of a cruel and passionate men over their slaves, sometimes operates."

JEFFERSON'S EFFORTS TO ABOLISH SLAVERY

The Founders had some significant missteps regarding slavery, but not all of their actions were failures. Jefferson, Madison, Franklin, and others laid the foundation for the evil practice of slavery to be eliminated, and so further institutionalize the natural law principles they so strongly promoted. An examination of Jefferson's contribution seems appropriate. He has received the most modern criticism for his ability to write that "all men are created equal" while owning slaves.

In his original draft of the Declaration of Independence, the longest and most forceful grievance was regarding slavery:

He has waged cruel war against human nature itself, violating it's [sic] most sacred rights of life & liberty in the persons of a distant people who never offended him, captivating & carrying them into slavery in another hemisphere, or to incur miserable death in their transportation thither. This piratical warfare, the opprobrium of infidel powers, is the warfare of the Christian king of Great Britain, determined to keep open a market where MEN should be bought & sold, he has

> *prostituted his negative for suppressing every legislative attempt to prohibit or to restrain this execrable commerce: and that this assemblage of horrors might want no fact of distinguished die, he is now exciting those very people to rise in arms among us, and to purchase that liberty of which he has deprived them, by murdering the people upon whom he also obtruded them; thus paying off former crimes committed against the liberties of one people, with crimes which he urges them to commit against the lives of another.[93]*

Of the Declaration of Independence, and specifically the slavery grievance, John Adams said:

> *I was delighted with its high tone, and the flights of oratory with which it abounded, especially that concerning Negro Slavery, which though I knew his Southern brethren would never suffer to pass in Congress, I certainly never would oppose.[94]*

Jefferson's draft of the Declaration was not published until years later. John Adams speculated as to the reason.

> *I have long wondered that the original [draft] has not been published. I suppose the reason is, [Jefferson's] vehement phillipic against negro slavery.[95]*

Jefferson continued to promote the "proposition that all men are created equal"[96] throughout his life. In 1779 he proposed a law for emancipation in Virginia.[97] In 1783 he drafted a new constitution for Virginia that included a provision for freeing the slaves and outlawing the practice.[98] In Congress, in 1794, he was one vote shy of banning slavery in the whole Western Territory.[99] Query 18 in his

---

[93] Slavery Grievance, Jefferson's draft of the Declaration of Independence, 1776
[94] Letter from John Adams to Timothy Pickering, 6 August 1822
[95] Ibid.
[96] Abraham Lincoln, Gettysburg Address, 1863
[97] A Bill Concerning Slaves, 18 June 1779
[98] May–June 1783
[99] *Plan of Government for the Western Territory, Report of the Committee*, 1 March 1784

Notes on the State of Virginia denounced slavery.[100] In 1806, as president, he publicly supported abolition with words that echoed the slavery grievance. He urged Congress to:

> *. . . withdraw the citizens of the United States from all further participation in those violations of human rights which have been so long continued on the unoffending inhabitants of Africa, and which the morality, the reputation, and the best interests of our country, have long been eager to proscribe.[101]*

Congress agreed and passed the Act Prohibiting Importation of Slaves. Jefferson signed the bill into law on March 2, 1807, and it took effect, as per the Constitution, January 1, 1808.

The Founders believed that all people are created equal, and that each person is born with inherent, unalienable rights of life, liberty, property, and the pursuit of happiness. They backed up these declarations with natural laws and codified them in our founding documents. Those documents may not have eliminated slavery as quickly as nature demanded, but the natural laws upon which they are built permeated American society until they purged the evil practice.

With words meant to criticize the Founders and the Constitution, Confederate Vice President Alexander Stephens unintentionally complimented their achievement of founding a nation upon an idea that "rested upon the assumption of the equality of races." He unintentionally condemns the Confederacy by declaring that their new constitution was specifically "founded upon. . . the great truth that the negro is not equal to the white man; that slavery, subordination to the superior race, is his natural and normal condition."

In his criticism of the "old Constitution" and the principles it was founded on, and his declaration that his "new government, is the first, in the history of the world," he inadvertently declared that the

---

[100] Thomas Jefferson, *Notes on the State of Virginia*, Query XVIII: Manners, 1781
[101] Thomas Jefferson, Sixth Annual Message to Congress, 2 December 1806

U.S. Constitution was NOT founded upon the arrogance of superiority, but upon natural law principles of equality. The Constitution did not institutionalize slavery. In "all men are created equal," there is no room for "superiority" thought. Equally endowed rights of life, liberty, and property are ours and ours alone. Slavery is a gross violation of those rights. All of the natural law principles promoted by the Founders, declared in the Declaration and codified in the Constitution conclude, like the Greek sophist Alcidamas preached, "God has left all men free; nature has made no man a slave."[102]

Tocqueville's *Democracy in America* and Olmstead's *Cotton Kingdom* revealed that the antebellum South more closely resembled Plato's *Republic* with its "superior" class that thought themselves justified in enslaving others simply because of their pompous hubris. It more closely resembled King James' doctrine of the Divine Right of Kings in which a divinely appointed elite class thought themselves superior enough to govern others without their consent. The slave South did not resemble Adam Smith's free market capitalism or John Locke's and Thomas Jefferson's idea that "all men are created equal."

Natural law is scientific law. It is observable and measurable. Tocqueville and Olmstead observed, measured, and concluded that slavery was supported by an aristocratic, feudal system that produced the immorality of slavery on one end and an idle, pleasure-loving society on the other. The southern condition produced little human progress. That was in stark contrast to the North, where individual freedom was championed and the opportunity to pursue happiness in a free market capitalistic society flourished. For human progress, human dignity, and human rights, the North won the primitive-versus-sophisticated natural law battle. Plato was wrong—Thomas Jefferson was right.

Sophisticated natural laws for human interaction and happiness require that each individual is born with the unalienable right to life

---

[102] Alcidamas, *Messeniakos*, 4th century B.C.

and liberty. They are born with the exclusive right to govern their life and liberty. No one is born with the inherent right to govern another without their consent. What they do with their life and liberty is an extension of themselves. It is their property.

Under these laws, every individual is equal. These laws and rights are antithetical to the idea that some are born superior to others, and that that superiority complex gives them the right to take others' life, liberty, and property for themselves. Slavery is a violation of the natural law of property.

Now that we have explored what property is and what it is not, and have established that natural law does not support the institution of slavery, we can move on to protecting and preserving property for the preservation and perpetuation of liberty in society.

PROTECTING PROPERTY IS ESSENTIAL TO LIBERTY

We have certain unalienable rights. To protect those rights, we establish government by our consent. Because government is created by our consent, government can only do that which we have the right to do ourselves. We cannot delegate to the government anything that would be illegal if we were to do it ourselves.

Our fundamental rights are life, liberty, and property. These three rights are inseparably connected. In other words, we cannot be deprived of one without being deprived of the others. The fundamental purpose of government is to protect our life and liberty by protecting our property. That protection of property should be from other individuals, groups of people, or from governments.

Property rights are essential to liberty. John Adams summed it up beautifully. He saw private property as the most important single foundation undergirding human liberty and human happiness. He said:

> *The moment the idea is admitted into society that property is not as sacred as the laws of God, and that there is not a force of law and public justice to protect it, anarchy and tyranny commence.*

Property must be secured or liberty cannot exist.[103]

Property is the most tangible of the three fundamental rights—life, liberty, and property. The tangible part of life, i.e., our bodies, is defined more as property than life. John Locke declared, "every man has a 'property' in his own 'person.'" What gives us life? Not just a living body, but thinking, reasoning, emotional, passionate life? Some say life comes from a Creator, some say nature, chemicals, chance, design, etc. The dictionary confirms its ambiguous definition by the multiple delineations of the word. Life, actual life, is not as tangible as we may think.

Liberty is even more elusive than life. We have a difficult time defining what it really is, yet we fight to the death to preserve it for ourselves and for others. The dictionary defines liberty as "freedom from. . . ," followed by any number of words—captivity, control, etc. But what about freedom from freedom? Too much freedom can cause anarchy, which is one of society's greatest oppressors. So how can liberty be equated so closely to freedom? Liberty, actual liberty, is not as tangible as we may think.

Property, on the other hand, is very tangible—and not just physical property. Anything that we have used our life and liberty for is our property. Property is the real-world manifestation of what we have done with our life and liberty. It is difficult to know exactly how to protect the elusive concepts of life and liberty. But we can more easily determine how to protect property, and in protecting property, life and liberty are protected. As explained in previous sections, taking property is the same as taking life and liberty. Likewise, protecting property is the same as protecting life and liberty. Hence, "property must be secured or liberty cannot exist."[104]

---

[103] John Adams, *Defense of the Constitutions of Government of the United States*, 1787
[104] Ibid.

THE PRESERVATION OF PROPERTY BEING THE END OF GOVERNMENT

John Locke sums up the importance of protection of property and the intellectual reasoning behind limiting government in its ability to take property on a whim, as well as or better than any other philosopher of freedom:

> *Thirdly, The Supreme Power cannot take from any Man any part of his Property without his own consent. For the preservation of Property being the end of Government, and that for which Men enter into Society, it necessarily supposes and requires, that the People should have Property, without which they must be suppos'd to lose that by entring into Society, which was the end for which they entered into it, too gross an absurdity for any Man to own. Men therefore in Society having Property, they have such a right to the goods, which by the Law of the Community are theirs, that no Body hath a right to take their substance, or any part of it from them, without their own consent; without this, they have no Property at all. For I have truly no Property in that, which another can by right take from me, when he pleases, against my consent. . .*

> *. . . For if any one shall claim a Power to lay and levy Taxes on the People, by his own Authority, and without such consent of the People, he thereby invades the Fundamental Law of Property, and subverts the end of Government. For what property have I in that which another may by right take, when he pleases to himself?[105]*

The protection and preservation of property, then, should be the end of government—its sole purpose. If laws exceed the protection of property, they contradict the very purpose of making laws in the first

---

[105] John Locke, *Second Treatise on Civil Government*, Chapter 11: "Of the Extent of the Legislative Power," 1689

place. If laws and government do not protect property than they do not protect life and liberty.

> *If there be a government then which. . . directly violates the property which individuals have in their opinions, their religion, their persons, and their faculties; nay more, which indirectly violates their property, in their actual possessions, in the labor that acquires their daily subsistence, and in the hallowed remnant of time which ought to relieve their fatigues and soothe their cares. . . that such a government is not a pattern for the United States.*
>
> *If the United States mean to obtain or deserve the full praise due to wise and just governments, they will equally respect the rights of property, and the property in rights: they will rival the government that most sacredly guards the former; and by repelling its example in violating the latter, will make themselves a pattern to that and all other governments.*[106]

The pattern for government, according to James Madison, is to protect property of all kinds. In doing so, such a government will "deserve the full praise due to wise and just governments."

THE RIGHT TO ESTABLISH, ALTER, AND ABOLISH GOVERNMENT

A majority of the people have the right to establish, alter, and abolish their own form of government with authority delegated only by their consent. The Declaration of Independence puts it this way:

> *. . . to secure. . . rights, Governments are instituted among Men, deriving their just powers from the consent of the governed, —That whenever any Form of Government becomes destructive of these ends, it is the Right of the People to alter or to abolish it, and to*

---

[106] James Madison, "Property," *National Gazette*, 29 March 1792

institute new Government, laying its foundation on such principles and organizing its powers in such form, as to them shall seem most likely to effect their Safety and Happiness. . . when a long train of abuses and usurpations, pursuing invariably the same Object evinces a design to reduce them under absolute Despotism, it is their right, it is their duty, to throw off such Government, and to provide new Guards for their future security.[107]

At the Pennsylvania ratifying convention, James Wilson underscored the doctrine that the authority to establish, alter, and abolish government comes from the people, stating on October 28, 1787:

. . . the supreme power resides in the people. This Constitution, Mr. President, opens with a solemn and practical recognition of that principle: —"We, the people of the United States, in order to form a more perfect union, establish justice, etc., do ordain and establish this Constitution for the United States of America." It is announced in their name—it receives its political existence from their authority: they ordain and establish.[108]

John Locke presented the same concept in his *Essay Concerning Civil Government.*

The reason why men enter into society is the preservation of their property. . . [therefore] whenever the legislators endeavour to take away and destroy the property of the people, or reduce them to slavery under arbitrary power, they [the officials of government] put themselves into a state of war with the people, who are there-upon absolved from any further obedience, and are left to the common refuge which God hath provided for all men

---

[107] Declaration of Independence, 4 July 1776
[108] James Wilson, Pennsylvania ratifying convention, 28 October 1787

> *against force and violence. Whensoever, therefore, the legislative shall transgress this fundamental rule of society, and either by ambition, fear, folly, or corruption, endeavour to grasp themselves, or put into the hands of any other, an absolute power over the lives, liberties, and estates of the people, by this breach of trust they [the government officials] forfeit the power the people put into their hands . . . and it devolves to the people, who have a right to resume their original liberty, and. . . provide for their own safety and security. . .[109]*

While John Locke is focused on the right to abolish, the unalienable right to establish our own form of government is the underlying right; the ability to abolish is secondary. After all, we cannot abolish that which we have not first established.

It is important to note that the establishment of a new form of government must be done by a majority. Therefore, if the government was established by a majority, it can only be altered or abolished by its creator—the majority. Locke points out that:

> *. . . when any number of men have, by the consent of every individual, made a community, they have thereby made that community one body, with a power to act as one body, which is only by the will and determination of the majority. . . . And thus every man, by consenting with others to make one body politic under one government, puts himself under an obligation to every one of that society to submit to the determination of the majority, and to be concluded by it. . .[110]*

Once a government is established, all individuals still retain the right to establish, alter, and abolish their own form of government. That right is unalienable. They cannot be compelled to be governed without their consent. The government was created by the right to

---

[109] John Locke, *Second Treatise on Civil Government*, "Of the Dissolution of Government," 1689
[110] Ibid.

establish, alter, and abolish. That right is the government's creator, so to speak. Once created, the created cannot destroy its creator. That is to say, the established government cannot eliminate the very right that brought it into existence in the first place.

However, if the individual chooses not to be governed by the established government, they cannot expect to reap the protection and safety provided by that governmental system. An individual that declares independence from a government system, for example, does not have the right to travel on roads paid for and maintained by the very system from which they have severed themselves. They may have the unalienable right to travel, but not on property that they do not own, which includes public roads.

When exercising the right to establish our own form of government, there is an obvious need for that government to possess the ability to govern. To do so, certain powers, and people appointed to control those powers, are necessary. The authority to make law, for example, exists in Article I of the U.S. Constitution, which grants that power to representatives and senators chosen by the people. So exactly how is legislative power distributed to the legislative branch? The Declaration of Independence states that "governments are instituted among Men, deriving their just powers from the consent of the governed."

The United States Government gets its "just power," and those in Congress get the authority to control those powers, from the consent of the governed. Authority is delegated, or distributed, by consent. Without consent, government is impotent. It has no power, no control, and no authority.

It is imperative, when considering the idea of consent in the Declaration, that the word *just* not be overlooked. *Just* means correct, lawful, right, guided by truth and reason, and principled. In short, *just* means according to natural law. The power that is delegated to government and the control that is delegated to governors must be based on natural law. The people cannot delegate to government the power to reverse the effects of gravity, or any other principle of natural law. Attempting to do so would result in society fleeing from itself, only to suffer a worse penalty.[111] We may have the unalienable right to establish our own form of government, but care should be taken to base that government on natural law.

Humankind has always been plagued with powers that seem to trample on and abuse their rights. Tyrants always seek to have power over others. The way they gain that power is by taking away the rights of others—our life, liberty, or property. To protect their rights, people establish laws and appoint agents or governments to carry out those laws.

DELEGATING POWER BY THE CONSENT OF THE PEOPLE

Governments are instituted among Men, deriving their just powers from the consent of the governed. . .[112]

Once the idea is established that government gets its authority from the consent of the governed, the question becomes, what authority can the people delegate to government? Can they delegate any authority they wish? These questions are necessary for any nation that desires to implement principles of self-government.

To answer these questions, we first must understand that our government is established to protect individual rights. This is primarily done by determining how multiple individuals can exercise their liberty without invading the liberty of others. The right to travel on public roads provides a good example as to how we handle this challenge.

We have the unalienable right to move from point A to point B. The problem is, we cannot take any path we want from A to B because we may trample on the rights of others in the process. It would be completely unreasonable, on the other hand, for all 330 million people in the United States to negotiate their own routes to work,

---

[111] ". . . and by reason of this very fact he will suffer the worst penalties. . ." Marcus Tullius Cicero, *The Republic*, 54 to 51 B.C.
[112] Declaration of Independence, 4 July 1776

school, the store, etc. with all the various property owners along the way. To solve this problem, we collectively purchase and pave tracts of land for the purpose of driving from point A to point B.

Our newly created roads are fine until we come to an intersection. At an intersection, there is a high probability that our natural right to travel will directly interfere with someone else's right to travel. That interference can be deadly if the intersection is not governed. If there is an accident, if there is serious injury or death, one or both parties can lose the ability to exercise their unalienable right to travel. The solution is to govern the intersection with some type of traffic control. This example depicts exactly what government and laws are for—the governance of the intersection of our natural rights. We may need to yield the use of our rights temporarily to let our neighbor use their rights, then we continue on with using our rights. We may yield use of them temporarily, but we never lose them; they are unalienable.

To manage the usage of the roads more effectively and consistently, we make rules for driving on them. We then create a test to see if everyone knows the rules. If we can pass a test, we get the vested (legal) right to drive on those roads. Our driver's license is our credential to prove we have that vested right.

We have the right to delegate to government the authority to govern the intersection of rights. We also have the right to delegate authority to others to enforce that governance—speed limits, traffic controls, etc. We do this in an attempt to yield as few rights as necessary in order to protect our rights when they intersect with the rights of others.

In addition to the right to travel, so long as we do not trample the rights of others, we have the right to stand at our doorstep with a garden hose in hand just in case our home catches fire, so we can put it out. And we have the right to stand at our doorstep with a gun in our other hand just in case someone comes to assault our family.

Do you want to stand at your doorstep with a hose in one hand and a gun in the other 24 hours a day to protect your home? Probably not. You need to go to work or school, you want to spend time with family and friends, you do not want to sit at your doorstep all day. So, what can you do?

As a community we can get together and hire firefighters, purchase the necessary equipment, build fire stations and task this new fire department with protecting our property from fire. We can then hire and outfit a police department and task them with the responsibility of protecting our lives and property. What have we just created? Government.

What gave us the right or authority to create that government? Because we have the right to protect our homes from fire and assault, we have the right to delegate the administration of those rights to our agent, the government. That is all government is, the delegation of the administration of our rights to another through law.

Once we delegate those rights to our agent, the government, have we lost the right to protect our homes? No, we still have the right to stand at our doorstep with a garden hose and gun to protect it.

The problem arises when we begin to ask government to do things that we ourselves do not have the authority to do. Frederic Bastiat said, "Government is a great fiction where everybody seeks to live at the expense of everybody else."[113]

The exploration of the ability to delegate the governance of rights continues with the right of consent, which will be covered in Part 2 in the sections on the Third Amendment and the protection of property in the Fifth Amendment. Those discussions will answer the question of just how far we can go in delegating authority to the government.

Along with further discussions on consent and property rights, additional natural law principles of liberty are covered in each of the first ten amendments of the United States Constitution, known as the Bill of Rights.

---

[113] Frederic Bastiat, *Government*, 1848

PART 2

The Bill of Rights

CONGRESS OF THE UNITED STATES

begun and held at the City of New-York, on Wednesday the fourth of March, one thousand seven hundred and eighty-nine.

THE Conventions of a number of the States, having at the time of their adopting the Constitution, expressed a desire, in order to prevent misconstruction or abuse of its powers, that further declaratory and restrictive clauses should be added: And as extending the ground of public confidence in the Government, will best ensure the beneficent ends of its institution.

Frederick Augustus Muhlenberg
Speaker of the House of Representatives

John Adams
Vice-President and President of the Senate

*The headings provided on each of the following amendments are not part of the original text. They have been added here for the convenience of the reader.

Amendment 1
FREEDOM OF RELIGION, SPEECH, AND THE PRESS

Congress shall make no law respecting an establishment of religion, or prohibiting the free exercise thereof; or abridging the freedom of

121

speech, or of the press; or the right of the people peaceably to assemble, and to petition the government for a redress of grievances.

Amendment 2
THE RIGHT TO BEAR ARMS

A well-regulated Militia, being necessary to the security of a free State, the right of the people to keep and bear Arms, shall not be infringed.

Amendment 3
THE HOUSING OF SOLDIERS

No soldier shall, in time of peace be quartered in any house, without the consent of the owner, nor in time of war, but in a manner to be prescribed by law.

Amendment 4
PROTECTION FROM UNREASONABLE SEARCHES AND SEIZURES

The right of the people to be secure in their persons, houses, papers, and effects, against unreasonable searches and seizures, shall not be violated, and no warrants shall issue, but upon probable cause, supported by oath or affirmation, and particularly describing the place to be searched, and the persons or things to be seized.

Amendment 5
PROTECTION OF RIGHTS TO LIFE, LIBERTY, AND PROPERTY

No person shall be held to answer for a capital, or otherwise infamous crime, unless on a presentment or indictment of a Grand Jury, except in cases arising in the land or naval forces, or in the Militia, when in actual service in time of War or public danger; nor shall any person be subject for the same offense to be twice put in jeopardy of life or limb; nor shall be compelled in any criminal case to be a witness against himself, nor be deprived of life, liberty, or property, without due process of law; nor shall private property be taken for public use, without just compensation.

Amendment 6
RIGHTS OF ACCUSED PERSONS IN CRIMINAL CASES

In all criminal prosecutions, the accused shall enjoy the right to a speedy and public trial, by an impartial jury of the state and district wherein the crime shall have been committed, which district shall have been previously ascertained by law, and to be informed of the nature and cause of the accusation; to be confronted with the witnesses against him; to have compulsory process for obtaining witnesses in his favor, and to have the assistance of counsel for his defense.

Amendment 7
RIGHTS IN CIVIL CASES

In suits at common law, where the value in controversy shall exceed twenty dollars, the right of trial by jury shall be preserved, and no fact tried by a jury, shall be otherwise re-examined in any court of the United States, than according to the rules of the common law.

Amendment 8
EXCESSIVE BAIL, FINES, AND PUNISHMENTS FORBIDDEN

Excessive bail shall not be required, nor excessive fines imposed, nor cruel and unusual punishments inflicted.

Amendment 9
MISINTERPRETING THE CONSTITUTION

The enumeration in the Constitution, of certain rights, shall not be construed to deny or disparage others retained by the people.

Amendment 10
UNDELEGATED POWERS KEPT BY THE STATES AND THE PEOPLE

The powers not delegated to the United States by the Constitution, nor prohibited by it to the states, are reserved to the states respectively, or to the people.

THE BILL OF RIGHTS

First Amendment

"CONGRESS SHALL MAKE NO LAW RESPECTING AN ESTABLISHMENT OF RELIGION, OR PROHIBITING THE FREE EXERCISE THEREOF; OR ABRIDGING THE FREEDOM OF SPEECH, OR OF THE PRESS; OR THE RIGHT OF THE PEOPLE PEACEABLY TO ASSEMBLE, AND TO PETITION THE GOVERNMENT FOR A REDRESS OF GRIEVANCES."

The First Amendment is not a list of single, disconnected subjects; it is a logical progression of rights. Freedom of religious expression is often referred to as our first right. This is because our individual rights begin with the ability to think and believe. No other person has control over our thoughts and beliefs. The next logical step is our freedom to speak and to publish, or print, those thoughts—the freedom of speech and of the press. Next comes the right to assemble with other citizens to discuss what we have spoken and printed. Last, we have the right to assemble for the purpose of expressing our thoughts to our delegated representatives in government. If we have a right to think, we have a right to petition, and a right to every step in between.

BROAD CONCEPTS

- Freedom of Religious Expression

- Freedom of Speech and of the Press

- Right to Assemble

- Right to Petition

THE FREEDOM OF RELIGIOUS EXPRESSION

"CONGRESS SHALL MAKE NO LAW RESPECTING AN ESTABLISHMENT OF RELIGION, OR PROHIBITING THE FREE EXERCISE THEREOF..."

KEY QUOTES FROM THE FOUNDING ERA

"for I have sworn upon the altar of God eternal hostility against every form of tyranny over the mind of man."[1]
—Thomas Jefferson

"Religion. . . must be left to the conviction and conscience of every man; and it is the right of every man to exercise it as these may dictate. This right is in its nature an unalienable right."[2] —James Madison

"[Government intervention] tends only to corrupt the principles of that very religion it is meant to encourage."[3] —Virginia, An Act for establishing religious Freedom

The rights that form the basis for the freedom of religious expression are the rights to our own thoughts and beliefs. To deny these basic rights would prohibit an individual from using their own mind. Even in his youth, Benjamin Franklin understood the benefit of protecting the freedom of thought. At sixteen he said, "Without freedom of thought, there can be no such thing as wisdom."[4]

Along with the freedom of thought is the freedom of belief or the freedom of opinion. After the right to life, these are the first rights that every person is free to exercise. The freedom of expression is the right to think, believe, and form an opinion.

The freedom of religious expression, therefore, is the right to express our thoughts and beliefs in whatever way we wish, as long as we do not infringe upon the rights of others. James Madison explains this connection between thought and religious expression:

This right is in its nature an unalienable right. It is unalienable, because the opinions of men, depending only on the evidence contemplated by their own minds

---

[1] Letter from Thomas Jefferson to Benjamin Rush, 23 September 1800
[2] James Madison, *Memorial and Remonstrance against Religious Assessments*, 1785
[3] Virginia, An Act for establishing religious Freedom, 16 January 1786
[4] Benjamin Franklin, *Silence Dogood* No. 8, 1722

cannot follow the dictates of other men. . . We maintain therefore that in matters of Religion, no man's right is abridged by the institution of Civil Society and that Religion is wholly exempt from its cognizance.[5]

Notice Madison's strong language at the end. He states that government should not have matters of religion in its jurisdiction at all. The Founders discovered that without the freedom of religious expression, the government of a free people cannot be maintained.

From the Pilgrims' journey to America in 1620 to the Constitutional Convention in 1787, early Americans struggled to discover just how deep the freedom of religious expression ran. They discovered that like life and liberty, the freedom of thought is an unalienable right.

James Madison expressed that the freedom of religion stems from the underlying unalienable right to think and form opinions, and that no other person or institution possesses the right to abridge this natural right.

The term *free exercise* was adopted by colonial America as the best description of the freedom of religion. The idea of free exercise evolved from, first, the right of the "church"; second, to religious rights; third, to "tolerance"; and finally to "free exercise." Each stage of this evolution brought us closer to the idea that each individual has the right to their own thoughts and beliefs without oppression from any other individual, group, or government. Free exercise, then, does not necessarily mean a church or even a belief in a superior being. Free exercise is the ability to form your own opinions and guiding beliefs without the interference of another.

THE FOUNDERS' VIEW ON RELIGION

The Founders wanted separation between government and religion not because they thought religion unnecessary in society, but because they did not want government interfering with religion, so that religious influence could be felt throughout society. They felt the common, golden threads of all sound religions, not

---

[5] James Madison, *Memorial and Remonstrance against Religious Assessments*, 1785

denominational doctrine, must be maintained in a society in order for freedom to exist. The Supreme Court has observed that, to most people, freedom of religion is the most precious of all the unalienable rights, next to life itself. These concepts are found extensively throughout the writings of most of the Founders:

> *Of all the dispositions and habits which lead to political prosperity, religion and morality are indispensable supports.*[6] —George Washington

> *Our Constitution was made only for a moral and religious people. It is wholly inadequate to the government of any other.*[7] —John Adams

> *. . . assert for ourselves a freedom to embrace, to profess and to observe the Religion which we believe to be of divine origin, we cannot deny an equal freedom to those whose minds have not yet yielded to the evidence which has convinced us.*[8] —James Madison

THE FOUNDERS' CAMPAIGN FOR EQUALITY OF ALL RELIGIONS

One of the most remarkable efforts of the American Founders was their attempt to do something no other nation had ever successfully achieved—provide legal equality for all religions. Jefferson and Madison were undoubtedly the foremost among the Founders in that effort. They pushed through the first "freedom of religion" statutes in Virginia. Jefferson sought to disestablish the official church of Virginia in 1776, but this effort was not completely successful until ten years later.

Meanwhile, in 1784, Patrick Henry was so enthusiastic about strengthening the whole spectrum of Christian churches that he introduced a bill *"Establishing a Provision for Teachers of the Christian Religion."* It was the intention of this bill to allow each taxpayer to designate "to what society of Christians" his money

---

[6] George Washington, Farewell Address, 17 September 1796
[7] Letter from John Adams to the Officers of the Militia of Massachusetts, 11 October 1798
[8] James Madison, *Memorial and Remonstrance against Religious Assessments*, 1785

would go. The funds collected by this means were to make "provision for a minister or teacher of the Gospel. . . or the providing of places of divine worship [for that denomination], and to none other use whatever."[9]

Madison immediately reacted with his famous "Memorial and Remonstrances," in which he proclaimed with the greatest possible energy the principle that the state government should not prefer one religion over another. Equality of religions was the desired goal. He wrote:

> *Who does not see that the same authority which can establish Christianity, in exclusion of all other religions, may establish with the same ease any particular sect of Christians, in exclusion of all other sects?. . . The bill violates that equality which ought to be the basis of every law.[10]*

It was not easy for the colonists to retrain their thinking to truly understand and accept the ideas of the free exercise of religion. They thought they had achieved civility by becoming religiously tolerant, but they soon realized that tolerance is not necessarily good thinking.

THE PARADOX OF TOLERANCE

Early Americans learned that tolerance is a form of captivity as they wrestled with the concept of free exercise.

The term *religious tolerance* was used by the early colonists. While that was an improvement from a state-established religion, it was not liberty. Tolerance is a form of oppression. Thomas Paine stated it clearly:

> *Toleration is not the opposite of intoleration, but is the counterfeit of it. Both are despotisms. The one assumes*

---

[9] Virginia, Establishing a Provision for Teachers of the Christian Religion, 1 January 1784
[10] James Madison, *Memorial and Remonstrance against Religious Assessments*, 1785

> *to itself the right of withholding liberty of conscience,*
> *and the other of granting it. . .[11]*

Paine continues to explain that, in essence, tolerance is declaring that one group is determining the acceptability of another group's beliefs. In other words, they are determining whether God should be tolerant and accept their lesser belief system. Paine illustrated the absurdity:

> *Were a bill brought into Parliament, entitled, "An act to tolerate or grant liberty to the Almighty to receive the worship of a Jew or a Turk," or "to prohibit the Almighty from receiving it," all men would startle, and call it blasphemy. . .[12]*

To tolerate someone's religion, or worse, to pass a law that tolerates their religion, is a form of state establishment. Such a law would be declaring that one religion, the presumed correct one, would be, by law, tolerating the other religion. Toleration assumes an established religion that grants toleration. If the power to grant exists, then the power to revoke must exist as well. Can you see the paradox?

The Framers began to change their outlook. James Madison felt that toleration was not compatible with liberty, falling woefully short of its intended goal: freedom of conscience.

George Mason's draft of the Virginia Declaration of Rights used the word *toleration.*

> *. . . all men should enjoy the fullest toleration in the exercise of religion, according to the dictates of conscience. . .[13]*

James Madison amended the Declaration of Rights to read:

---

[11] Thomas Paine, *Rights of Man,* 1791
[12] Ibid.
[13] George Mason, Virginia Declaration of Rights Draft, May 1776

> *. . . all men are equally entitled to the free exercise of religion, according to the dictates of conscience. . .*[14]

Reverend John Leland said:

> *Government should protect every man in thinking and speaking freely, and see that one does not abuse another. The liberty I contend for is more than toleration. The very idea of toleration is despicable; it supposes that some have a pre-eminence above the rest to grant indulgence, whereas all should be equally free, Jews, Turks, Pagans and Christians.*[15]

It is interesting to see the evolution—the attempt to find balance with the freedom of conscience from toleration by those members of state-established religions toward the non-established religions to the recognition of the despicable nature of the idea of toleration. They were moving from captivity to liberty. It was an important evolution for the cause of liberty. George Washington summed up the benefits of removing toleration from our conscience:

> *It is now no more that toleration is spoken of, as if it was by the indulgence of one class of people, that another enjoyed the exercise of their inherent natural rights. For happily the Government of the United States, which gives bigotry no sanction, to persecution no assistance, requires only that they who live under its protection, should demean themselves as good citizens, in giving it on all occasions their effectual support.*[16]

The idea of toleration once again plagues us today. From religious tolerance to sexual preference tolerance, we have returned to the habit of presuming our belief is better than others, therefore, we must be "tolerant."

---

[14] Virginia Declaration of Rights, June 1776

[15] Reverend John Leland, *The Rights of Conscience Inalienable*, 1791

[16] George Washington, letter to the Hebrew Congregation of Newport, Rhode Island, 17 August 1790

The following 1945 quote by Karl R. Popper, an Austrian-British philosopher and professor, contemplated what he called the Paradox of Tolerance. Popper is serious, but in his seriousness, he misses the ridiculousness of his position. He seems never to consider that perhaps the idea of tolerance is the problem, and that tolerance and intolerance are really the same thing. Because they are the same, they have the same results—captivity.

> *Unlimited tolerance must lead to the disappearance of tolerance. If we extend unlimited tolerance even to those who are intolerant, if we are not prepared to defend a tolerant society against the onslaught of the intolerant, then the tolerant will be destroyed, and tolerance with them. —In this formulation, I do not imply, for instance, that we should always suppress the utterance of intolerant philosophies; as long as we can counter them by rational argument and keep them in check by public opinion, suppression would certainly be unwise. But we should claim the right to suppress them if necessary even by force; for it may easily turn out that they are not prepared to meet us on the level of rational argument, but begin by denouncing all argument; they may forbid their followers to listen to rational argument, because it is deceptive, and teach them to answer arguments by the use of their fists or pistols. We should therefore claim, in the name of tolerance, the right not to tolerate the intolerant. We should claim that any movement preaching intolerance places itself outside the law, and we should consider incitement to intolerance and persecution as criminal, in the same way as we should consider incitement to murder, or to kidnapping, or to the revival of the slave trade, as criminal.*[17]

Based on Popper's thesis, tolerance must be intolerant to intolerance. But who is to say that the tolerant is superior to the so-called intolerant? Perhaps, in reality, the intolerant is actually

---

[17] Karl R. Popper, *The Open Society and Its Enemies*, Volume 1, 1945

superior to the tolerant—making the intolerant the actual tolerant and the tolerant the intolerant—in which the newly declared tolerant must now be intolerant to the newly declared intolerant lest they be destroyed. It is hard to follow. Not because people are not smart enough to understand it, but because Popper's concept is an absurd paradox.

The Founders had evolved beyond the oppressive nature of tolerance to the idea of free exercise. They concluded that religion and government must be separated for free exercise to exist and flourish.

GOVERNMENT AND RELIGION WILL CORRUPT EACH OTHER IF NOT SEPARATED

In centuries past, the religious community thought government support was necessary for religion to survive or thrive. History proved that mixing church and state caused great tyranny and oppression and eventually corrupted both. The problem was not in the state, nor in the religion; it was the marriage of the two to which many historical tragedies can be traced.

The American colonists recognized that combining church and state corrupted both. James Madison said:

> *. . . it tends only to corrupt the principles of that very Religion it is meant to encourage. . .* [18]

> *. . . the old error, that without some sort of alliance or coalition between Government and Religion neither can be duly supported. Such indeed is the tendency to such a coalition, and such its corrupting influence on both parties.* [19]

The Baptist Reverend John Leland put it this way:

---

[18] Virginia, An Act for establishing religious Freedom, 1786
[19] Letter from James Madison to Edward Livingston, 10 July 1822

> *. . . it is not possible in the nature of things to establish religion by human laws without perverting the design of civil law and oppressing the people.*[20]

John Adams observed that ambition, when mixed with freedom, brought forth much good in the world. But when not restrained, it resulted in tyranny. When government has been attached to a single religion, it has caused the worst form of tyranny and human ignorance.

> *[Clergy] even persuading mankind to believe. . . that God Almighty had entrusted them with the keys of heaven, whose gates they might open and close at pleasure;. . . with a power of procuring or withholding the rain of heaven and the beams of the sun; with the management of earthquakes, pestilence, and famine. . . All these opinions. . . spread. . . among the people by reducing their minds to a state of sordid ignorance. . . Thus was human nature chained fast for ages in a cruel, shameful, and deplorable servitude to. . . tyrants. . .*

> *Thus, as long as. . . the people were held in ignorance, liberty. . . seem to have deserted the earth, and one age of darkness succeeded another. . . From the time of the Reformation to the first settlement of America, knowledge gradually spread. . . ecclesiastical and civil tyranny. . . lost their strength. . .*[21]

The solution to despotism, tyranny, and corruption was to establish free exercise. This was done with two policies:

> 1. ". . . no religious Test shall ever be required as a Qualification to any Office or public Trust under the United States."[22]

---

[20] Reverend John Leland, *The Rights of Conscience Inalienable*, 1791

[21] Adams, *A Dissertation on the Canon and Feudal Law*, 1765

[22] United States Constitution, Article 6, Clause 3, 1787

2. "Congress shall make no law respecting the establishment of religion or prohibiting the free exercise thereof. . .."[23]

Government is not only unnecessary to keep religion, but would be a poor keeper of religion, too, says Thomas Jefferson:

Reason and free enquiry are the only effectual agents against error. . . Was the government to prescribe to us our medicine and diet, our bodies would be in such keeping as our souls are now. . . . It is error alone which needs the support of government. Truth can stand by itself.[24]

THE FOUNDERS WANTED THE NATIONAL GOVERNMENT EXCLUDED FROM RELIGION

In his famous *Commentaries on the Constitution*, Justice Joseph Story of the Supreme Court pointed out why the Founders, as well as the states themselves, felt the national government should be absolutely excluded from any authority in the field of settling questions on religion. He explained:

In some of the states, Episcopalians constituted the predominant sect; in others, Presbyterians; in others, Congregationalists; in others, Quakers; and in others again, there was a close numerical rivalry among contending sects. It was impossible that there should not arise perpetual strife and perpetual jealousy on the subject of ecclesiastical ascendancy, if the national government were left free to create a religious establishment. The only security was in extirpating the power. But this alone would have been an imperfect security, if it had not been followed by a declaration of the right of the free exercise of religion, and a prohibition (as we have seen) of all religious tests. Thus the whole power over the subject of religion is left

---

23 United States Constitution, Amendment 1, 1789
24 Thomas Jefferson, *Notes on the State of Virginia*, 1785

> *exclusive to the state governments, to be acted upon according to their own sense of justice, and the state constitutions.*[25]

This is why the First Amendment of the Constitution provides the clear prohibition against Congress.

> "CONGRESS shall make NO law respecting an establishment of religion or prohibiting the free exercise thereof."[26]

Because the Founders recognized from experience that religion and government do not make good companions, they set out to keep the two separate, especially on a national level.

Jefferson and Madison encouraged states to eliminate their established religions, but during their terms as president, neither sought legislation to force the elimination of state established religions because the First Amendment prohibited any law from Congress in regard to religion.

The phrase "Congress shall make no law" was a restriction on Congress, not on the states or local municipalities. Varying degrees of "establishment" existed in the states well into the 1860s, without national authorities eliminating them. South Carolina, for example, did not remove the following language from their Constitution until 1868:

> *The Christian Protestant religion shall be deemed, and is hereby constituted and declared to be, the established religion of this State.*[27]

When the United States was founded, there were many Americans who were not enjoying freedom of religion to the fullest extent possible. At least seven states had officially established religions or

---

[25] Joseph Story, *Commentaries on the Constitution*, 1873
[26] United States Constitution, Amendment 1, 1789, emphasis added
[27] Charter of Carolina, 24 March 1663

denominations at the time the Constitution was adopted. These included:

Connecticut (Congregational Church)

New Hampshire (Protestant faith)

Delaware (Christian faith)

New Jersey (Protestant faith)

Maryland (Christian faith)

South Carolina (Protestant faith)

Massachusetts (Congregational Church)

Under these circumstances the Founders felt it would have been catastrophic, and might have precipitated civil strife, if the national government had tried to establish a policy on religion or disestablish the denominations which the states had adopted. Nevertheless, the Founders were anxious to eventually see complete freedom of all faiths and an equality of all religions, both Christian and non-Christian.

When Thomas Jefferson was serving in the Virginia legislature, he introduced a bill to have a day of fasting and prayer; but when he became president, Jefferson said there was no authority in the national government to proclaim religious holidays.

In matters of religion, I have considered that its free exercise is placed by the Constitution independent of the powers of the general government. I have therefore undertaken, on no occasion, to prescribe the religious exercises suited to it; but have left them as the Constitution found them, under the direction and discipline of State or Church authorities acknowledged by the several religious societies.[28]

---

[28] Thomas Jefferson, Second Inaugural Address, 4 March 1805

THE "WALL" BETWEEN CHURCH AND THE NATIONAL STATE

The Founders' intention, to the disappointment of many religious people today, was a complete separation. However, to the disappointment of many secular people today, the desired result was not a secular society, but a more thoughtful, religious society—using the separation of church and state as the solution. Jefferson explained the benefit separation would provide to specific religions—Christianity in this case:

> *If the freedom of religion, guaranteed to us by law in theory, can ever rise in practice under the overbearing inquisition of public opinion, truth will prevail over fanaticism, and the genuine doctrines of Jesus, so long perverted by his pseudo-priests, will again be restored to their original purity.*[29]

It may surprise some that Jefferson felt pure Christianity was a friend to liberty, and therefore important to the expansion of the human condition.

> *The Christian religion. . . brought to the original purity and simplicity of it's* [sic] *benevolent institutor, is a religion. . . friendly to liberty, science, and the freest expansion of the human mind.*[30]

But, Jefferson noted, it was the pure Christian religion that was a friend to liberty, not one that had been corrupted by the mixing of church and state for centuries. How do you achieve a pure version of Christianity, or any other religion for that matter? Jefferson's and Madison's solution was simple: liberty.

Jefferson's resolution for disestablishing the Church of England in Virginia was not to set up a wall between the state and the church, but for

---

[29] Letter from Thomas Jefferson to Jared Sparks, 4 November 1820
[30] Letter from Thomas Jefferson to Moses Robinson, 23 March 1801

taking away the privilege and preeminence of one religious sect over another, and thereby [establishing] . . . equal . . . rights among all.[31]

The famous correspondence between Thomas Jefferson and the Danbury Baptist Association underscores the First Amendment's prohibition to Congress. This correspondence is the origin of the phrase "separation of church and state." The Danbury Baptist Association was a coalition of churches in Connecticut, where Congregationalism was the official state church. Under these conditions, Baptists felt the weight of religious oppression.

. . . What religious privileges we enjoy (as a minor part of the state) we enjoy as favors granted, and not as inalienable rights; and these favors we receive at the expense of such degrading acknowledgements as are inconsistent with the rights of freemen.[32]

They were seeking President Jefferson's help, although they knew he had no authority to assist legally. They instead were seeking his influential support only.

Sir, we are sensible that the president of the United States is not the national legislator, and also sensible that the national government cannot destroy the laws of each state; but our hopes are strong that the sentiments of our beloved president, which have had such genial effect already, like the radiant beams of the sun, will shine and prevail through all these states and all the world, till hierarchy and tyranny be destroyed from the earth.[33]

Jefferson took his reply so seriously that he had the U.S. Attorney General, Levi Lincoln, review it before he sent it. He felt the letter would have the effect of "sowing useful truths and principles among

---

[31] Thomas Jefferson, rough draft of Resolutions for Disestablishing the Church of England and for Replacing Laws Interfering with Freedom of Worship, 1776
[32] Letter from the Danbury Baptist Association to Thomas Jefferson, 7 October 1801
[33] Ibid.

the people, which might germinate and become rooted among their political tenets."[34]

In his letter to the Danbury Baptist Association, Jefferson re-invoked his belief in religious liberty, expressed his satisfaction with the First Amendment, then asserted his desire that the idea of religious liberty would continue to spread, presumably to the state and local levels. He made no mention of any attempt to have Congress enforce that idea, because that too would have been a breach of the separation wall that "Congress shall make no law. . ."

> *Believing with you that religion is a matter which lies solely between man and his God, that he owes account to none other for his faith or his worship, that the legislative powers of government reach actions only, and not opinions, I contemplate with sovereign reverence that act of the whole American people which declared that their legislature should "make no law respecting an establishment of religion, or prohibiting the free exercise thereof," thus building a wall of separation between Church and State. Adhering to this expression of the supreme will of the nation in behalf of the rights of conscience, I shall see with sincere satisfaction the progress of those sentiments which tend to restore to man all his natural rights, convinced he has no natural right in opposition to his social duties.[35]*

Thomas Jefferson said that because religion is only between God and man, the American people built "a wall of separation between church and state." But how complete should the separation be? James Madison wrote:

> *There is not a shadow of right in the general government to intermeddle with religion. Its least interference with it would be the most flagrant usurpation.[36]*

---

34 Letter from Thomas Jefferson to Levi Lincoln, 1 January 1802
35 Letter from Thomas Jefferson to the Danbury Baptist Association, 1 January 1801
36 James Madison, Virginia ratifying convention, 1788

Jefferson pointed out one exception when government interference might be necessary and proper. Government can interfere when one person's exercise of their rights intersects with the rights of others.

> *It is time enough, for the rightful purposes of civil government, for its officers to interfere when principles break out into overt acts against peace and good order.*[37]

What was James Madison's opinion regarding religious activity in the public square? In 1817, Congress hired a chaplain to begin each session with a mandatory prayer. Madison felt this violated the Constitution because Congress was using tax dollars to pay for the chaplain and because the mandatory prayer "shut the door of worship against the members whose creeds and consciences forbid a participation..."[38] Instead, Madison recommended the representatives pay for the chaplain themselves and make the prayer voluntary. This, he felt, would be a better example to the people. Madison was not against prayer in Congress, just against coercion and taxes being used as instruments.

FROM PRINCIPLE TO POLICY—THE UNIVERSITY OF VIRGINIA

Jefferson established the University of Virginia—a public university. Madison participated in its founding as a member of the Board of Visitors. Recognizing religion as an important science to be studied, they devised a plan that would allow religion to be taught at this public school while adhering to constitutional principles.

The first policy was to have no Professor of Divinity, a position traditionally held by clergy of the dominant or state-sponsored religion. This policy took the science of religion out of the hands of a particular sect and placed it in the hands of the Professor of Ethics, an academic rather than a religious position.

> *[We] have proposed no Professor of Divinity; and the rather, as the proofs of the being of a God. The creator,*

---

[37] Thomas Jefferson, Statute of Religious Freedom, 1779
[38] James Madison, Detached Memoranda, 1817

preserver, and supreme ruler of the universe, the author of all the relations of morality, and of the laws and obligations these infer, will be within the province of the professor of ethics. . . Proceeding thus far without offence to the constitution, we have thought it proper at this point, to leave every sect to provide as they think fittest, the means of further instruction in their own peculiar tenets.[39]

The Board of Visitors wanted to make it clear that this policy was not intended to strip religion from public discourse, but to enhance the study of religion by making that study more free.

It was not, however, to be understood that instruction in religious opinion and duties was meant to be precluded by the public authorities, as indifferent to the interests of society. On the contrary, the relations which exist between man and his Maker, and the duties resulting from those relations, are the most interesting and important to every human being, and the most incumbent on his study and investigation. . .[40]

Jefferson made it clear that the actions of the Board of Visitors were not to establish a public institution of no religion, but rather one that promoted the study of religion while avoiding an establishment of religion.

A handle has been made. . . to disseminate an idea that this is an institution, not merely of no religion, but against all religion. Occasion was taken at the last meeting of the Visitors, to. . . silence this calumny. . . after stating the constitutional reasons against a public establishment of any religious instruction, we suggest the expediency of encouraging the different religious sects to establish, each for itself, a professorship of their own tenets, on the confines of the

---

³⁹ Report of the Commissioners for the University of Virginia, 1818
⁴⁰ Minutes of the Board of Visitors, University of Virginia, 1822

university, so near as that their students may attend the lectures there, and have the free use of our library, and every other accommodation we can give them; preserving, however, their independence of us and of each other. This fills the chasm objected to ours, as a defect in an institution professing to give instruction in all useful sciences. . .[41]

To encourage religious studies by college students of different faiths, Jefferson proposed the university do the following:

- **Teach** "the proofs of the being of a God, the creator, preserver, and supreme ruler of the universe, the author of all the relations of morality, and of the laws and obligations these infer, will be within the province of the professor of ethics."[42]

- **Show** "the developments of these moral obligations, of those in which all sects agree, [together with] a knowledge of the languages, Hebrew, Greek, and Latin, a basis will be formed common to all sects."[43]

- **Encourage** "the different religious sections to establish, each for itself, a professorship of their own tenets, on the confines [campus] of the university, so near. . . that their students may attend the lectures there, and have the free use of our library, and every other accommodation we can give them; preserving, however, their independence of us and of each other."[44]

- **Enable** "students of the University to attend religious exercises with the professor of their particular sect, either in the rooms of the buildings still to be erected [by each

---

[41] Letter from Thomas Jefferson to Dr. Thomas Cooper, 2 November 1822
[42] Report of the Commissioners for the University of Virginia, 1818
[43] Ibid.
[44] Ibid.

denomination on campus] or. . . in the lecturing room of such professor."[45]

- **Urge** students to participate in regular religious exercises, but do so without conflicting with the established schedule of the university. "Should the religious sects of this State, or any of them, according to the invitation held out to them, establish within or adjacent to, the precincts of the University, schools for instruction in the religion of their sect, the students at the University will be free, and expected to attend religious worship at the establishment of their respective sects. . . in time to meet their school in the University at its stated hour."[46]

In referring to the university campus and its immediate environs, where all faiths would be invited to provide facilities, Jefferson wrote:

> *By bringing the sects together, and mixing them with the mass of other students, we shall soften their aspirates, liberalize and neutralize their prejudices and make the general religion a religion of peace, reason and morality.*[47]

THE RESULTS OF RELIGIOUS EXPRESSION

The separation of church and state resulted in a pluralistic society. Benjamin Franklin reported on the results of free exercise in Pennsylvania:

> *It was wonderful to see the Change soon made in the Manners of our Inhabitants; from being thoughtless or indifferent about Religion, it seem'd as if all the World were growing Religious; so that one could not walk thro' the Town in an Evening without Hearing Psalms sung in different Families of every Street. . .*[48]

---

[45] Ibid.
[46] Ibid.
[47] Letter from Thomas Jefferson to Dr. Thomas Cooper, 2 November 1822
[48] Benjamin Franklin, *Auto Biography*, 1771

After forty years of separation and free exercise, James Madison observed:

That there has been an increase. . . Religious instruction is now diffused throughout the Community. . . The qualifications of the Preachers. . . are understood to be improving. On a general comparison of the present and former times, the balance is certainly and vastly on the side of the present, as to the number of religious teachers, the zeal which actuates them, the purity of their lives, and the attendance of the people on their instructions. It was the universal opinion of the Century preceding the last, that Civil Govt. could not stand without the prop of a Religious establishment, and that the [Christian] religion itself, would perish if not supported by a legal provision for its Clergy. The experience of Virginia conspicuously corroborates the disproof of both opinions. The Civil Govt. . . possesses the requisite Stability and performs its functions with complete success: Whilst the number, the industry, and the morality of the priesthood and the devotion of the people have been manifestly increased by the total separation of the Church from the State.[49]

James Madison was one of the most effective public servants at applying the idea of separation. As its author, he strictly observed the First Amendment in most cases. He promoted separation because he had "no doubt that every new example, will succeed, as every past one has done, in shewing that religion and Government will both exist in greater purity, the less they are mixed together."[50]

In the same letter, he said:

[It] is impossible to deny that Religion prevails with more zeal, and a more exemplary priesthood than it ever did when established and patronized by Public authority.

---

[49] Letter from James Madison to Robert Walsh, 2 March 1819
[50] Letter from James Madison to Edward Livingston, 10 July 1822

> *We are teaching the world the great truth that Governments do better without Kings & Nobles than with them. The merit will be doubled by the other lesson that Religion flourishes in greater purity, without. . . the aid of Government.*[51]

While religion was to be kept out of the reach of Congress, the Founders believed religion in society was essential. In his 1796 Farewell Address, George Washington said:

> *Of all the dispositions and habits which lead to political prosperity, religion and morality are indispensable supports. . .*

> *. . . And let us with caution indulge the supposition that morality can be maintained without religion. . . . Reason and experience both forbid us to expect that national morality can prevail to the exclusion of religious principle.*

> *It is substantially true that virtue or morality is a necessary spring of popular government.*[52]

The Founders said that, even though religion was not directly a part of our government, it was important because human beings tended to behave the way they believe. The tremendous influence of these beliefs on the American culture was immediately apparent to Alexis de Tocqueville when he visited the United States in 1831. He wrote:

> *On my arrival in the United States the religious aspect of the country was the first thing that struck my attention; and the longer I stayed there, the more I perceived the great political consequences resulting from this new state of things.*[53]

He described the situation as follows:

---

[51] Ibid.
[52] George Washington, Farewell Address, 1796
[53] Alexis de Tocqueville, *Democracy in America*, 1835

Religion in America takes no direct part in the government of society, but it must be regarded as the FIRST[54] of their political institutions; . . . I am certain that they hold it to be indispensable to the maintenance of republican institutions. This opinion is not peculiar to a class of citizens or to a party, but it belongs to the whole nation and to every rank of society.[55]

FREEDOM OF SPEECH AND OF THE PRESS

"CONGRESS SHALL MAKE NO LAW. . . ABRIDGING THE FREEDOM OF SPEECH, OR OF THE PRESS. . ."

KEY QUOTES FROM THE FOUNDING ERA

Without freedom of thought, there can be no such thing as Wisdom; and no such thing as public liberty, without Freedom of Speech.[56]   —Benjamin Franklin

Every freeman has an undoubted right to lay what sentiments he pleases before the public. . . But if he publishes what is improper, mischievous, or illegal, he must take the consequence of his temerity."[57]
—William Blackstone

In those wretched countries where a man cannot call his tongue his own, he can scarce call anything his own. Whoever would overthrow the liberty of a nation must begin by subduing the freeness of speech."[58]
—Benjamin Franklin

No government ought to be without censors, and, where the press is free, no one ever will."[59]
—Thomas Jefferson

---

[54] Emphasis added

[55] Alexis de Tocqueville, *Democracy in America*, 1835

[56] Benjamin Franklin, *Silence Dogood* No. 8, 9 July 1722

[57] William Blackstone, *Commentaries on the Laws of England*, 1769

[58] Benjamin Franklin, *Silence Dogood* No. 8, 9 July 1722

[59] Letter from Thomas Jefferson to George Washington, 9 September 1792

The freedom of speech and the press is a continuation of the freedom of religion because it relates to the freedom of thought and the freedom of expression. Speech and the press are how people communicate their thoughts.

History has shown that when government restricts the right to speak and the right to print, tyranny is free to oppress. The freedom of speech and of the press allows the people to keep each other informed of the actions of their government—good or bad.

The *press* means the printing press, although that is metaphorical: a hand-written document has all the same First Amendment protections as a printed document. Freedom of the press does not exclusively mean journalists, although journalists are included in the definition of the "freedom of the press." It means the ability of all people to be free to publish what they wish. However, this right does not release an author from suffering consequences of publishing false or inflammatory information about another person or speech that endangers life.

Almost from the moment that the art of printing began to be a significant cultural influence, efforts were exerted to gain control of its use by the king or the central government. For example, Henry VIII took absolute control of the press, determining who could print and what could be printed. When Cromwell ruled during the period of the Lone Parliament, the same control continued. By 1758, however, freedom of the press had been established to the point where Blackstone could say:

> *Every freeman has an undoubted right to lay what sentiments he pleases before the public; to forbid this is to destroy the freedom of the press, but if he publishes what is improper, mischievous, or illegal, he must take the consequence of his own temerity. To subject the press to the restrictive power of a licenser, as was formerly done, both before and since the revolution, is to subject all freedom of sentiment to the prejudices of one man, and make him the arbitrary and infallible judge of all*

controverted points in learning, religion, and government.[60]

THE TRIAL OF JOHN PETER ZENGER

The freedom of speech and the press got an early start in America in 1735 via the celebrated legal case of John Peter Zenger. Gouverneur Morris, delegate to the Constitutional Convention of 1787 and author of the preamble to the Constitution, said:

The trial of Zenger in 1735 was the germ of American freedom, the morning star of that liberty which subsequently revolutionized America.[61]

Gouverneur Morris was the great-grandson of Lewis Morris, the chief justice of the New York Supreme Court in 1733. Justice Morris was removed from his post by the governor of New York, William Cosby, because he was a dissenting vote against the governor in an earlier case. Among other things, that action by the governor motivated Zenger to establish a newspaper, the *New York Weekly Journal*, for the express purpose of publishing articles critical of the governor.

James Alexander, a lawyer and statesman, helped Zenger with the *New York Weekly Journal*. In a letter to his old friend, former Governor Robert Hunter, he revealed:

Our Governor, who came here but last year, has long ago given more distaste to the people than I believe any Governor that ever this Province had during his whole government. . . It would be tedious to give a detail of them. . .

Enclosed is also the first of a newspaper designed to be continued weekly, chiefly to expose [Governor Cosby] and those ridiculous flatteries with which Mr Harison

---

[60] William Blackstone, *Commentaries on the Laws of England*, 1758

[61] "Dr. John W. Francis tells us, in his description of the city of New York, that the late Gouverneur Morris told him that, 'The trial of Zenger in. . .,'" William Dunlap, *History of the New Netherlands, Province of New York, and State of New York*, 1839

> *loads our other newspaper, which our Governor claims
> and has the privilege of suffering nothing to be in but
> what he and Mr Harison approve of.[62]*

After publishing his newspaper for just over a year, Zenger was arrested, jailed for eight months, and tried for seditious libel. Andrew Hamilton, Zenger's attorney, admitted to the court that Zenger had, in fact, published the content that he was accused of, but argued he should not be convicted because the published content could be proved. The judge refused to allow Hamilton to provide evidence that the content was true because the law at the time made it clear that libel was libel, even if it could be proved.

> *You cannot be admitted, Mr. Hamilton, to give the truth
> of a libel in evidence. A libel is not to be justified; for it
> is nevertheless a libel that it is true.[63]*

Being forbidden to prove the truth of the libel, Hamilton instead pled to the hearts of the jury. He pled the cause of liberty in writing and speaking—freedom of speech and the press.

> *No, it is natural, it is a privilege, I will go farther, it is a
> right, which all free men claim, that they are entitled to
> complain when they are hurt. They have a right publicly
> to remonstrate against the abuses of power in the
> strongest terms, to put their neighbors upon their guard
> against the craft or open violence of men in authority,
> and to assert with courage the sense they have of the
> blessings of liberty, the value they put upon it, and their
> resolution at all hazards to preserve it as one of the
> greatest blessings heaven can bestow. . .*

> *If, then, this is the nature of power, let us at least do our
> duty, and like wise men who value freedom use our
> utmost care to support liberty, the only bulwark against
> lawless power, which in all ages has sacrificed to its wild*

---

[62] Letter from James Alexander to Robert Hunter, 1733
[63] John Peter Zenger, *A Brief Narrative of the Case and Trial of John Peter Zenger*, 1736

lust and boundless ambition the blood of the best men that ever lived. . .

The question before the Court and you, Gentlemen of the jury, is not of small or private concern. It is not the cause of one poor printer, nor of New York alone, which you are now trying. No! It may in its consequence affect every free man that lives under a British government on the main of America. It is the best cause. It is the cause of liberty. And I make no doubt but your upright conduct this day will not only entitle you to the love and esteem of your fellow citizens, but every man who prefers freedom to a life of slavery will bless and honor you as men who have baffled the attempt of tyranny, and by an impartial and uncorrupt verdict have laid a noble foundation for securing to ourselves, our posterity, and our neighbors, that to which nature and the laws of our country have given us a right to liberty of both exposing and opposing arbitrary power (in these parts of the world at least) by speaking and writing truth.[64]

The jury withdrew and quickly returned with their verdict. When asked by the clerk whether Zenger was guilty of printing and publishing the libels in the information, Thomas Hunt, the jury foreman replied: "Not guilty." Zenger wrote that with those two words, "there were three huzzas in the hall, which was crowded with people; and the next day I was discharged from my imprisonment."[65]

As a court trial and not a legislative deliberation, the Zenger trial did not create a new law regarding seditious libel, but it did send the message that the public was in support of the freedom of speech and of the press. After the trial, other newspapers began to publish more opposition content with less fear of repercussions by the government.

---

[64] Ibid.
[65] Ibid.

THE FOUNDERS' THOUGHTS ON THE FREEDOM OF SPEECH AND PRESS

In a letter written to Edward Carrington in 1787, Thomas Jefferson expressed his view on the importance of the freedom of speech. He did so from the view that when the people exercise their right of free speech, it keeps the government within its original bounds, even if the views of the people are in error.

> *The interposition of the people themselves on the side of government has had a great effect on the opinion here. I am persuaded myself that the good sense of the people will always be found to be the best army. They may be led astray for a moment, but will soon correct themselves. The people are the only censors of their governors: and even their errors will tend to keep these to the true principles of their institution. To punish these errors too severely would be to suppress the only safeguard of the public liberty. The way to prevent these irregular interpositions of the people is to give them full information of their affairs thro' the channel of the public papers, and to contrive that those papers should penetrate the whole mass of the people. The basis of our governments being the opinion of the people, the very first object should be to keep that right; and were it left to me to decide whether we should have a government without newspapers, or newspapers without a government, I should not hesitate a moment to prefer the latter. But I should mean that every man should receive those papers and be capable of reading them. . . Cherish therefore the spirit of our people, and keep alive their attention. Do not be too severe upon their errors, but reclaim them by enlightening them. If once they become inattentive to the public affairs, you and I, and Congress, and Assemblies, judges and governors shall all become wolves.*[66]

---

[66] Letter from Thomas Jefferson to Edward Carrington, 16 January 1787

Jefferson indicated that he would rather have a society with newspapers and no government than one with government and no newspapers. This is interesting in light of Jefferson's disdain for newspapers and is a testament to his views on the freedom of speech and the press. In his view, a newspaper full of lies is better than government without the ability of the people to speak and print freely. His letter to John Norvell highlights this point:

> *To your request of my opinion of the manner in which a newspaper should be conducted. . . I should answer. . . I really look with commiseration over the great body of my fellow citizens, who, reading newspapers, live & die in the belief, that they have known something of what has been passing in the world in their time. . . I will add, that the man who never looks into a newspaper is better informed than he who reads them; inasmuch as he who knows nothing is nearer to truth than he whose mind is filled with falsehoods & errors. He who reads nothing will still learn the great facts. . .*

> *Perhaps an editor might begin a reformation in some such way as this. Divide his paper into 4 chapters, heading the 1st, Truths. 2d, Probabilities. 3d, Possibilities. 4th, Lies. The first chapter would be very short, as it would contain little more than authentic papers, and information from such sources as the editor would be willing to risk his own reputation for their truth. The 2d would contain what, from a mature consideration of all circumstances, his judgment should conclude to be probably true. This, however, should rather contain too little than too much. The 3d & 4th should be professedly for those readers who would rather have lies for their money than the blank paper they would occupy.*[67]

---

[67] Letter from Jefferson to John Norvell, 14 June 1807

In 1787, James Wilson clarified what was meant by the freedom of the press at the Pennsylvania ratifying convention:

What is meant by the liberty of the press is, that there should be no antecedent restraint upon it; but that every author is responsible when he attacks the security or welfare of the government, or the safety, character, and property of the individual.[68]

THE SEDITION ACTS

In 1798, Congress passed four famously controversial laws known as the Alien and Sedition Acts. Even more surprisingly, John Adams, the president at the time, signed the acts into law. The Sedition Acts were a direct attack against the freedom of speech and of the press. These acts made it illegal to criticize Congress, the president, or any laws. Thomas Jefferson and James Madison responded to this attack in what became known as the Virginia and Kentucky Resolutions of 1798. The historical lesson that played out seems to strengthen the argument for the need of a bill of rights. Even John Adams, the fiery voice of the Revolution, could not resist the temptation to limit free speech and press when he was the one being criticized.

An Act in Addition to the Act, Entitled An Act for the Punishment of Certain Crimes Against the United States, approved July 14, 1798

SEC. 2. And be it farther enacted, That if any person shall write, print, utter or publish, or shall cause or procure to be written, printed, uttered or published, or shall knowingly and willingly assist or aid in writing, printing, uttering or publishing any false, scandalous and malicious writing or writings against the government of the United States, or either house of the Congress of the United States, or the President of the United States, with intent to defame the said government,

---

[68] James Wilson, Pennsylvania ratifying convention, 1 Dec. 1787

or either house of the said Congress, or the said President, or to bring them, or either of them, into contempt or disrepute; or to excite against them, or either or any of them, the hatred of the good people of the United States, or to stir up sedition within the United States, . . . for opposing or resisting any law of the United States, or any act of the President of the United States. . . or to resist, oppose, or defeat any such law or act. . . then such person, being thereof convicted before any court of the United States having jurisdiction thereof, shall be punished by a fine not exceeding two thousand dollars, and by imprisonment not exceeding two years.

SEC. 4. And be it further enacted, That this act shall continue and be in force until the third day of March, one thousand eight hundred and one, and no longer. . .[69]

One might be curious as to why March 3, 1801, was chosen as the date the law would expire. It just so happens that the next presidential term and the next Congress would begin March 4, 1801. The authors of the law, and the president who signed it into law, were only concerned about sedition for as long as they were in office.

Thomas Jefferson and James Madison drafted resolutions for Virginia and Kentucky to adopt in opposition to the Alien and Sedition Acts. These resolutions give the reader insight into the thinking of the Founders—at least into the thinking of Madison and Jefferson—as it relates to the freedom of speech and the press.

VIRGINIA AND KENTUCKY RESOLUTIONS OF 1798

Virginia Resolutions, 21 December 1798

That the General Assembly doth particularly PROTEST against the palpable and alarming infractions of the Constitution, in the two late cases of the "Alien and

---

[69] An Act in Addition to the Act, Entitled An Act for the Punishment of Certain Crimes Against the United States, 14 July 1798

Sedition Acts," passed at the last session of Congress; the first of which exercises a power nowhere delegated to the federal government, and which, by uniting legislative and judicial powers to those of executive, subverts the general principles of free government, as well as the particular organization and positive provisions of the Federal Constitution; and the other of which acts exercises, in like manner, a power not delegated by the Constitution, but, on the contrary, expressly and positively forbidden by one of the amendments thereto,—a power which, more than any other, ought to produce universal alarm, because it is leveled against the right of freely examining public characters and measures, and of free communication among the people thereon, which has ever been justly deemed the only effectual guardian of every other right.

That this state having, by its Convention, which ratified the Federal Constitution, expressly declared that, among other essential rights, "the liberty of conscience and the press cannot be canceled, abridged, restrained, or modified, by any authority of the United States," and from its extreme anxiety to guard these rights from every possible attack of sophistry and ambition, having, with other states, recommended an amendment for that purpose, which amendment was, in due time, annexed to the Constitution—it would mark a reproachful inconsistency, and criminal degeneracy, if an indifference were now shown to the most palpable violation of one of the rights thus declared and secured, and to the establishment of a precedent which may be fatal to the other.[70]

Kentucky Resolutions, 10 November 1798

---

[70] Virginia Resolutions, 21 December 1798

Resolved, That it is true, as a general principle, . . . that, no power over the. . . freedom of speech, or freedom of the press, being delegated to the United States by the Constitution, nor prohibited by it to the states, all lawful powers respecting the same did of right remain, and were reserved to the states, or to the people; that thus was manifested their determination to retain to themselves the right of judging how far the licentiousness of speech, and of the press, may be abridged without lessening their useful freedom, and how far those abuses which cannot be separated from their use, should be tolerated rather than the use be destroyed; and thus also they guarded against all abridgment, by the United States. . . and that, in addition to this general principle and express declaration, another and more special provision has been made by one of the amendments to the Constitution, which expressly declares, that "Congress shall make no laws. . . abridging the freedom of speech, or of the press," thereby guarding, in the same sentence, and under the same words, the freedom. . . of speech, and of the press, insomuch that whatever violates either throws down the sanctuary which covers the others—and that libels, falsehood, and defamation, equally with heresy and false religion, are withheld from the cognizance of federal tribunals. That therefore the act of the Congress of the United States, passed on the 14th of July, 1798, entitled "An Act in Addition to the Act entitled An Act for the Punishment of certain Crimes against the United States," which does abridge the freedom of the press, is not law, but is altogether void, and of no force.[71]

The year after the Virginia and Kentucky Resolutions, the people of Kentucky enshrined their views on the freedom of speech and the press in their Constitution of 1799.

---

[71] Kentucky Resolutions, 10 November 1798

> *Sec. 7. That printing-presses shall be free to every person who undertakes to examine the proceedings of the legislature or any branch of government, and no law shall ever be made to restrain the right thereof. The free communication of thoughts and opinions is one of the invaluable rights of man, and every citizen may freely speak, write, and print on any subject, being responsible for the abuse of that liberty.*
>
> *Sec. 8. In prosecutions for the publication of papers investigating the official conduct of officers or men in a public capacity, or where the matter published is proper for public information, the truth thereof may be given in evidence. And in all indictments for libels, the jury shall have a right to determine the law and the facts, under the direction of the court, as in other cases.* [72]

It is intriguing to imagine what would have happened if the First Amendment did not exist when the Alien and Sedition acts were passed in 1798. What arguments would Jefferson and Madison have used? Fortunately, they had the First Amendment to fall upon to protest the acts as a violation of natural law and a violation of the freedom of speech protected by the Constitution. This is an early testament for the need for a bill of rights and why the study of our unalienable rights in the Bill of Rights continues to be essential for the preservation of liberty.

A DIFFERENCE OF OPINION IS NOT A DIFFERENCE OF PRINCIPLE

The presidential election between Thomas Jefferson and John Adams was one of the most heated in American history. Two longtime friends became bitter political enemies. Their friendship was rekindled in their sunset years, but in 1800 they did not see eye to eye. Jefferson won the election; in his inaugural address he petitioned the people to enter into a united discourse, something lost during the course of the election.

---

[72] Kentucky Constitution, 1799

The remarkable thing about Jefferson's inaugural speech is that he strongly endorses the freedom of speech even though he had been obliterated in the press. Worse yet, he and his likeminded Americans were the ones specifically targeted by the Alien and Sedition Acts. After all that, he still believed that the freedom of speech was the best method of combating falsehood and discord.

Jefferson begins his speech by acknowledging that a stranger to the idea of liberty as it exists in America might not understand the purpose of public debate, even if that debate is heated. But once an election is decided according to the rules of the Constitution, Americans should reunite in the spirit of common liberty. To not do so would defeat the purpose of protecting liberty—harmony.

> *During the contest of opinion through which we have passed the animation of discussions and of exertions has sometimes worn an aspect which might impose on strangers unused to think freely and to speak and to write what they think; but this being now decided by the voice of the nation, announced according to the rules of the Constitution. . . Let us, then, fellow-citizens, unite with one heart and one mind. Let us restore to social intercourse that harmony and affection without which liberty and even life itself are but dreary things. And let us reflect that, having banished from our land that religious intolerance under which mankind so long bled and suffered, we have yet gained little if we countenance a political intolerance as despotic, as wicked, and capable of as bitter and bloody persecutions. . . that this should be more felt and feared by some and less by others, and should divide opinions as to measures of safety. But every difference of opinion is not a difference of principle. We have called by different names brethren of the same principle. We are all Republicans, we are all Federalists.*[73]

---

[73] Thomas Jefferson, First Inaugural Address, 4 March 1801

Jefferson draws a parallel between religious freedom and political freedom and expresses that promoting one and not the other would indicate little social progress. Differences of policy between Republicans and Federalists in 1800 was not necessarily a difference of principle, just as differences in religious creeds are not often differences of morality. Like the fact that liberty is common among us, we have a federal republic in common too. In a dark time of discord, Jefferson sought the light of common ground. Rights protected by the Constitution are the one thing all Americans have in common. This includes the freedom of speech. Speech should be protected even if it goes so far as to express the opinion that the nation should be abolished. In fact, to allow that speech would show how important the protection of speech is.

> *If there be any among us who would wish to dissolve this Union or to change its republican form, let them stand undisturbed as monuments of the safety with which error of opinion may be tolerated where reason is left free to combat it.*[74]

Most importantly, protecting all speech is the only way to guarantee that correct opinions are free to rebut errors. Humans are imperfect. No person or group of people has a monopoly on truth. If one group is allowed to silence the speech of others, not only will tyranny result, but truth may also be censored too. If some people can be in error, it is likely that other people are in error as well. Therefore, all must be free to express their opinions if truth is to find its way into the light.

> *Sometimes it is said that man can not be trusted with the government of himself. Can he, then, be trusted with the government of others? Or have we found angels in the forms of kings to govern him? Let history answer this question.*[75]

---

[74] Ibid.
[75] Ibid.

Americans have been free to express their ideas and document their findings with fewer censors than history's other examples. The United States of America has been a significant leader in the world in advances in civil government, in religious commitment in the form of charity, in medicine, transportation, manufacturing, science, agriculture, and virtually every modern achievement. This is not because Americans are more capable than other nations, but because the freedom of speech and the freedom of the press are protected and enshrined in the Bill of Rights.

THE RIGHT TO ASSEMBLE

"CONGRESS SHALL MAKE NO LAW. . . ABRIDGING. . . THE RIGHT OF THE PEOPLE PEACEABLY TO ASSEMBLE. . ."

KEY QUOTE FROM THE FOUNDING ERA

It is beyond debate that freedom to engage in association for the advancement of beliefs and ideas is an inseparable aspect of. . . "liberty."[76] —
Justice John Marshall Harlan II

The right to assemble begins with the freedom of association. Each individual is free to choose with whom to associate and to be a part of any organization. This freedom includes religious association, employment, entertainment, etc.

The right to assemble is the right to associate with whomever we wish. For example:

- For a relationship with whomever we choose.

- Religious gatherings—associated with the freedom of expression.

- Business exchanges—the right to buy, sell, employ, or be employed with those of our choice.

---

[76] John Marshall Harlan, *NAACP v. Alabama*, 1958

- Entertainment gatherings with family, friends, or anyone with whom we choose to engage in any form of entertainment.

- Education for the purposes of furthering various sciences in cooperation with others.

- Assembling with like-minded people for the purpose of petitioning the government.

THE RIGHT TO ASSEMBLE TO PETITION

One of the foremost complaints of the American colonies against King George III, in the Declaration and Resolves of 1774, was that "assemblies have been frequently dissolved, contrary to the rights of the people, when they attempted to deliberate on grievances."[77]

They further complained that their "petitions to the Crown for redress have been repeatedly treated with contempt by his Majesty's Minister of State."[78]

The right to assemble has not been easy to preserve, even in the United States. During the debate of highly inflammatory issues, the tendency of government officials is to look with grave suspicion upon public assemblies, and sometimes ignore petitions which run contrary to current administrative policy. President Van Buren's administration was marked by a struggle to prevent the receipt and consideration by Congress of numerous petitions for the abolition of slavery. Senator John C. Calhoun even declared such petitions to be "a violation of the Constitution."[79]

Difficult cases have arisen in connection with the enforcement of sedition laws. For example, it is a violation of the law, in some cases, to assemble for the purpose of conspiring to commit a crime or to

---

[77] Continental Congress, Declaration and Resolves, 1774
[78] Ibid.
[79] John C. Calhoun, remarks on the Right of Petition, delivered in the Senate, 13 February 1840

use violence in overthrowing constituted authority. However, a peaceable assembly for lawful discussion cannot be made a crime.

The right to assemble for the purpose of petitioning government for a redress of grievances leads us to the obvious next right—the right to petition.

RIGHT TO PETITION

"CONGRESS SHALL MAKE NO LAW. . . ABRIDGING. . . THE RIGHT OF THE PEOPLE. . . TO PETITION THE GOVERNMENT FOR A REDRESS OF GRIEVANCES. . ."

KEY QUOTES FROM THE FOUNDING ERA

No government ought to be without censors.[80]
—Thomas Jefferson

[The right to petition] would seem unnecessary to be expressly provided for in a republican government, since it results from the very nature of its structure and institutions. It is impossible, that it could be practically denied, until the spirit of liberty had wholly disappeared, and the people had become so servile and debased, as to be unfit to exercise any of the privileges of freemen.[81] —
Joseph Story

HISTORY OF THE RIGHT TO PETITION THE GOVERNMENT

This provision guarantees the people the right to petition the government without intervention or prohibition by government authorities. Joseph Story suggests that this provision "was probably borrowed from the declaration of rights in England, on the revolution of 1688, in which the right to petition the king for a redress of grievances was insisted on."[82]

English history is full of examples in which kings and rulers refused to address the grievances of the people. This frequently resulted in

---

[80] Letter from Thomas Jefferson to George Washington, 9 September 1792
[81] Joseph Story, *Commentaries on the Constitution*, 1887
[82] Joseph Story, *Commentaries on the Constitution*, 1888

rebellion and even revolution and was codified in declaratory documents such as:

Magna Carta

Petition of Right

English Bill of Rights

Declaration of Resolves

The Declaration of Independence

King John's oppressive reign resulted in the barons forcing him to sign the Magna Carta, which concluded with a

> *COMMAND that the English Church shall be free, and that men in our kingdom shall have and keep all these liberties, rights, and concessions, well and peaceably in their fullness and entirety for them and their heirs. . . in all things and all places for ever.*[83]

In 1628, the English Parliament sent the Petition of Right to King Charles I. Parliament demanded that the king recognize four main provisions: no taxation without Parliament's consent; no imprisonment without cause; no quartering of soldiers in private homes; and no martial law in peacetime.

The English Bill of Rights was the result of King James II endeavoring "to subvert and extirpate the Protestant religion and the laws and liberties of [his] kingdom."[84] After the Glorious Revolution, when William and Mary took power, the lords and commoners reestablished some of their basic rights, among which was "the right of the subjects to petition the King."[85]

After Parliament passed the Coercive Acts, the colonial legislature responded with the Declaration of Resolves in which they claimed

---

[83] Magna Carta, 1215
[84] English Bill of Rights, 1689
[85] Ibid.

the "right peaceably to assemble, consider of their grievances, and petition the king."[86]

The Declaration of Independence denounced in the strongest possible terms the refusal of the king to give respectful consideration to the petitions of the people.

> *In every stage of these oppressions we have petitioned for redress in the most humble terms: Our repeated petitions have been answered only by repeated injury. A prince, whose character is thus marked by every act which may define a tyrant, is unfit to be the ruler of a free people.*[87]

King George III responded to this petition by refusing to read it. He did not make any public statement about the Declaration until October 31, 1776, when he mentioned the separation in a speech to Parliament.

Governments throughout the ages have resented petitions for the simple reason that they usually itemize the sins of government and the dereliction of administration by government offices. Nevertheless, this is the safety valve by which governments survive. Unless administrators are sensitive to the grievances of the people, the hostility of rebellious forces can reach a boiling point. King George III learned this too late. So did Louis XVI of France. Constant communication between the government and its people is fundamental to efficient administration.

PROTECTING THE UNALIENABLE RIGHT OF EXPRESSION

The logical progression of rights in the First Amendment helps clarify our responsibility as citizens to preserve free expression. Who can deny that each individual has a right to think? If this basic undeniable right exists, which of us can rightfully restrain another from expressing their thoughts? Our collective expression of thought is what moves society forward. As we assemble to discuss

---

[86] Declaration and Resolves of the First Continental Congress, October 1774
[87] Declaration of Independence, 4 July 1776

our thoughts, varying opinions arise. Inevitably, one group in society will try to silence another, first by intimidation and then by the force of government. This repeated pattern is the reason the Framers wisely included the First Amendment. Our undeniable right to free expression exists so long as we petition our government for redress against any attempts to subvert it.

Second Amendment

"A WELL-REGULATED MILITIA, BEING NECESSARY TO THE SECURITY OF A FREE STATE, THE RIGHT OF THE PEOPLE TO KEEP AND BEAR ARMS, SHALL NOT BE INFRINGED."

KEY QUOTES FROM THE FOUNDING ERA

Conceived it to be the privilege of every citizen, and one of his most essential rights, to bear arms, and to resist every attack upon his liberty or property, by whomsoever made.[1] —Roger Sherman

To preserve liberty, it is essential that the whole body of the people always possess arms, and be taught alike, especially when young, how to use them.[2]
—Richard Henry Lee

The said Constitution shall never be construed to authorize Congress to. . . prevent the people of the United States who are peaceable citizens from keeping their own arms.[3] —Samuel Adams

A well regulated militia, composed of the body of the people, trained to arms, is the best and most natural defense of a free country.[4]
—James Madison

What, Sir, is the use of a militia? It is to prevent the establishment of a standing army, the bane of liberty. . . Whenever Governments mean to invade the rights and liberties of the people, they always attempt to

---

[1] Roger Sherman, Debates on 1790 Militia Act
[2] Richard Henry Lee, *Federal Farmer* No. 18, 1788
[3] Samuel Adams, Massachusetts ratifying convention, 1788
[4] James Madison, Annals of Congress, 1789

> *destroy the militia, in order to raise an army upon their ruins.*[5]
>
> —Elbridge Gerry

Self-preservation is the fundamental principle behind the Second Amendment. It is no different than the right to protect our bodies from hunger and the elements. We do this by working to secure food, clothing, and shelter.

We could end there, but that line between self-preservation and infringing upon the rights of others is not as clear as we would hope. This is not helped by the fact that the Second Amendment is written with such ambiguity, which contributes to the fact that it is perhaps the most debated amendment in the Bill of Rights.

There are many reasons why the Second Amendment is so debated. The two most significant are that first, it is looked at by people on both sides of the debate through a twenty-first century lens, and second, it is taken at face value. The words are evaluated, and punctuation is debated based on its words, not what it means. Many attempts have been made to interpret its meaning before considering its history.

Adding to the ambiguity of the Second Amendment was the Supreme Court's silence on the subject for nearly two centuries. It was not until the 2008 *District of Columbia v. Heller* case that the court engaged in its "first in-depth examination of the Second Amendment."[6] But don't get too excited; the court's opinion in that case stated that "one should not expect it to clarify the entire field."[7] We'll get into that case later.

Navigating how the Second Amendment came to be written in its current form can be a bit confusing. To help along that lengthy path, here are the key points along the way:

- We have the right to life and, by extension, the right of self-preservation, by force if necessary.

---

[5] Elbridge Gerry, Annals of Congress, 1789
[6] United States Supreme Court, *District of Columbia v. Heller*, 2008
[7] Ibid.

- In order to forcefully preserve our lives from powers stronger than us, we must have the right to use arms (weapons) for that preservation.

- The idea of self-preservation had been self-evident for hundreds of years prior to the founding era. By then each state already secured the right in their declarations of rights and constitutions.

- The Second Amendment was not written for the express purpose of protecting the individual right to keep and bear arms, even though it does exactly that.

- Societies also have the right of self-preservation. Through experience, the Founders knew that countries needed to be able to protect themselves from foreign invasion, rogue standing armies, and excessively tyrannical governments. They knew that the best method for protecting a country from those forces is a militia, which consists of every able-bodied person.

- The states, out of fear of foreign invasion, standing armies, and tyranny, wanted to ensure that the militia would always be available to protect the country or the states if needed.

- The primary way to ensure the existence of the militia is to make sure that the unalienable right to keep and bear arms exists among individuals.

That is the path. Without that understanding, the Second Amendment seems remarkably unclear. Now, let's get into the details, beginning with the fundamental right behind the Amendment.

THE RIGHT OF SELF-PRESERVATION

Because we have a right to life, it is logical to conclude that we have a right to preserve that life. Likewise, we have a right to liberty and the preservation of that liberty.

We have an inherent right to life and liberty, which includes the right to preserve our life and liberty. If we do not have the right to preserve a right, we do not have the right in the first place. And if we do not have the absolute, arbitrary power to destroy our life and liberty,[8] then we not only have the right to preserve them, we have a duty to do so as well.

We preserve our life and liberty by working to acquire the means of preserving them. We work to plant, cultivate, and harvest food. We construct shelter and produce clothing. If we don't directly do those things, we work for others to acquire them. We use our life and liberty to accumulate property for our sustenance, leisure, pleasure, and improve upon our ability to acquire more property.

We only have the right to use, or govern, property that we have acquired by the sweat of our own brow. This includes the right to exchange our property for the property of another with their consent. We do not have the right to take another's property without their consent, and they do not have a right to ours. The unalienable right we have to our life, liberty, and property gives each of us the right and the duty to preserve them, by force if necessary. The right and duty to preserve may require defense, and in turn the means to do so. The means to defend requires arms: our own hands, a rock, a stick, a sword, a bow, a gun, etc.

We have the right to protect our property almost as aggressively as our lives. This is because we used our life and liberty to obtain that property. In defending our property, we are defending the life and liberty we spent to obtain it. The earlier equation, LIFE + LIBERTY = PROPERTY, illustrates the rationale of defending property by force.

Individuals do not have the right to govern another without their consent. Likewise, they do not have the right to destroy the life, liberty, and property of others. They may have the natural ability and could do so based on primitive natural law. But if we want to

---

[8] "Nobody has an absolute arbitrary power over himself. . . to destroy his own life." John Locke, *The Second Treatise on Civil Government*, 1689

live in a peaceful, civil society, adherence to sophisticated natural law tells us that we do not have the right to destroy another's rights. In fact, to preserve civility, we have a duty not to do so.

Throughout history, defensive weapons have changed as technology has advanced. Today, firearms are the most common and accessible weapons. Regardless of many regulations meant to prevent otherwise, criminally-minded people can obtain guns almost as easily as law-abiding citizens. Imagine what would happen if law-abiding citizens were denied access to the same weapons that law-breaking citizens obtained through illegal means. They would essentially be denied the right of self-preservation.

This is not to illustrate a cynical view of the world in which an individual must defend themselves against every one of their neighbors, but rather a practical principle we currently practice on a state and national level. It is a principle of peace through strength. For example, as a nation we have a strong military, and this discourages neighboring countries from invading. This principle applies on a community and individual level as well. If it is known that the law-abiding residents of your community own guns and are trained in their use, crime in that community should, in theory, be low.

The fact that we have a right to bear arms does not mean we are required to. People are free to not own a weapon for any reason they choose, including a fear of guns. However, a single destructive individual can cause havoc among an entire community that is unarmed. Each individual has the right to choose to prepare themselves against that danger in the name of self-preservation. Likewise, an individual may choose to stockpile food in preparation for a famine while others may see no need.

The right to bear arms as an individual is the right to preserve our own life and liberty, and by extension, our property. In the Founders' era, and nearly a thousand years of English history before them, the right of self-preservation was a self-evident truth—a no-brainer, in modern terms. It was never questioned whether an individual could work to obtain food, clothing, and shelter. It was never questioned whether an individual could bear arms for hunting, and rarely questioned whether they could bear arms for their individual and collective preservation.

The Founders felt little need to codify such an obvious right in the Constitution, especially since it was considered up to the states to codify it in their declarations of rights and constitutions. Specific language recognizing the right to life and liberty was not in the 1787 Constitution, and neither was language expressing the right to preserve life and liberty.

The people of Pennsylvania affirmed in their 1776 Declaration of Rights:

> *That the people have a right to bear arms for the defence of themselves and the state. . .*

And reiterated that affirmation in stronger terms, in their 1790 Constitution:

> *The right of the citizens to bear arms in defense of themselves and the State shall not be questioned.*

Not until the addition of the Second Amendment was the principle of self-preservation codified, and that was in terms of state preservation—but we'll get to that later.

We have the right of self-preservation, but do we have the right or duty to preserve the rights of others? Do we have a collective right of self-preservation?

THE RIGHT OF COLLECTIVE PRESERVATION

Similar to individual self-preservation, the citizens of a state or country have a collective right to protect the society they create. The majority in a society has the right to establish, alter, and abolish their form of government. Interestingly, citizens who form a society have the absolute arbitrary power over their form of government. A majority can completely abolish it if they wish. Once abolished, they can create a new society in its place. By contrast, individuals do not have absolute power over their own life and liberty. An individual cannot create another life if they abolish theirs.

Society is established by individuals, collectively, to collectively protect their individual rights. When people join in a society, they benefit from the specialized labor of others. The shoemaker makes shoes, the butcher provides cut meats, the farmer grows fruits and vegetables, and so on. Each individual works their craft and trades their goods for the goods of others. Rules and laws are put in place to govern society and the exchange of those goods—all for the purposes of collective preservation and for the ultimate purpose of individual self-preservation.

In addition to establishing and governing a society for the exchange of goods and services, the citizens have a right to defend their country from enemies foreign and domestic. A criminal justice system is created to defend society from enemies domestic. Standing armies and militia are formed to defend from enemies foreign.

The debate over the Second Amendment has produced two general sides, the "individual rights" side and the "collective rights" side. The individualist side believes the Second Amendment protects the right of the individual to keep and bear arms. The collectively minded side believes the Amendment only protects the right to keep and bear arms for militia or military service only.

BRIEF HISTORY OF THE RIGHT TO BEAR ARMS

To more fully appreciate the right to bear arms, a brief history of English armament helps illustrate the struggle that the English went through to keep this right and what happens when it is denied. As discussed previously, the right to self-preservation is a self-evident human right. It would be impossible to compile a complete history of this right. For the purposes of this book, we will take a brief look at some of the significant events in English history which led the Founding Fathers to the conclusion that bearing arms is a right of the people.

The right to bear arms predates the Constitution. It is well established in English history and, in fact, predates the invention of firearms.

Prior to the reign of Alfred the Great (871–899 A.D.), the citizen army, or the "fyrd," consisted of freemen, who were required to be armed. During Alfred's reign, all his subjects, including the peasants, were required to purchase weapons and ready themselves for military service.

The Norman Conquest in 1066 brought elements of feudal law to England and many of the Anglo-Saxons' rights to land and personal property were denied. They did, however, manage to retain possession of their arms, which limited the power of the monarchy. In fact, kings regularly appealed to their subjects for military assistance. William Rufas, who reigned as the second Norman king (1087–1100), called on his English subjects to quell a rebellion against his feudal barons. He obtained their assistance only after promising better laws and to rescind taxes instituted under his reign, among other things.

The Assize of Arms in 1181 by Henry II (1154–1189), and its expansion in 1253 by his successor Henry III, compelled every able-bodied freeman to arm themselves according to their possessions. Strict laws were enforced upon anyone who did not pledge to defend the crown.

During the reign of the four Edwards, the bow increased in popularity and effectiveness. By the reign of Edward IV, "every Englishman or Irishman dwelling in England [was required to] have a bow of his own height" and made of specific types of wood "according to their power."[9]

Every township in England was required to have an archery range where all citizens must practice their skill with the bow. With few exceptions, the law required all commoners to be armed with the deadliest military weapons and imposed only minimal restraints on

---

[9] Robert Hardy, *The Longbow: A Social and Military History*, 1977

their use, such as specific locations where armament was not allowed—the royal courts, at tournaments with spectators, or in the presence of the king's ministers, to name a few.

Experimentation with firearms began in England as early as the 1300s, but the new technology advanced very slowly. In the early 1500s the longbow was still favored over the wheellock, which was considered to be a major breakthrough in firearm technology. It operated by friction from a wheel mechanism, which ignited the gunpowder with a spark. As firearms improved during the 16th century, many European countries attempted to control weaponry by imposing bans upon their manufacture or restricting the sale of firearms and ammunition. Henry VIII experimented with this practice briefly in England, but it was short-lived, as it was found to be incompatible with English customs and laws.

The long-standing requirement of armament in England was so well established in the minds and practices of the people that Henry had little choice but to ease the restrictions he had imposed on gun manufacture and sale. He eventually ended restrictions on firearms through an official proclamation.

Sir John Fortescue, a Tudor legal commentator, would later compare the

> *. . . happy state of peasants in England, with its limited monarchy, and the unhappy state of peasants in France, with absolute monarchy, that the French peasants were so poorly off that they not only starved but could not have any 'Wepen' or the means to obtain it. The consciousness of English as a weapons owning and using people, in contrast to the French and other Continentals, was beginning to take form.*[10]

During the reign of Queen Elizabeth, the militia system was further developed. In fact, it was during her reign that the term *militia* was first used. This term described the armed body of citizens who were

---

[10] The Right to Keep and Bear Arms, Report of the Senate Subcommittee on the Constitution, 1982

trained to stand ready in defense of their nation. Lieutenants from each county formally mustered the militia to regular practice and to display their weapons. Because militia members were private citizens who purchased their own weapons and not part of an army that was paid and armed by the crown, the queen or king had less control over them.

This began to change under the reign of James I, who believed that kings were "God's lieutenants upon earth" and "accountable to none but God only."[11]

His reign was hotly contested by Parliament's rising power, and they clashed incessantly. However, peace prevailed in England until his son, Charles I, came to power in 1625. Charles inherited his father's views of absolute monarchy and was intensely disliked by Parliament, which ultimately resulted in civil war. Charles was forced to gather what troops he could and flee the city.

Because of policy changes in regulating the militia under the two monarchs, the militia had become less effective, resulting in Parliament creating the New Model Army. This army was led by Sir Thomas Fairfax, with Oliver Cromwell as second in command. At the end of the English Civil War, Charles was beheaded for treason and the British monarchy was abolished in favor of the Commonwealth of England, with Oliver Cromwell as Lord Protector. In this capacity, Cromwell's army eventually disbanded Parliament and became a military dictatorship.

Not long after Cromwell's death in 1658, Charles II, the son of Charles I, took the throne. He was followed by James II, who was the second surviving son of Charles I. Both kings ruled as absolute monarchs and enforced many disarmament laws. James II sought to expand the standing army and

> *hoped that every Body would be convinced that the Militia, which had hitherto been to [sic] much depended on, was not sufficient for such Occasions, and that there*

---

[11] James I speech before Parliament, 1609

*was nothing but a good Force of well-diciplined Troops,
in constant Pay, that could defend us.*[12]

Parliament blocked these efforts, but he did manage to cause warrantless searches:

*complaining; that; "a great; many persons not qualified
by law. . . keep muskets or other guns in their houses."*[13]

Having converted to Catholicism earlier in his life, James relentlessly persecuted the Protestants, directing much of his disarmament efforts towards them.

Several prominent Englishmen wrote to William of Orange, the son-in-law of James II, and convinced him to bring his army and march on London. Two of James's most loyal supporters, his daughter Anne and General John Churchill, sided with William, at which point James fled to France. Parliament allowed William and his wife Mary to take the throne on condition that they sign the English Bill of Rights. Among other things, this declaration criticized James for "raising and keeping a standing army within this kingdom in time of peace without consent of Parliament." It further asserted "their ancient rights and liberties," including their right to "have arms for their defence suitable to their conditions and as allowed by law."[14]

This written declaration of rights was a huge move toward individual liberty, and a standard that British subjects appealed to on many occasions thereafter. Even the colonists appealed to it for a protection of their rights. For example, in 1768, when the British troops began occupying Boston, the town government urged its citizens to arm themselves. Some of the colonists who were loyal to the king, also known as Tories, denounced this action as illegal, saying the people had no individual right to possess arms. Several of the colonial newspapers, including the *Boston Evening Post*, claimed armament as a "natural right":

---

[12] Journals of the House of Commons, Volumes 8–11, 1780

[13] The Right to Keep and Bear Arms, Report of the Senate Subcommittee on the Constitution, 1982

[14] English Bill of Rights, 1689

> *. . . it is certainly beyond human art and sophistry, to prove that the British subjects, to whom the privilege of possessing arms is expressly recognized by the Bill of Rights, and to live in a province where the law requires them to be equipped with arms, are guilty of an illegal act, in calling upon one another to be provided with them, as the law directs.*[15]

The *New York Journal Supplement* pointed out that it "was a measure as prudent as it was legal," and that "it is a natural right which the people have reserved to themselves, confirmed by the Bill of Rights to keep arms for their own defense."[16]

From the English history of collective preservation and the right to bear arms, two armed protectors emerged, the standing army and the militia. A standing army is a country's permanent military force to protect the nation from external invasion. Historically, the militia is made up of every able-bodied male. They must keep arms and be trained and prepared to bear them in defense of themselves and their country.

THE MILITIA IN EARLY AMERICA

As tensions were mounting between Britain and the American colonies in 1774–1776, ten of the thirteen colonies established provincial congresses. These were de facto government bodies established to govern their respective colonies independent of king and Parliament.

In response to the Boston Tea Party, Parliament altered the Massachusetts colonial government in 1774. Rejecting the premise that Parliament had the authority to take such action, Massachusetts resisted by establishing the Massachusetts Provincial Congress. That new body immediately called for the militia to begin training for looming hostilities. It was that militia that received word that the British were marching on Lexington and Concord to seize the

---

[15] *Boston Evening Post*, 1769
[16] *New York Journal Supplement*, 1769

weapons and gunpowder stored in magazines. The militia engaged the British, killing 73 and suffering 49 deaths.

Recalling the first battles of the American Revolution is important to understanding how the militia is used. The militia, in 1775, was not a loose band of private citizens that took it upon themselves to organize, train, and fight. Rather, they were called up by the new Massachusetts Congress; leaders were appointed; training occurred to make them "well regulated"; and they fought only upon the order to do so. The militia was comprised of private citizens called up, organized, and trained by their established government.

Once the colonies declared their independence, the separate states continued using militia systems on the Massachusetts model. As the newly-independent states began creating their own constitutions, many of them also declared certain rights of the people. Virginia, being one of the first to write a constitution, included with it a declaration of rights. Among other things, it declared:

> *That a well-regulated militia, composed of the body of the people, trained to arms, is the proper, natural, and safe defense of a free state; that standing armies, in time of peace, should be avoided as dangerous to liberty; and that in all cases the military should be under strict subordination to, and governed by, the civil power.*[17]

Just over a year later, the states united under the Articles of Confederation, which gave some power to a national government. It required that:

> *No vessel of war. . . [or] body of forces [shall] be kept up by any State in time of peace, except such number only, as in the judgement of the United States in Congress assembled. . . but every State shall always keep up a well-regulated and disciplined militia,*

---

[17] Virginia Declaration of Rights, 1776

sufficiently armed and accoutered. . . and a proper quantity of arms, ammunition and camp equipage.[18]

It is evident from these and other documented sources that the newly independent states were leery of standing armies, having experienced the king's standing army among them. The Revolutionary War began with small militia enlistments, and the Articles of Confederation provided very little power to raise money to pay them. The small bands of militia were essentially held together by a common threat and a conviction of the cause of liberty. At a critical point in the war, an account written by an unidentified sergeant describes the difficulty caused by the circumstances. In a beautiful and touching way, it also illustrates the capacity of the human soul in insurmountable odds.

While we were at Trenton, on the last of December, 1776, the time for which I and most of my regiment had enlisted, expired. At this trying time General Washington, having now but a little handful of men and many of them new recruits in which he could place but little confidence, ordered our regiment to be paraded, and personally addressed us, urging that we should stay a month longer. He alluded to our recent victory at Trenton; told us that our services were greatly needed, and that we could now do more for our country than we ever could at any future period; and in the most affectionate manner entreated us to stay. The drums beat for volunteers, but not a man turned out. The soldiers, worn down with fatigue and privations, had their hearts fixed on home and the comforts of the domestic circle, and it was hard to forego the anticipated pleasures of the society of our dearest friends.

The General wheeled his horse about, rode in front of the regiment, and addressing us again said, "My brave fellows, you have done all I asked you to do, and more

---

[18] Articles of Confederation, 1777

than could be reasonably expected; but your country is at stake, your wives, your houses, and all that you hold dear. You have worn yourselves out with fatigue and hardships, but we know not how to spare you. If you will consent to stay only one month longer, you will render that service to the cause of liberty, and to your country, which you probably never can do under any other circumstances. The present is emphatically the crisis, which is to decide our destiny." The drums beat the second time. The soldiers felt the force of the appeal. One said to another, "I will remain if you will." Others remarked "We cannot go home under such circumstances." A few stepped forth, and their example was immediately followed by nearly all who were fit for duty in the regiment, amounting to about two hundred volunteers. An officer enquired of the General if these men should be enrolled. He replied,—"No! Men who will volunteer in such a case as this, need no enrolment to keep them to their duty."[19]

Early American history is full of stories like this, where the fate of the country lay in the hands of a few ordinary people who did extraordinary things. There were two important lessons learned from this experience. First, the strength of the nation lies in the hearts of the people. When push comes to shove, the instinct for freedom and survival prevails. Second, these trying experiences gave George Washington a unique vantage point, a front-row seat, if you will, to problems of the militia as it was then regulated. Just a few months before the war ended, Washington committed to paper some of his thoughts on "a peace establishment for the United States of America," in which he suggested four policies.

First. A regular and standing force. . . as shall be deemed necessary to awe the Indians, protect our Trade,

---

[19] *The Phenix*, 1832

prevent the encroachment of our Neighbours... and guard us at least from surprizes;

Secondly. A well organized Militia; upon a Plan that will pervade all the States, and introduce similarity in their Establishment Manoeuvres, Exercise and Arms.

Thirdly. Establishing Arsenals of all kinds of Military Stores.

Fourthly. Academies... for the Instruction of the Art Military; particularly those Branches of it which respect Engineering and Artillery, which are highly essential, and the knowledge of which, is most difficult to obtain. Also Manufactories of some kinds of Military Stores.[20]

He expressed his dislike for "large standing Arm[ies] in time of Peace," believing they are "dangerous to the liberties of a Country," but also recognizing that "a few Troops, under certain circumstances, are not only safe, but indispensably necessary."[21]

When the Founders met at Independence Hall in 1787 and ultimately drafted an entirely new Constitution, they delegated to Congress the power:

To raise and support Armies...

To provide and maintain a Navy;

To make Rules for the Government and Regulation of the land and naval Forces;

To provide for calling forth the Militia to execute the Laws of the Union, suppress Insurrections and repel Invasions;

To provide for organizing, arming, and disciplining, the Militia, and for governing such Part of them as may be employed in the Service of the United States, reserving

---

[20] George Washington, "Sentiments on a Peace Establishment," 1783
[21] Ibid.

> *to the States respectively, the Appointment of the Officers, and the Authority of training the Militia according to the discipline prescribed by Congress;*[22]

They further delegated to the president the role of "Commander in Chief. . . of the Militia of the several States, when called into the actual Service of the United States."[23]

The national Constitution, ratified in 1789, gave Congress and the president more power over the state militias than the states felt comfortable with. In their recommendations for amendments, the states sent a clear message to the national government not to interfere with their right of self-preservation.

The states were already leery of a standing army; now they were concerned that the national government had too much control over the militias of each state. With that control, the national government could either fail to properly fund and train the militia in favor of a larger standing army or confiscate the arms of the people—thereby weakening the militia out of existence. The feared result would be the inability of each state to defend themselves from invasion by a foreign country, or by the national government if it grew to tyrannical proportions.

DEVELOPING THE SECOND AMENDMENT

When the proposed Constitution was released to the public to review and for the states to ratify, many people must have raised an eyebrow at the clause concerning the training of the militia, particularly as it put the law-making power for disciplining the state militias in the hands of Congress. Although it closely resembled Washington's thoughts from several years earlier, the people were concerned that if the entire body of the militia were under the authority of the national government, it would pose a great threat to their liberty. In attempting to address this concern, Alexander Hamilton posed the question:

---

[22] The United States Constitution; Article 1, Section 8, 1787
[23] The United States Constitution; Article 2, Section 2, Clause 1, 1787

> *Where in the name of common-sense, are our fears to end if we may not trust our sons, our brothers, our neighbors, our fellow-citizens? What shadow of danger can there be from men who are daily mingling with the rest of their countrymen and who participate with them in the same feelings, sentiments, habits and interests?[24]*

He further rested their fears by pointing out that the proposed constitution required the *states* "to have the SOLE AND EXCLUSIVE APPOINTMENT OF THE OFFICERS."[25] This was one of the vital checks in the system.

In the same article, he also addressed the concern that some Americans had regarding the training and disciplining of the entire militia. At that time, the militia generally consisted of all males 17 to 45 years of age. How much military training could reasonably be expected of the common militia member? Questions like this must have been prevalent because Alexander Hamilton reasoned that:

> *The project of disciplining all the militia of the United States is as futile as it would be injurious, if it were capable of being carried into execution. A tolerable expertness in military movements is a business that requires time and practice. It is not a day, or even a week, that will suffice for the attainment of it. To oblige the great body of the yeomanry, and of the other classes of the citizens, to be under arms for the purpose of going through military exercises and evolutions, as often as might be necessary to acquire the degree of perfection which would entitle them to the character of a well-regulated militia, would be a real grievance to the people, and a serious public inconvenience and loss.*

> *Little more can reasonably be aimed at, with respect to the people at large, than to have them properly armed and equipped; and in order to see that this be not*

---

[24] Alexander Hamilton, *Federalist* No. 29, 1788
[25] Ibid.

neglected, it will be necessary to assemble them once or twice in the course of a year.

But though the scheme of disciplining the whole nation must be abandoned as mischievous or impracticable; yet it is a matter of the utmost importance that a well-digested plan should, as soon as possible, be adopted for the proper establishment of the militia.[26]

This concept of a small standing army and a well-regulated militia was the goal of the Framers and the balance that was needed, but it is understandable why the newly independent states were leery of this plan. After all, they had just fought for their independence and did not what to lose it to another power-hungry government.

The states ultimately consented to ratification, but only with the agreement "that further declaratory and restrictive clauses should be added"[27] as amendments to the Constitution. Congress met for the first time on March 4, 1789, with the daunting task of making laws and procedures for themselves and the nation. By June, James Madison began compiling and condensing a list of nearly 200 proposed amendments submitted by the states. Among these proposed amendments was language prohibiting Congress from passing legislation that would disarm the people, arguing that the militia was "the proper, natural and safe defence of a free state."[28] Several states patterned their "right to bear arms" proposals after Section 13 of the Virginia Declaration of Rights. A few of these proposals have been included to show the evolution of thought.

Massachusetts, February 6, 1788:

. . . the said Constitution be never construed to authorize Congress to. . . prevent the people of the United States, who are peaceable citizens, from keeping their own

---

[26] Ibid.

[27] Preamble to the Bill of Rights, 1789

[28] Virginia ratifying convention, 1788

arms; or to raise standing armies, unless when necessary for the defence of the United States.[29]

North Carolina, August 1, 1788:

That the people have a right to keep and bear arms; that a well regulated militia composed of the body of the people, trained to arms, is the proper, natural and safe defence of a free state. That standing armies in time of peace are dangerous to Liberty, and therefore ought to be avoided, as far as the circumstances and protection of the community will admit; and that in all cases, the military should be under strict subordination to, and governed by the civil power.

That any person religiously scrupulous of bearing arms ought to be exempted upon payment of an equivalent to employ another to bear arms in his stead.[30]

Maryland, April 26, 1788:

That no standing army shall be kept up in time of peace, unless with the consent of two thirds of the members present of each branch of congress.[31]

New Hampshire, June 21, 1788:

Congress shall never disarm any Citizen unless such as are or have been in Actual Rebellion.[32]

New York, July 26, 1788:

That the People have a right to keep and bear Arms; that a well regulated Militia, including the body of the People capable of bearing Arms, is the proper, natural and safe defence of a free State.

---

[29] Massachusetts ratifying convention, 1788
[30] North Carolina ratifying convention, 1788
[31] Maryland ratifying convention, 1788
[32] New Hampshire ratifying convention, 1788

> *That the Militia should not be subject to Martial Law except in time of War, Rebellion or Insurrection.*
>
> *That standing Armies in time of Peace are dangerous to Liberty, and ought not to be kept up, except in Cases of necessity; and that at all times, the Military should be under strict Subordination to the civil Power.*[33]

From these suggested amendments, it is evident that the legislatures of the various states wanted to rein in some of the military power granted to Congress in the Constitution and use the militia to provide the majority of the nation's defense. Madison's original draft of the Second Amendment pulled heavily from these suggestions and read as follows:

> *The right of the people to keep and bear arms shall not be infringed; a well armed and well regulated militia being the best security of a free country: but no person religiously scrupulous of bearing arms shall be compelled to render military service in person.*[34]

The "religiously scrupulous" clause, or "conscientious objector" clause as it is often referred to today, was debated in the House of Representatives, but ultimately removed. Elbridge Gerry was concerned "that this clause would give an opportunity to the people in power to destroy the constitution itself. They can declare who are those religiously scrupulous, and prevent them from bearing arms."[35] Thomas Scott "observed that if this becomes part of the constitution, such persons can neither be called upon for their services, nor can an equivalent be demanded; it is also attended with still further difficulties, for a militia can never be depended upon."[36] Due to these and other concerns, it was omitted.

---

[33] New York ratifying convention, 1788
[34] James Madison, Annals of Congress, 1789
[35] Elbridge Gerry, Annals of Congress, 1789
[36] Thomas Scott, Annals of Congress, 1789

MILITIA ACTS

During the first Congress, which began March 4, 1789, George Washington urged them to pass legislation for the organizing of the militia. Despite his repeated requests, Congress didn't address it until the very end of the first Session of the Second Congress—three years after they first met. On May 2, 1792, they approved a Militia Act and then a few days later, on May 8, they amended it and adjourned that same day.

These acts closely aligned with Hamilton's thought of assembling the militia for an annual inspection of arms and maneuvers. After the inspection, the adjutant general of each state was to "make a return of all militia of the state, to the Commander in Chief of the said state, and a duplicate of the same to the president of the United States."[37]

He was to report "the actual situation of their arms, accoutrements, and ammunition, their delinquencies, and every other thing which relates to the general advancement of good order and discipline."[38]

Being part of the militia did not mean they were full-time soldiers, but it did mean that they had to be properly armed and trained in the event they were called into service.

The acts required every able-bodied free male in their respective states, from "eighteen years, and under the age of forty-five years," to enlist in the militia. Upon enlistment, each member had six months to obtain "a good musket or firelock, a sufficient bayonet and belt, two spare flints, and a knapsack, a pouch, with a box therein, to contain not less than twenty four cartridges" attached to his musket or firelock. He was required to have "a proper quantity of powder and ball" or a rifle with "twenty balls. . . and a quarter of a pound of powder."[39]

---

[37] Militia Act of 1792
[38] Ibid.
[39] Ibid.

The United States Constitution outlines who can call forth the militia and for what purposes. On the national level Congress was given the power of "calling forth the Militia to execute the Laws of the Union, suppress Insurrections and repel Invasions,"[40] and "The President shall be Commander in Chief. . . of the Militia of the several States, when called into the actual Service of the United States."[41]

On a state level, the governor may call forth the militia of the respective state in accordance with the laws of that state. For example, Illinois's Constitution says:

> *The Governor is commander-in-chief of the organized militia, except when they are in the service of the United States. He may call them out to enforce the laws, suppress insurrection or repel invasion.*[42]

The first time the militia was called into service by the national government was in 1794, during George Washington's second administration. Due to the expenses incurred during the Revolutionary War, the new United States carried significant debt. Their attempts to pay it off through tariffs were insufficient and Congress began looking for other ways to generate revenue. Alexander Hamilton suggested a tax on whiskey, and Congress ultimately passed it in February 1791. Violent protests and riots ensued over the next few years, especially in western Pennsylvania, where grain-producing farmers felt the brunt of this tax. Pennsylvania's vote in the House and the Senate had been divided, giving no glaring warning of the ensuing conflict. The fines imposed on tax dodgers were particularly stiff.

By the fall of 1794, the rebellion had grown serious. In a proclamation dated September 25, 1794, President Washington denounced those who would set the government at defiance and

---

[40] The United States Constitution; Article 1, Section 8, Clause 15, 1787
[41] The United States Constitution; Article 2, Section 2, Clause 1, 1787
[42] Illinois Constitution, Article 12, Section 4, 1970

contested "whether a small portion of the United States shall dictate to the whole Union. . . at the expense of those who desire peace."[43]

He proclaimed,

> *[In] obedience to that high and irresistible duty consigned to me by the Constitution to "take care that the laws be faithfully executed. . ." and considering it unfortunate ". . . that the American name should be sullied by the outrages of citizens on their own Government. . ."[44]*

and summoned the militia from New Jersey, Pennsylvania, Maryland, and Virginia.[45]

Almost 13,000 militia members from the four states responded to the call, each group being led by their governor. As "Commander in Chief," George Washington headed the militia, making it the only time an acting president personally led troops to battle. As it turned out, a torrential rainstorm delayed the army, and by the time they reached the rebel leaders, cooler heads had prevailed, greatly minimizing the conflict.

The War of 1812 again saw the militia called upon to assist the small military army that Congress had approved in their first legislative session. With only 7,000 military enlistments at the beginning of the war, the state militias were indispensable in protecting their infant country from defeat. By the end of the war, militia enlistments reached 458,000, though most engaged in little, if any, combat.

A WELL-REGULATED MILITIA

After the War of 1812, the militia would not be called into service again by the national government until the Civil War. During this extended period of peace, the states had become lax in regulating their militias, and as a result the knowledge of war began to decay.

---

43 George Washington, Proclamation of September 25, 1794
44 Ibid.
45 Ibid.

The adjutant general of each state was to file an annual report to the governor and to the president of the United States, detailing the condition of the militia. After sending his 1823 report, Adjutant General William Sumner of Massachusetts wrote a letter to John Adams, including a copy of this report. The report expressed his concern that "a change in the opinions of the people seems to be commencing, founded on the erroneous notion that the militia is a military institution [and] of no use in time of peace."[46]

Realizing that "no man, who valued his popularity, would have dared to express [these sentiments] even five years ago," Sumner recommended "that the public attention should be roused."[47]

He listed several objections that were commonly voiced against the militia, particularly with regard to training. Some felt that preparation for war was ungrateful in time of peace. Training frequently occurred during the busy season and in the opinion of some "introduce[d] too much frolicking." Business owners complained that training "deprive[d them] of the use of [their] servants" and "impede[d] their operations."[48]

Having laid out the inconveniences of militia training, Sumner got to the heart of the matter, explaining the principle upon which the militia should operate.

> *One of the designs of keeping the militia constantly organized, armed and trained, was to save the expense of maintaining a large regular force. The plan was predicated upon the principle that the people should defend their own homes; not that they should be called away for the defence of others. It teaches them their dependence upon their own exertions, and makes them ever watchful of danger to those interests, for the protection of which, none feel so great a solicitude as themselves. Thus it is, that, always prepared to resist*

---

[46] Letter from William Sumner to John Adams, 1823
[47] Ibid.
[48] Ibid.

> *aggression, they are able to pursue their domestic avocations and agricultural pursuits, for the support of their families, upon the very soil which they may be required to defend.*[49]

He then explains the principle of peace through strength previously mentioned.

> *If it be asked how the militia protected us, when they were never engaged? I will ask, in turn, whether it is not better to have one's power so respected by an enemy, that he dare not encounter it, than, by its weakness, to encourage him to assail it, with a confidence, or even a hope, of its overthrow. In the one case, there is a triumph without a battle; in the other, if it be gained, it must be attended with at least some sacrifices.*[50]

He reasoned that abolishing the militia

> *because there is no war, would be absurd. That reason is applicable to the reduction of the army; but, the army and militia are raised from different causes; and are supported upon different principles. They both contribute to the same end, in war, [but] In free governments . . . that kind of force should be maintained in peace, which is not dangerous to liberty.*[51]

Ten years later, Joseph Story, then serving as a U.S. Supreme Court Justice, emphasized similar views and concerns.

> *The importance of [the Second Amendment] this article will scarcely be doubted by any persons, who have duly reflected upon the subject. The militia is the natural defence of a free country against sudden foreign invasions, domestic insurrections, and domestic usurpations of power by rulers. It is against sound policy*

---

[49] Ibid.
[50] Ibid.
[51] Ibid.

for a free people to keep up large military establishments and standing armies in time of peace, both from the enormous expenses, with which they are attended, and the facile means, which they afford to ambitious and unprincipled rulers, to subvert the government, or trample upon the rights of the people. The right of the citizens to keep and bear arms has justly been considered, as the palladium of the liberties of a republic; since it offers a strong moral check against the usurpation and arbitrary power of rulers; and will generally, even if these are successful in the first instance, enable the people to resist and triumph over them. And yet, though this truth would seem so clear, and the importance of a well regulated militia would seem so undeniable, it cannot be disguised, that among the American people there is a growing indifference to any system of militia discipline, and a strong disposition, from a sense of its burthens, to be rid of all regulations. How it is practicable to keep the people duly armed without some organization, it is difficult to see. There is certainly no small danger, that indifference may lead to disgust, and disgust to contempt; and thus gradually undermine all the protection intended by this clause of our national bill of rights.[52]

Story's words almost seem prophetic. By the time of the Civil War in 1861, militia training had all but ceased. The trainings that remained had been "reduced to rude assemblies and disorderly bands"[53] as Sumner had predicted. When Abraham Lincoln called out the militia, it was immediately apparent that they were ill prepared. Volunteers responded, greatly exceeding Lincoln's 75,000 quota, but the first battle at Bull Run revealed a serious lack of training.

---

[52] Joseph Story, *Commentaries on the Constitution of the United States*, 1833
[53] Letter from William Sumner to John Adams, 1823

He acknowledged that "military power, of some sort, must always be at the command of the civil authority [and] if the militia is to be abolished, the army [of necessity] should be increased."[54]

Sumner attributed the failures of the militia to two primary causes, the first of which was "the failure to train the men" and the second more important was "the omission to train the officers."[55] This was partly due to the 1792 Militia Acts not outlining penalties for lack of proper training.

THE MILITIA TODAY

What is the militia and what is it not? As defined by national statute:

> (a) The militia of the United States consists of all able-bodied males at least 17 years of age and, except as provided in section 313 of title 32, under 45 years of age who are, or who have made a declaration of intention to become, citizens of the United States and of female citizens of the United States who are members of the National Guard.

> (b) The classes of the militia are—

>> (1) the organized militia, which consists of the National Guard and the Naval Militia; and

>> (2) the unorganized militia, which consists of the members of the militia who are not members of the National Guard or the Naval Militia.[56]

The militia is not only the National Guard, as some people presume or advocate. It is not a group of citizens who have self-labeled themselves a militia either. According to the Constitution, the militia is paid for, organized, trained, and called up by state and national governments.

---

[54] Ibid.

[55] Ibid.

[56] U.S. Code: Title 10: Armed Forces, Chapter 12, Section 246: Militia: Composition and Classes

It is confusing when private groups organize and call themselves the militia, and that confusion is compounded by media who parrot that militia label.

The militia is the general population of able-bodied individuals from the public at large. It is not a private group of citizens. It's okay if a group of individuals gather to practice shooting and share an enthusiasm for weapons. They have freedom of speech, the right to assemble, and the right to bear arms. However, it is illegal, or heavily regulated, in most states to form a private military group.

A private group of citizens are not authorized to form a military group for the purpose of protecting the rights of others without their consent. Private military groups are not authorized to establish their own governments to replace any segment of the United States republic. They cannot establish courts or tribunals that subpoena or charge a non-consenting citizen from the United States or any other state. Those private groups, like any other private organization, can establish whatever organized structure they wish. But that structure can enforce their rules upon their members only.

The clarification of what a private group can and cannot do is relevant to the Second Amendment. Throughout our history, groups have formed, called themselves militia, and appointed themselves as guardians over the liberty of others, even without their consent. They have also formed tribunals and have drawn up charges against various local, state, and federal officials. These groups should not be confused with the militia spoken of by the Founders and codified in the Constitution and Bill of Rights.

The militia is made up of able-bodied citizens. They can only be called up by the consent of the people. That consent must be acquired the same way all consent is acquired—by a majority. That majority comes from the people through their elected representatives. Constitutionally, the militia is called up by a majority of Congress and many state constitutions allow for their legislatures or governors to call up the militia.

The militia held off the redcoats in Lexington and Concord in 1775 not because they called themselves up, but because they were called up by the Massachusetts Provincial Congress.

IS THE MILITIA NEEDED TODAY?

The question has been asked, do we still need a militia today? With law enforcement, the National Guard, and our standing army, do we really need the militia? Perhaps that question is being asked because of the confusion that we have already cleared up regarding private groups that call themselves militia. If it is thought that these private groups are the militia, the question of their necessity is a good one. But they are not the militia, even if they identify themselves as such or are described as such. We'll leave the subject of their validity up to the reader and focus the question on the militia of the Constitution and Bill of Rights.

The question as to the modern necessity of the militia would be like asking if we should abandon civilian control of the military because we have never had a military coup. Perhaps the reason why we have never had a military coup is because we have civilian control over the military. Civilian control has worked well up to now. It is not worth the risk to remove civilian control and see what happens next. Likewise, do we want to strip Americans of the right to bear arms, thus eliminating the militia, just to see if they are needed today?

The militia is an enormous body of approximately 60 million[57] Americans. That dwarfs the 1.4 million-person United States military and China, the largest military in the world at 2.2 million.[58] Perhaps this has contributed to only a handful of minor mainland United States invasions by warring countries. Repelling invasion is one reason for the militia. Repelling tyranny is another.

---

[57] Approximate number of male citizens 17 to 45 and women in the National Guard, which constitutes the militia according to U.S. Code: Title 10: Armed Forces, Chapter 12, Section 246: Militia: Composition and Classes.

[58] Although China's military is larger in number, the United States has the largest military in terms of percentage of population.

It is often mentioned that the right to bear arms is necessary to repel tyranny, but James Madison placed that purpose in the militia. In *Federalist* No. 46, he attempts to ease concerns of the national government expanding to the elimination of the states. He does so by explaining how difficult it would be to eliminate the states so long as the militia exists.

The only refuge left for those who prophesy the downfall of the State governments is the visionary supposition that the federal government may previously accumulate a military force for the projects of ambition. The reasonings contained in these papers must have been employed to little purpose indeed, if it could be necessary now to disprove the reality of this danger. That the people and the States should, for a sufficient period of time, elect an uninterrupted succession of men ready to betray both; that the traitors should, throughout this period, uniformly and systematically pursue some fixed plan for the extension of the military establishment; that the governments and the people of the States should silently and patiently behold the gathering storm, and continue to supply the materials. . .

Extravagant as the supposition is, let it however be made. Let a regular army, fully equal to the resources of the country, be formed; and let it be entirely at the devotion of the federal government; still it would not be going too far to say, that the State governments, with the people on their side, would be able to repel the danger. The highest number to which, according to the best computation, a standing army can be carried in any country, does not exceed one hundredth part of the whole number of souls; or one twenty-fifth part of the number able to bear arms. This proportion would not yield, in the United States, an army of more than twenty-five or thirty thousand men. To these would be opposed a militia amounting to near half a million of citizens with arms in their hands, officered by men chosen from among

> *themselves, fighting for their common liberties, and united and conducted by governments possessing their affections and confidence. It may well be doubted, whether a militia thus circumstanced could ever be conquered by such a proportion of regular troops. . . Besides the advantage of being armed, which the Americans possess over the people of almost every other nation, the existence of subordinate governments, to which the people are attached, and by which the militia officers are appointed, forms a barrier against the enterprises of ambition, more insurmountable than any which a simple government of any form can admit of. . .*[59]

Is the overthrow of the states by the national government likely? No, we think not. But, like civilian control over the military, perhaps the militia is the reason why a national overthrow is unlikely. Today the militia lays dormant. Its existence is causing no harm, but its elimination could have detrimental effects. Perhaps not tomorrow, but a century from now our descendants could ask, after it is too late for them, why did they eliminate the militia? History is full of "civilized" societies that fell to tyranny after they thought themselves beyond such things.

If the question as to the modern necessity of the militia is being asked to soften the real question of the necessity of the right to bear arms, that is a whole different thing. If that is really the question, then let that be asked, rather than making the waters of the Second Amendment any murkier than they already are. That question would be answered by answering the question do individuals have the right of self-preservation? We hope that has already been answered in this chapter on the Second Amendment. That brings from the militia back to self-preservation. As to the connection between the militia and the right to bear arms, we'll examine a landmark case by the Supreme Court.

---

[59] James Madison, *Federalist* No. 46, 1788

DISTRICT OF COLUMBIA V. HELLER, 2008

In 2008 the Supreme Court produced an opinion based on its "first in-depth examination of the Second Amendment"[60] for *District of Columbia v. Heller*. But, as the court said:

> *It should be unsurprising that such a significant matter has been for so long judicially unresolved. For most of our history, the Bill of Rights was not thought applicable to the States, and the Federal Government did not significantly regulate the possession of firearms by law-abiding citizens. Other provisions of the Bill of Rights have similarly remained unilluminated for lengthy periods. This Court first held a law to violate the First Amendment's guarantee of freedom of speech in 1931, almost 150 years after the Amendment was ratified, and it was not until after World War II that we held a law invalid under the Establishment Clause.[61]*

In 2008, in the District of Columbia, better known as Washington, D.C., handgun possession was illegal. The chief of police was authorized to issue yearly licenses. After being denied a license, Heller, a D.C. special policeman, sued the District. He claimed that they had violated his Second Amendment rights to keep and bear arms.

In weighing the validity of Heller's suit, the court sought to determine if the right to bear arms was an individual right or whether it only existed in connection with militia or military service. Because the court was focused on that question only, it disclosed that "one should not expect it to clarify the entire field." The militia, for instance, is not defined in the ruling because that was not relevant to the question. Notwithstanding the court's fractional examination, the Heller case has become the standard for Second Amendment cases since.

---

[60] United States Supreme Court, *District of Columbia v. Heller*, 2008
[61] Ibid.

The portion of the Second Amendment that was examined was such a thorough review of the right to keep and bear arms by the court, its opinion is presented in the following pages.

Once again, the Second Amendment reads in full:

> *A well-regulated Militia, being necessary to the security of a free State, the right of the people to keep and bear Arms, shall not be infringed.*

The court begins by acknowledging the very different interpretations of the Second Amendment. The petitioners and the dissenting justices "believe that it protects only the right to possess and carry a firearm in connection with militia service."[62] In contrast, the respondent argued "that it protects an individual right to possess a firearm unconnected with service in a militia, and to use that arm for traditionally lawful purposes, such as self-defense within the home."[63]

Next, the court does a beautiful job dissecting the amendment with simple precision to begin its examination.

> *The Second Amendment is naturally divided into two parts: its prefatory clause and its operative clause. The former does not limit the latter grammatically, but rather announces a purpose. The Amendment could be re-phrased, "Because a well regulated Militia is necessary to the security of a free State, the right of the people to keep and bear Arms shall not be infringed."*
>
> *Although this structure of the Second Amendment is unique in our Constitution, other legal documents of the founding era, particularly individual-rights provisions of state constitutions, commonly included a prefatory statement of purpose.*

---

[62] Ibid.
[63] Ibid.

Logic demands that there be a link between the stated purpose and the command. The Second Amendment would be nonsensical if it read, "A well regulated Militia, being necessary to the security of a free State, the right of the people to petition for redress of grievances shall not be infringed."[64]

If the operative clause is plagued with ambiguity, it may be clarified by the language of the prefatory clause. In that case, the operative clause is reliant upon the prefatory clause.

But apart from that clarifying function, a prefatory clause does not limit or expand the scope of the operative clause.[65]

It is a matter of settled law, the court claimed, and gave precedent opinions to back up their claim, that preambles or prefatory clauses cannot control the enacting portion of a statute when the enacting clause is clear. Prefatory clauses neither add to nor take away from the meaning and purpose of the operative clause.

To further clarify, the prefatory clause, "A well-regulated Militia being necessary to the security of a free State," is stating a purpose. To accomplish that purpose, the prefatory clause announces the tool it will use to provide for a well-regulated militia that secures the free state—the right of the people to keep and bear arms. The purpose cannot add to or take away from the tool. The tool is the tool, before and after it is used for a purpose. A hammered nail does not change the nature of the hammer.

If one were to declare a purpose—"to keep our bellies full of bread," and then declare the tool to make it happen—"the right to drive to the store must be preserved," the stated purpose does not bind the tool. The prefatory clause about bread does not bind the right to drive to getting bread alone. The right to drive to any other destination still exists. Likewise, the right to keep and bear arms is

---

[64] Ibid.
[65] Ibid.

not limited to militia and military service alone simply because that happens to be the one stated purpose of the Second Amendment.

Although it is second to the prefatory clause, the court first examined the operative clause. They did so because:

> . . . *if a prologue can be used only to clarify an ambiguous operative provision, surely the first step must be to determine whether the operative provision is ambiguous. It might be argued, we suppose, that the prologue itself should be one of the factors that go into the determination of whether the operative provision is ambiguous—but that would cause the prologue to be used to produce ambiguity rather than just to resolve it.*[66]

Now, the thorough examination of the operative clause:

> *The first salient feature of the operative clause is that it codifies a "right of the people." The unamended Constitution and the Bill of Rights use the phrase "right of the people" two other times, in the First Amendment's Assembly-and-Petition Clause and in the Fourth Amendment's Search-and-Seizure Clause. The Ninth Amendment uses very similar terminology ("The enumeration in the Constitution, of certain rights, shall not be construed to deny or disparage others retained by the people"). All three of these instances unambiguously refer to individual rights, not "collective" rights. . . (the right to assemble cannot be exercised alone, but it is still an individual right, and not one conditioned upon membership in some defined "assembly," as [Justice Stevens] contends the right to bear arms is conditioned upon membership in a defined militia. And JUSTICE STEVENS is dead wrong to think that the right to petition is "primarily collective in nature."*

---

[66] Ibid.

Three provisions of the Constitution refer to "the people" in a context other than "rights"—the famous preamble ("We the people"), §2 of Article I (providing that "the people" will choose members of the House), and the Tenth Amendment (providing that those powers not given the Federal Government remain with "the States" or "the people"). Those provisions arguably refer to "the people" acting collectively—but they deal with the exercise or reservation of powers, not rights. Nowhere else in the Constitution does a "right" attributed to "the people" refer to anything other than an individual right. . .

We start therefore with a strong presumption that the Second Amendment right is exercised individually and belongs to all Americans. . .

We move now from the holder of the right—"the people"—to the substance of the right: "to keep and bear Arms."

Before addressing the verbs "keep" and "bear," we interpret their object: "Arms." The 18th-century meaning is no different from the meaning today. The 1773 edition of Samuel Johnson's dictionary defined "arms" as "weapons of offence, or armour of defence." Timothy Cunningham's important 1771 legal dictionary defined "arms" as "any thing that a man wears for his defence, or takes into his hands, or useth in wrath to cast at or strike another."[67]

The opinion of the court references frivolous argument that some have expressed, that only 18th century arms are protected by the Second Amendment because those are what existed when the Amendment was written. They combat that illogical argument by pointing out that the First Amendment protects modern forms of speech and communication just as strongly as 18th century forms.

---

[67] Ibid.

The Second Amendment extends to all bearable arms, even those that did not exist in 1789.

After that tangential observation, the court turned to the phrases "keep arms" and "bear arms." Based on dictionary definitions, they conclude that "the most natural reading of 'keep Arms' in the Second Amendment is to 'have weapons.'"[68]

They further determined that the right to keep and bear arms is an individual right unconnected with militia service. William Blackstone, for example, wrote that Catholics were not permitted to "keep arms in their houses" as a penalty if they were convicted of not attending service in the Church of England.

The District's attorneys in the Heller case argued that because there were founding-era militia laws that required members to "keep" arms, the phrase "keep Arms" is only connected to militia service. In response to that assertion, the court said:

> *This is rather like saying that, since there are many statutes that authorize aggrieved employees to "file complaints" with federal agencies, the phrase "file complaints" has an employment-related connotation. "Keep arms" was simply a common way of referring to possessing arms, for militiamen and everyone else.[69]*

James Wilson, delegate to the Constitutional Convention of 1787, co-author of the Pennsylvania Constitution, and one of the first Supreme Court Justices, not only made it clear that the individual has the right to bear arms, but the duty to do so in the defense of his country. In the Heller opinion, the court excerpts from the following words of Wilson:

> *[It] is the great natural law of self preservation, which, as we have seen, cannot be repealed, or superseded, or suspended by any human institution. This law, however, is expressly recognised in the constitution of*

---

[68] Ibid.
[69] Ibid.

Pennsylvania. "The right of the citizens to bear arms in the defence of themselves shall not be questioned." This is one of our many renewals of the Saxon regulations. "They were bound," says Mr. Selden, "to keep arms for the preservation of the kingdom, and of their own persons."

With regard to the second; every man's house is deemed, by the law, to be his castle; and the law, while it invests him with the power, enjoins on him the duty, of the commanding officer. "Every man's house is his castle," says my Lord Coke, in one of his reports, "and he ought to keep and defend it at his peril; and if any one be robbed in it, it shall be esteemed his own default and negligence." For this reason, one may assemble people together in order to protect and defend his house." (The Works of the Honorable James Wilson, *by James Wilson and Bird Wilson, 1804)*[70]

The court concluded that the right to keep arms is an individual right. But what of the right to "bear" arms?

At the time of the founding, as now, to "bear" meant to "carry." When used with "arms," however, the term has a meaning that refers to carrying for a particular purpose—confrontation. In Muscarello v. United States, *524 U. S. 125 (1998), in the course of analyzing the meaning of "carries a firearm" in a federal criminal statute, JUSTICE GINSBURG wrote that "[s]urely a most familiar meaning is, as the Constitution's Second Amendment . . . indicate[s]: "wear, bear, or carry. . . upon the person or in the clothing or in a pocket, for the purpose. . . of being armed and ready for offensive or defensive action in a case of conflict with another person."*

---

[70] Ibid.

> *We think that JUSTICE GINSBURG accurately captured the natural meaning of "bear arms." Although the phrase implies that the carrying of the weapon is for the purpose of "offensive or defensive action," it in no way connotes participation in a structured military organization.*[71]

After reviewing founding-era sources, the court concluded that the use of the term *bear arms* was unambiguous. The many references reviewed used the term outside of a military or militia context. The clearest examples were found in early state constitutions, which recognized the individual right to bear arms as a matter of self-preservation.

Pennsylvania

> *The right of the citizens to bear arms in defense of themselves and the State shall not be questioned.*

Vermont

> *That the people have a right to bear arms for the defence of themselves and the State. . .*

Kentucky

> *That the right of the citizens to bear arms in defence of themselves and the State shall not be questioned. . .*

Ohio

> *That the people have a right to bear arms for the defence of themselves and the State. . .*

Indiana

> *That the people have a right to bear arms for the defense of themselves and the State. . .*

---

[71] Ibid.

Mississippi

Every citizen has a right to bear arms, in defence of himself and the State.

Connecticut

Every citizen has a right to bear arms in defence of himself and the state.

Alabama

Every citizen has a right to bear arms in defence of himself and the State.

Missouri

[T]hat their right to bear arms in defence of themselves and of the State cannot be questioned. . .

The court further expounded on the logic of the meaning "bear arms" as an individual right versus the idea that it is connected to military service only:

If "bear arms" means, as we think, simply the carrying of arms, a modifier can limit the purpose of the carriage ("for the purpose of self defense" or "to make war against the King"). But if "bear arms" means, as the petitioners and the dissent think, the carrying of arms only for military purposes, one simply cannot add "for the purpose of killing game." The right "to carry arms in the militia for the purpose of killing game" is worthy of the mad hatter. Thus, these purposive qualifying phrases positively establish that "to bear arms" is not limited to military use.[72]

Justice Stevens, a dissenting judge in the Heller case, concluded that Madison's original language for the Second Amendment was evident of an exclusive military connection in connection to the right

---

[72] Ibid.

to bear arms. Madison's original proposal to Congress included: ". . . but no person religiously scrupulous of bearing arms, shall be compelled to render military service in person."[73]

The court's first response to that conclusion was that it is unwise to put too much weight on portions of an amendment or any statute that were not passed. Those portions were removed for a purpose, and that purpose could very well be that the language struck may not have fulfilled the intended purpose of the amendment.

Second, the court clarified that the deleted portion was not meant to exempt from military service a person who objected to war, but who had a problem with personal gunfights.

> *Thus, the most natural interpretation of Madison's deleted text is that those opposed to carrying weapons for potential violent confrontation would not be "compelled to render military service," in which such carrying would be required.*[74]

After putting all of the textual elements together, the court concluded that:

> *[They] guarantee the individual right to possess and carry weapons in case of confrontation. This meaning is strongly confirmed by the historical background of the Second Amendment. We look to this because it has always been widely understood that the Second Amendment, like the First and Fourth Amendments, codified a pre-existing right. The very text of the Second Amendment implicitly recognizes the pre-existence of the right and declares only that it "shall not be infringed." As we said in United States v. Cruikshank, 92 U. S. 542, 553 (1876), "[t]his is not a right granted by the Constitution. Neither is it in any manner dependent upon*

---

[73] James Madison, Annals of Congress, 1789
[74] United States Supreme Court, *District of Columbia v. Heller*, 2008

that instrument for its existence. The Second amendment declares that it shall not be infringed. . ."[75]

The Second Amendment is ambiguous, not because of the operator clause, but because of the prefatory clause. At first glance it may appear to many to be solely about militia or military service, especially looking at it through a twenty-first century lens. The historical definition of the militia is rarely referenced today, let alone the fact that the unorganized militia is virtually nonexistent. Few people are prepared and trained to take up arms if the unorganized militia were to be called up. We don't look at the militia and the right to bear arms the same as the people of 1789 did.

By the time of the founding, the right to have arms had become fundamental for English subjects:

> *the right secured in 1689 as a result of the Stuarts' abuses was by the time of the founding understood to be an individual right protecting against both public and private violence. . . In the tumultuous decades of the 1760s and 1770s, the Crown began to disarm the inhabitants of the most rebellious areas. That provoked polemical reactions by Americans invoking their rights as Englishmen to keep arms. A New York article of April 1769 said that "[i]t is a natural right which the people have reserved to themselves, confirmed by the Bill of Rights, to keep arms for their own defence."[76] . . . They understood the right to enable individuals to defend themselves. . . . Americans understood the "right of self-preservation" as permitting a citizen to "repe[l] force by force" when "the intervention of society in his behalf, may be too late to prevent an injury."[77]*

The individual right to bear arms in founding-era America was self-evident. The people did not question that right in the least. There

---

[75] Ibid.
[76] A Journal of the Times: Mar. 17, 1769 New York
[77] United States Supreme Court, *District of Columbia v. Heller*, 2008

was little need, in their mind, to place such an obvious right and truth in the national Constitution. In light of that understanding, it is not surprising that the Second Amendment would focus on immediately pressing concerns—the strength of the militia to defend the states from enemies foreign and domestic.

Next, the court sought to determine if the prefatory clause comported with its interpretation of the operative clause.

Again, the prefatory clause reads:

> *A well-regulated Militia, being necessary to the security of a free State. . .*

In *United States v. Miller* (1939), the Supreme Court explained that "the Militia comprised all males physically capable of acting in concert for the common defense."[78] As evidence of that statement, the court quotes Webster's 1828 dictionary, a quote from Madison's *Federalist* No. 46, and an excerpt of a letter from Thomas Jefferson:

> *The militia of a country are the able bodied men organized into companies, regiments and brigades, with officers of all grades, and required by law to attend military exercises on certain days only, but at other times left to pursue their usual occupations.*[79]

> *. . . a militia amounting to near half a million of citizens with arms in their hands. . .*[80]

> *. . . the militia of the State, that is to say, of every man in it able to bear arms. . .*[81]

The petitioners in the Heller case took a narrower view of the militia. They stated that "militias are the state- and congressionally regulated military forces described in the Militia clause." They then referenced Article I of the Constitution where it reads:

---

[78] Ibid.
[79] *American Dictionary of the English Language*, Noah Webster, 1828
[80] James Madison, *Federalist* No. 46, 1788
[81] Letter from Thomas Jefferson to Destutt de Tracy, 26 January 1811

To provide for calling forth the Militia to execute the Laws of the Union, suppress Insurrections and repel Invasions;

To provide for organizing, arming, and disciplining, the Militia, and for governing such Part of them as may be employed in the Service of the United States, reserving to the States respectively, the Appointment of the Officers, and the Authority of training the Militia according to the discipline prescribed by Congress... [82]

Although the court agreed with the petitioners that "militia" means the same thing in Article I and the Second Amendment, they disagreed with the rest.

[We] believe that petitioners identify the wrong thing, namely, the organized militia. Unlike armies and navies, which Congress is given the power to create ("to raise... Armies"; "to provide... a Navy,") the militia is assumed by Article I already to be in existence. Congress is given the power to "provide for calling forth the militia," and the power not to create, but to organize it— and not to organize "a" militia, which is what one would expect if the militia were to be a federal creation, but to organize "the" militia, connoting a body already in existence. This is fully consistent with the ordinary definition of the militia as all able-bodied men. [83]

From that pool of "able-bodied men," Congress has power to organize the units that will comprise the trained fighting force. They do so by providing funding and training so they will be "well regulated." Well regulated does not mean that they have control over the militia by regulation. It simply means that they are an effective military force. And all of that is referring to the "organized" militia, not the "unorganized militia," which can only be "well regulated" to the extent that their right to bear arms is not infringed.

---

[82] United States Constitution, Article I, section 8, clauses 15–16, 1787
[83] United States Supreme Court, *District of Columbia v. Heller*, 2008

Now we'll move on to the phrase "security of a free state," meaning "security of a free polity," not security of each of the several states. Joseph Story wrote in his treatise on the Constitution that:

> *the word "state" is used in various senses. In its most enlarged sense it means the people composing a particular nation or community. In this sense the state means the whole people, united into one body politic. . .*[84]

The Constitution, including the Bill of Rights, uses the word *state(s)* 140 times. Those instances can be categorized into three different definitions:

State: a condition of being[85]

The Constitution uses *state* in this context only once, "[The president] shall from time to time give to the Congress Information of the *State of the Union*"

State: one of the constituent units of a nation having a federal government[86]

Of the 140 usages of the word *state(s)*, 136 of them are in the context of this definition. Each use under this definition is apparent. It is difficult to interpret these usages as anything other than referring to one of the fifty states. The plural is used 89 times—a clear reference to one or more states. Words used in conjunction with most occurrences of the word *state* support this definition: united, each, several, particular, nine, etc.

State: a) a politically organized body of people usually occupying a definite territory, especially one that is sovereign; b) the political organization of such a body of people[87]

---

[84] Joseph Story, *Commentaries on the Constitution of the United States*, 1833
[85] *Merriam-Webster Dictionary*, 2021
[86] Ibid.
[87] Ibid.

State under this definition is used three times:

> *. . . and foreign States. . .*[88]

> *. . . or foreign State. . .*[89]

> *. . . a free state. . .*[90]

The first two instances are clearly using *state* in its most general form, to mean a body politic. The secretary of state, or a head of state, is not referring to the secretary or head of one of the fifty states, but the secretary or head of a body politic.

The third instance is from our current subject, the Second Amendment. It may seem clear to some, but not to others. Some argue that the reference here is to the fifty states, not to the general body politic.

The phrase *free state* predates the Founders by at least 200 years. It was used hundreds of times by authors who influenced the Founders, and they adopted the phrase. In each of those hundreds of occurrences, the phrase referred to a non-despotically governed country. There is not a single occurrence in which the phrase was used to describe one or all of the states within the union.[91]

Madison's original draft used the phrase "a free country," but the committee changed it to "a free state." It is not clear why the committee changed the word, but we can assume it was for one of a few reasons. It could have been done stylistically: the states wanted to make it clear that it was every body politic, including the several states, not just the country of the United States, or to specifically reference each state of the union. While the last reason is the least likely due to the common usage historically, it would not take away from the idea that the right to keep and bear arms as individuals is still independent of militia service.

---

[88] United States Constitution, Article III, Section 2
[89] United States Constitution, Article I, Section 9
[90] United States Constitution, Amendment 2
[91] Euguene Volokh, "Necessary to the Security of a Free State," *Notre Dame Law Review*, 2007

The definition of the word *state* may seem like hair-splitting; however, on that hair rests one of the main points made by those who consider the right for collective use and protection only. In the end, it matters little whether it is referring to a body politic or a state in the union. Either way, the prefatory clause cannot add to or take away from the operative clause. The court concludes the "free state" argument by outlining the reasons why the militia is necessary to secure a free state.

> *There are many reasons why the militia was thought to be "necessary to the security of a free state." First, of course, it is useful in repelling invasions and suppressing insurrections. Second, it renders large standing armies unnecessary—an argument that Alexander Hamilton made in favor of federal control over the militia.[92] Third, when the able-bodied men of a nation are trained in arms and organized, they are better able to resist tyranny.[93]*

After the court finished presenting the prefatory and operative clauses, they addressed the relationship between the two.

During the 1788 ratifying conventions, the states voiced their concern that the national government would disarm the people to impose tyrannical rule through a standing army or a select militia. Today some rule out that concern because there is little fear of that today. We are too "civilized," they say. It could be argued, however, that the reason why we have reduced that fear is because of the Second Amendment and civilian rule over the military and militia.

To the court's point, the states' fears of a standing army and the disarming of the people by the national government were pervasive in anti-federalist rhetoric.

> *John Smilie, for example, worried not only that Congress's "command of the militia" could be used to create a "select militia," or to have "no militia at all," but also, as a separate concern, that "[w]hen a select*

---

[92] Alexander Hamilton, *Federalist* No. 29, 1788
[93] United States Supreme Court, *District of Columbia v. Heller*, 2008

militia is formed; the people in general may be disarmed."[94]

Federalists responded that because Congress was given no power to abridge the ancient right of individuals to keep and bear arms, such a force could never oppress the people. . . It was understood across the political spectrum that the right helped to secure the ideal of a citizen militia, which might be necessary to oppose an oppressive military force if the constitutional order broke down. It is therefore entirely sensible that the Second Amendment's prefatory clause announces the purpose for which the right was codified: to prevent elimination of the militia. The prefatory clause does not suggest that preserving the militia was the only reason Americans valued the ancient right; most undoubtedly thought it even more important for self-defense and hunting. But the threat that the new Federal Government would destroy the citizens' militia by taking away their arms was the reason that right—unlike some other English rights—was codified in a written Constitution. JUSTICE BREYER's assertion that individual self-defense is merely a "subsidiary interest" of the right to keep and bear arms. . . is profoundly mistaken.[95]

If the Second Amendment right goes no further than the right to keep and bear weapons as an organized militia, then that right exists solely at the discretion of Congress. That interpretation leaves the unorganized citizen militia unarmed and unable to provide a safeguard against tyranny—one of the purposes of the militia in the first place.

Thus, if petitioners are correct, the Second Amendment protects citizens' right to use a gun in an organization from which Congress has plenary authority to exclude them. It guarantees a select militia of the sort the Stuart

---

[94] Merrill Jensen et al., *Documentary History of the Ratification of the Constitution*, 1976
[95] United States Supreme Court, *District of Columbia v. Heller*, 2008

kings found useful, but not the people's militia that was the concern of the founding generation.[96]

Disagreeing with the majority of the court in Heller, Justice Stevens, argued that the right to keep and bear arms is connected to military service only and no such individual right exists. The majority then went on to debunk that idea.

The court highlighted three important founding-era legal scholars who understood that the Second Amendment protects an individual right unconnected with militia service. The first was St. George Tucker's version of *Blackstone's Commentaries*. Tucker elaborated on the Second Amendment:

> *This may be considered as the true palladium of liberty. . . The right to self-defence is the first law of nature: in most governments it has been the study of rulers to confine the right within the narrowest limits possible. Wherever standing armies are kept up, and the right of the people to keep and bear arms is, under any colour or pretext whatsoever, prohibited, liberty, if not already annihilated, is on the brink of destruction.*[97]

In 1825, William Rawle, a prominent lawyer and a member of the Pennsylvania Assembly that ratified the Bill of Rights, said this about the Second Amendment:

> *In the second article, it is declared, that a well regulated militia is necessary to the security of a free state; a proposition from which few will dissent. . .*

> *The corollary, from the first position is, that the right of the people to keep and bear arms shall not be infringed.*

> *The prohibition is general. No clause in the constitution could by any rule of construction be conceived to give to*

---

[96] Ibid.

[97] St. George Tucker, *Blackstone's Commentaries: With Notes of Reference to the Constitution and Laws of the Federal Government of the United States and of the Commonwealth of Virginia*, 1803

congress a power to disarm the people. Such a flagitious attempt could only be made under some general pretence by a state legislature. But if in any blind pursuit of inordinate power, either should attempt it, this amendment may be appealed to as a restraint on both.[98]

In his famous *Commentaries on the Constitution of the United States*, Joseph Story compared the Second Amendment to a similar provision in the English Bill of Rights that had no connection to militia service. Recognizing Story's position, in 1871 the Tennessee Supreme Court said:

Story, shows clearly that this right was intended. . . and was guaranteed to, and to be exercised and enjoyed by the citizen as such, and not by him as a soldier, or in defense solely of his political rights.[99]

In an 1840 work Story wrote:

One of the ordinary modes, by which tyrants accomplish their purposes without resistance, is, by disarming the people, and making it an offence to keep arms, and by substituting a regular army in the stead of a resort to the militia.[100]

Adding to their argument that the right is an individual right unconnected to militia service, the court quoted an 1846 decision by the Supreme Court of Georgia:

The right of the whole people, old and young, men, women and boys, and not militia only, to keep and bear arms of every description, and not such merely as are used by the militia, shall not be infringed, curtailed, or broken in upon, in the smallest degree; and all this for the important end to be attained: the rearing up and qualifying a well-regulated militia, so vitally necessary

---

[98] William Rawle, *A View of the Constitution of the United States*, 1829
[99] *Andrews v. State*, 1871
[100] Joseph Story, *A Familiar Exposition of the Constitution of the United States*, 1840

> *to the security of a free State. Our opinion is, that any law, State or Federal, is repugnant to the Constitution, and void, which contravenes this right, originally belonging to our forefathers, trampled under foot by Charles I. and his two wicked sons and successors, re-established by the revolution of 1688, conveyed to this land of liberty by the colonists, and finally incorporated conspicuously in our own Magna Carta![101]*

In the aftermath of the Civil War, there was an increased interest in the Second Amendment. People debated whether and how to secure constitutional rights for the newly freed slaves. The court said:

> *Blacks were routinely disarmed by Southern States after the Civil War. Those who opposed these injustices frequently stated that they infringed blacks' constitutional right to keep and bear arms. Needless to say, the claim was not that blacks were being prohibited from carrying arms in an organized state militia. A Report of the Commission of the Freedmen's Bureau in 1866 stated plainly: '[T]he civil law [of Kentucky] prohibits the colored man from bearing arms. . . Their arms are taken from them by the civil authorities. . . Thus, the right of the people to keep and bear arms as provided in the Constitution is infringed.". . .*

> *A joint congressional Report said:*

> *"[In] some parts of [South Carolina], armed parties are, without proper authority, engaged in seizing all firearms found in the hands of the freemen. Such conduct is in clear and direct violation of their personal rights as guaranteed by the Constitution of the United States. . ."*

> *The view expressed in these statements was widely reported and was apparently widely held. For example,*

---

[101] *Nunn v. Georgia*, 1846

an editorial in The Loyal Georgian *(Augusta) on February 3, 1866, assured blacks that "[a]ll men, without distinction of color, have the right to keep and bear arms to defend their homes, families or themselves." Halbrook 19. Congress enacted the Freedmen's Bureau Act on July 16, 1866. Section 14 stated:*

"[T]he right. . . to have full and equal benefit of all laws and proceedings concerning personal liberty, personal security, and the acquisition, enjoyment, and disposition of estate, real and personal, including the constitutional right to bear arms, shall be secured to and enjoyed by all the citizens. . . without respect to race or color, or previous condition of slavery. . ."

The understanding that the Second Amendment gave freed blacks the right to keep and bear arms was reflected in congressional discussion of the bill, with even an opponent of it saying that the founding generation "were for every man bearing his arms about him and keeping them in his house, his castle, for his own defense."[102]

The next important point the Court brings up is the fact that the Constitution doesn't grant the natural right to keep and bear arms. The Constitution does not grant any natural right. It does not need to grant something that already existed prior to the Constitution. The Constitution was written to secure rights, not grant them. Quoting a previous Supreme Court opinion, the Court said:

The opinion explained that the right "is not a right granted by the Constitution [or] in any manner dependent upon that instrument for its existence.[103]

As in-depth as the Heller opinion is, especially compared to any other ruling, the Court still left a lot to be considered. They did,

---

[102] United States Supreme Court, *District of Columbia v. Heller*, 2008
[103] *United States v. Cruikshank*, 1875

however, make it clear that although the Second Amendment was inserted to protect the militia, it protects the individual right to keep and bear arms as well. A natural right that does not require militia service for an individual to exercise. A right that is derived from the unalienable right of self-preservation.

OUR DUTY TO TAKE ALL OTHER STEPS FIRST

This does not mean we have the right to be the aggressor. If someone offends, the return action cannot be greater than the offense. You become the offending aggressor. It is only to defend against the threat of loss of life and/or significant property.

Third Amendment

"NO SOLDIER SHALL, IN TIME OF PEACE BE QUARTERED IN ANY HOUSE, WITHOUT THE CONSENT OF THE OWNER, NOR IN TIME OF WAR, BUT IN A MANNER TO BE PRESCRIBED BY LAW."

KEY QUOTES FROM THE FOUNDING ERA

As the happiness of the people is the sole end of government, so the consent of the people is the only foundation of it, in reason, morality, and the natural fitness of things.[1] —John Adams

A Government is instituted to protect property of every sort. . . This being the end of government, that alone is a just government, which impartially secures to every man, whatever is his own.[2] —James Madison

Governments are instituted among men, deriving their just powers from the Consent of the governed.[3]
—Declaration of Independence

The Third Amendment is one of the least controversial amendments in the Bill of Rights. The Founders included this amendment because of a practice European kings, quartering troops in the homes of the people to save money or to quell a rebellion. Since it has received so little attention in the courts and the media, many scholars barely give it a passing glance, if they mention it at all. It is, however, important to our discussion because it helps reinforce some of our natural unalienable rights. In reading the Third Amendment, many miss that it is not just about quartering soldiers; it is, more importantly, about consent.

The Third Amendment guarantees the right of the people from being compelled to shelter soldiers in their homes without the

---

[1] John Adams, *A Proclamation by the General Court*, 19 January 1776
[2] James Madison, "Property," *National Gazette*, 29 March 1792
[3] Declaration of Independence, 4 July 1776

homeowners' consent, except in time of war as prescribed by law. This was a grievous practice in the colonies before they declared their independence, and the Founders wanted to ensure that their newly formed government would not follow the same pattern.

Most of the Framers believed "that a well-regulated militia," composed of the body of the people, trained to arms, is the "proper, natural, and safe defense of a free State,"[4] and that no standing armies in time of peace were needed. However, they recognized, as George Washington did, that though "a large standing Army in time of Peace hath ever been considered dangerous to the liberties of a Country, yet a few Troops, under certain circumstances, are not only safe, but indispensably necessary."[5]

Eventually the Founders came to a consensus that some standing armies in the more vulnerable parts of the country were necessary to discourage their enemies from coming upon them. Thus, they gave Congress the power to "raise and support Armies," but stipulated that money appropriated for this purpose shall not "be for a longer Term than two Years."[6] The states did not believe that a two-year term was sufficient to guard against the danger of quartering troops and thus recommended the Third Amendment.

HISTORY OF QUARTERING TROOPS

Standing armies were commonplace in England, notwithstanding the intense resistance against them. This and other practices became so oppressive during the reign of Charles I that in 1628 he was compelled to sign the Petition of Right, which listed the grievances of the people. One of these grievances complained that the king was sending "great companies of soldiers and mariners. . . into divers [sic] counties, and the inhabitants, against their wills, had been compelled to take them into their houses and allow them there to sojourn against the laws and customs of this realm."[7]

---

[4] *The Virginia Declaration of Rights*, 1776
[5] George Washington, "Sentiments on a Peace Establishment," 1 May 1783
[6] United States Constitution, Article 1, Section 8, Clause 12, 1787
[7] Petition of Right, 1628

When Louis XIV of France threatened to quarter troops in the homes of the Protestant Huguenots unless they returned to the state church, they fled in terror to various parts of the world rather than risk such an affliction.

Parliament attempted to enforce this same practice among the colonies by issuing various legislation known as the Coercive or Intolerable Acts. These acts were designed to punish the colonists and submit them to the will of the crown.

The first of these four acts was the Boston Port Act which closed the port of Boston until the city paid for the tea that was dumped into the harbor during what came to be known as the Boston Tea Party.

Next was the Massachusetts Government Act, which suspended the Massachusetts charter of 1691 and drastically limited its colonial legislature.

Parliament then revoked the colonists' ability to hold trials for British officials in the Administration of Justice Act.

Lastly, in an attempt to enforce the foregoing acts and to save money, Parliament passed the Quartering Act, which gave royal governors authority to house British soldiers in the homes of the colonists without the consent of the colonial legislature. King George not only ordered the colonists to quarter the troops in their homes, but attempted to force them to provide "fire, candles, vinegar and salt, bedding, utensils for dressing their victuals... without paying anything for the same."[8] It placed each home under martial law and the soldiers who took over the homes were notorious for assaulting the women, destroying the furniture, and abusing the owners.

When the colonies declared their independence from Britain, they included in their declaration similar grievances as were contained in the English Petition of Right. Among these grievances, they declared that the king had quartered "large bodies of armed troops

---

[8] Quartering Act, 24 March 1765

among" them and that he had kept "in times of peace standing armies without the consent of [their] Legislature."[9]

As the states drafted their Constitutions, some of them, including Delaware, added similar language, declaring "that no soldiers ought to be quartered in any house in time of peace without the consent of the owner, and in time of war in such manner only as the legislature shall direct."[10]

Notice the similar language that is now the Third Amendment. The Framers had good reason to include such a prohibition in the Bill of Rights, and we should be grateful that this amendment has not been put to the test.

THE RIGHT OF INDIVIDUAL CONSENT

In the Third Amendment we are guaranteed that "No Soldier shall, in time of peace be quartered in [our] house without [our] consent." Because we have the right to consent, we can protect our unalienable natural rights. We can choose how to use and dispose of the property we obtain. We can also choose who comes into our house and when. These are some of our natural rights that no one, including government, should violate.

The Declaration of Independence identifies "certain unalienable Rights [among which] are Life, Liberty and the pursuit of Happiness." If we did not have a right to give our consent for a soldier to live in our house, we would have neither liberty nor the right to property. In other words, what we choose to do with our life and property is what allows us to pursue those things in life that make us happy. If someone takes away our right to consent by forcing us to do something against our will, this is rightly termed tyranny and will impede our "pursuit of happiness." This right of consent is essential in a free society and must be considered a natural unalienable right belonging to all people.

---

[9] Declaration of Independence, 4 July 1776
[10] Delaware Declaration of Rights, 1776

This right of consent can intersect with another individual's rights. It is difficult to find the line between protecting one individual's rights while protecting another's rights at the same time. Consider Jefferson's definition of liberty presented earlier:

> *Liberty. . . is unobstructed action according to our will: but rightful liberty is unobstructed action according to our will, within the limits drawn around us by the equal rights of others.*[11]

Rightful liberty only goes as far as another person's liberty. The moment our liberty begins to encroach upon another's, it ends. He further clarifies that a civil law violates liberty if it allows one person to encroach upon another person's liberty. For example, seat belt laws can be argued to be an infringement on an individual's right to consent because not wearing a seatbelt does not infringe upon the rights of another. Mandatory automobile insurance, on the other hand, can be required because an uninsured driver could violate the rights of another in an accident.

THE RIGHT OF COLLECTIVE CONSENT

In addition to our individual right of consent, this amendment illustrates how the Founders chose to protect this right in a collective sense. It states that soldiers could be quartered in our home during times of war, but it would need to be done "in a manner to be prescribed by law." This qualifier, "to be prescribed by law," is critical as it illustrates how the Framers chose to protect our right to consent in our federal system. We can have confidence knowing that if were necessary, troops would be quartered in our homes "in a manner to be prescribed by law" and not by the arbitrary whims of a dictator. We do not lose our right to consent in time of war. Rather, we pre-consent through laws passed before the war. It is wise, especially regarding emergencies, that laws and procedures are created long before the emergency occurs—a time when calmer minds can craft sober legislation. Samuel Adams gave wise

---

[11] Letter from Thomas Jefferson to Isaac H. Tiffany, 4 April 1819

recommendation to that effect. In addition, he said it would be unwise to abandon existing law for the whims of individuals:

> *It is always safe to ADHERE TO THE LAW, and to keep every man of every denomination and character WITHIN ITS BOUNDS—Not to do this would be in the highest degree IMPRUDENT: Whenever it becomes a question in prudence, whether we shall make use of legal and constitutional methods to prevent the incroachments of ANY KIND OF POWER, what will it be but to depart from the straight line, to give up the LAW and the CONSTITUTION, which is fixed and stable, and is the collected and long digested sentiment OF THE WHOLE, and to substitute in its room the opinion of individuals, than which nothing can be more uncertain: The sentiments of men in such a case would in all likelihood be as various as their sentiments in religion or anything else; and as there would then be no settled rule for the publick to advert to, the safety of the people would probably be at an end.[12]*

While it is unlikely that we would be asked to quarter soldiers, this phrase adds extra emphasis to the wisdom of the Founders in placing "all [law-making] powers. . . in a Congress of the United States. . ."[13] In other words, since we have collectively consented to give Congress the authority to declare war, we have also consented that in a war emergency, troops could be quartered in our homes if needed. We consented to this because we know that laws affecting our life, liberty and property cannot be passed without first being thoroughly discussed by representatives of our choosing. According to the Constitution, not even the president of the United States can sign a law without it first being approved by Congress. Unfortunately, there are now more laws from the national government that don't go through Congress than do.[14] This should

---

[12] Samuel Adams, *Boston Gazette*, 17 Oct. 1768, emphasis from original quote.

[13] United States Constitution, Article 1, Section 1, Clause 1, 1787

[14] The president and executive department heads file regulations in the Federal Registry. If Congress does not object within a certain amount of time, it becomes law. Although this

be alarming to every American because it means that we have not consented to those laws. As citizens, we should be vigilant in protecting this process because it is the way we preserve our right to consent in society.

By virtue of the society we live in, we collectively give our consent to certain things. In a community, we consent to city or county ordinances, so long as we are fairly represented. On a state and national level, we consent to laws passed by our legislatures because we recognize that we can have a voice in the laws that are made. However, we should object when laws are passed that violate our natural unalienable rights such as the right to life, liberty, and property. We also may object if a law is written contrary to the authority we consented to give our elected representatives. Hence, "the right of the people peaceably to assemble, and to petition the Government for a redress of grievances"[15] is a mechanism that allows us to defend our individual natural right of consent. If we value our right of consent, we must engage, not only on election day, but every available opportunity.

CONCLUSION

The right to consent is fundamental to the relationship between individual and collective citizens and their government. After all, government derives its "just power from the consent of the governed." Without consent, the government cannot exist. The Third Amendment was created based on the natural right to consent to our form of government.

The amendment may seem unnecessary today because we have little trouble with the quartering of troops. But perhaps the reason why we have little trouble is because the Third Amendment exists. It created a parchment barrier that has protected citizens from the scourge of quartering troops. It also provides a preface to the Fourth Amendment, which is a more detailed protection of our property

---

process is not provided as a legitimate method of law-making in the Constitution, the courts have upheld the practice.

[15] United States Constitution, Amendment 1, 1789

through the power of consent. The Third Amendment protects our homes in general, and the Fourth protects every word on every paper, down to the paperclip that binds them together.

Fourth Amendment

"THE RIGHT OF THE PEOPLE TO BE SECURE IN THEIR PERSONS, HOUSES, PAPERS, AND EFFECTS, AGAINST UNREASONABLE SEARCHES AND SEIZURES, SHALL NOT BE VIOLATED, AND NO WARRANTS SHALL ISSUE, BUT UPON PROBABLE CAUSE, SUPPORTED BY OATH OR AFFIRMATION, AND PARTICULARLY DESCRIBING THE PLACE TO BE SEARCHED, AND THE PERSONS OR THINGS TO BE SEIZED."

KEY QUOTES FROM THE FOUNDING ERA

Now, one of the most essential branches of English liberty is the freedom of one's house. A man's house is his castle; and whilst he is quiet, he is as well guarded as a prince in his castle.[1] —James Otis

Every subject has a right to be secure from all unreasonable searches, and seizures, of his person, his houses, his papers, and all his possessions. All warrants, therefore, are contrary to this right, if the cause or foundation of them be not previously supported by oath or affirmation. . . and no warrant ought to be issued but in cases, and with the formalities prescribed by the laws.[2]
—Massachusetts Declaration of Rights

That general warrants, whereby an officer or messenger may be commanded to search suspected places without evidence of a fact committed, or to seize any person or persons not named, or whose offense is not particularly described and supported by evidence, are grievous and oppressive, and ought not to be granted.[3]
—Virginia Declaration of Rights

The Fourth Amendment was designed to protect individuals from the arbitrary interference of government officials in their personal lives. It was common for government officials, prior to 1776, to

---

[1] James Otis, John Adams's reconstruction of Otis's speech given in the writs of assistance case, 24 February 1761

[2] Massachusetts Declaration of Rights, Article 14, 25 October 1780

[3] Virginia Declaration of Rights, Article 1, Section 10, 12 June 1776

enter upon private property and search for and seize persons or things with little or no evidence of wrongdoing. After the colonies declared their independence, the newly formed states began drafting their own constitutions, many of which included a declaration of rights. Among these declarations, nearly everyone contained some kind of prohibition against such actions. Some went further, declaring that this was a "right" that the people possessed and not merely a privilege.

The doctrine of the divine right of kings was almost always present in the past. Under this doctrine, the king was considered the highest authority, second only to God. Like God, the king granteth and the king taketh away. In other words, the people had no rights, only privileges which could be granted or taken at the whim of the king. When the colonies declared their independence, the concept of individual, unalienable rights was proclaimed to the world.

The American colonists declared that there were certain privileges that not even a king could take away—privileges so basic in nature that they had to be considered natural rights inherent in all people. This was the declaration to the world in 1776 that all people "are endowed by their Creator with certain unalienable Rights." Those rights include life, liberty, property, and the pursuit of happiness. The Fourth Amendment protects those rights by applying practical policy that limits government interference in our "persons, houses, papers, and effects."

> **Persons**: the right to life.
>
> **Papers**: the liberty to read and write according to the dictates of your own conscience.
>
> **Houses**: the right to property.
>
> **Effects** (i.e., movable property): the right to pursue happiness in whatever form that may be.

Thus, the Fourth Amendment protects some of our most basic human rights—rights that millions have struggled to obtain over the centuries, as you will see in the coming pages.

PROTECTING UNALIENABLE RIGHTS BY POLICY

The Fourth Amendment has two parts. The first refers to "the right of the people." The second is the policy that was created to protect these rights. The Founders established this policy to ensure that the rights of the people were protected, while still allowing for investigation into criminal activity. This policy restricts a police officer, for example, from entering upon private property and searching or seizing persons or things even if probable cause dictates that a person is in violation of the law. Unless an officer sees a person in the act of committing a crime or has direct evidence to suggest that a crime is being committed, a warrant is required and can only be obtained "upon probable cause, supported by Oath or affirmation, and particularly describing the places to be searched, and the persons or things to be seized."[4]

In other words, for an officer to obtain a warrant of arrest, he must be able to show the judge:

- Probable cause that the person named in the warrant is responsible for the crime.

- Specific places to be searched and things to be seized.

- The officer must then take an oath or give an affirmation that what he has told the judge is true.

ORIGINS OF THE FOURTH AMENDMENT

The struggle to protect the rights that we enjoy in the Fourth Amendment has been a long and painful process. This struggle can be traced throughout human history, but for the purposes of this book we will only go back as far as the Magna Carta and proceed forward from there in exploring these basic human rights.

In 1215, King John became so oppressive that the barons rebelled and forced the king to sign a charter that protected their rights. Chapter 39 of the Magna Carta states that:

---

[4] United States Constitution, Amendment 4, 1789

> *No free man is to be arrested, or imprisoned, or disseised [deprived of property], or outlawed, or exiled, or in any other way ruined, nor will we go against him or send against him, except by the lawful judgment of his peers or by the law of the land.[5]*

Although the Magna Carta did not actually grant any protection or rights to the common people, over time it came to symbolize the basic desires of all people to feel secure in their person and property.

Leonard W. Levy gives one suggestion of how a common person may have come to believe that the Great Charter secured their rights. He quotes Robert Beale, a clerk of the Privy Council in the late 1500s. In 1589, Beale rhetorically asked:

> *[What] had happened to Chapter 39 of the great charter when agents of a prerogative court, acting under its warrant, could "enter into mens houses, break of their chests and chambers" and carry off as evidence whatever they pleased.[6]*

Beale's statement and others like it began giving hope that in some future day these same rights would be secured for all people. The Great Charter became a symbol of freedom from oppression, and in the early 1600s the famous notion that "a man's home is his castle" first began appearing.

The right to be secure in a person's house and property is a universal desire. By contrast, it is common that when a person gains a little power, they abuse the rights of others. It seems ironic that the very things we all desire are oft times not respected when a person obtains authority over another. Because of this natural tendency, abuses continued in the form of general warrants that remained a common practice in Britain. It became even more oppressive in the colonies, allowing searches and seizures to take place with little and sometimes no evidence of wrongful acts.

---

[5] Magna Carta, 1215
[6] Leonard Levy, *Origins of the Bill of Rights*, 1999

WRITS OF ASSISTANCE

One of the most oppressive general warrants which Parliament imposed on the colonies came about in the early 1760s. This type of warrant was called a writ of assistance. In general terms, a writ was an official letter or written statement from an admiralty court (in which there were no juries) giving authority to a customs official to conduct general searches for smuggled goods. Further, it allowed the official to require the assistance of constables and sheriffs in their searches and seizures of persons and things.

During the Seven Years' War and after the British army conquered Montreal in 1760, Parliament turned their attention more directly on the American colonies. Due to the war, Britain was deeply in debt and Parliament devised a plan to collect more tax revenue from the Americans.

Parliament sent orders to Charles Paxton, who served as collector of customs in Boston, to apply to the civil authority for writs of assistance. This would enable Paxton and his customs house officers

> *to command all Sheriffs & Constables, to attend and aid them, in breaking open houses, stores, Shops, Cellars, Ships Bales, trunks, chests, casks, packages of all sorts, to search for goods wares and Merchandizes, which had been imposed against the prohibitions, or without paying the taxes imposed by certain Acts of Parliament called "The Acts of Trade" [Navigation Acts]. . .[7]*

Although these acts had rarely been enforced in the colonies, nor was it probable that they could be enforced, Parliament saw this as an opportunity to raise money from confiscated items and to secure more control over the colonies.

Knowing that Stephen Sewall, who currently served as chief justice of the court, was against writs of assistance, Paxton was hesitant to apply. However, before the next court term in February of 1761, Sewall died, and Lieutenant Governor Hutchinson was appointed in

---

[7] Letter from John Adams to William Tudor, Sr., 29 March 1817

his place. Hutchinson was well known as a loyalist to the crown and word quickly spread among the merchants of the "menacing Monster, the Writ of Assistants *[sic]*."[8]

Earnestly seeking representation, merchants found James Otis, Jr., a lawyer of the court who had previously been asked by the court to argue in favor of writs of assistance. Being thus employed with the court and fearing that he would be compelled to argue in favor of the writ, Otis resigned his lucrative position. Risking his very life, he agreed to represent the merchants and refused pay, stating that "in such a Cause. . . I despise all fees."[9]

At the beginning of his address before the court, Otis declared:

> *I will to my dying day oppose, with all the powers and faculties God has given me, all such instruments of slavery on the one hand and villainy on the other as this Writ of Assistance is. It appears to me the worst instrument of arbitrary power, the most destructive of English liberty and the fundamental principles of law, that ever was found in an English law-book. . .*[10]

He then gave four reasons why he believes writs of assistance are illegal in English law:

> *In the first place, the writ is universal, being directed "to all and singular justices, sheriffs, constables, and all other officers and subjects"; so that, in short, it is directed to every subject in the King's dominions. Everyone with this writ may be a tyrant; if this commission be legal, a tyrant in a legal manner, also, may control, imprison, or murder anyone within the realm.*
>
> *In the next place, it is perpetual; there is no return. A man is accountable to no person for his doings. Every*

---

[8] Ibid.

[9] Ibid.

[10] James Otis, John Adams's reconstruction of Otis's speech given in the writs of assistance case, 24 February 1761

man may reign secure in his petty tyranny, and spread terror and desolation around him until the trump of the Archangel shall excite different emotions in his soul. In the third place, a person with this writ, in the daytime, may enter all houses, shops, etc., at will, and command all to assist him. Fourthly, by this writ not only deputies, etc., but even their menial servants, are allowed to lord it over us. . .[11]

He further cited the common belief that "a man's house is his castle":

One of the most essential branches of English liberty is the freedom of one's house. A man's house is his castle; and whilst he is quiet, he is as well guarded as a prince in his castle. This writ, if it should be declared legal, would totally annihilate this privilege.[12]

John Adams, who attended the proceedings, was so moved by Otis's speech that later in life he desired this scene to be memorialized on canvas. He wrote a letter to William Tudor, Sr., inquiring of him if he knew a painter and then proceeded to paint a verbal picture of Otis standing before the court. He recalled that:

Otis was a flame of fire! With a promptitude of Classical Allusions, a depth of research, a rapid summary of historical events & dates, a profusion of Legal Authorities, a prophetic glance of his eyes into futurity, and a rapid torrent of impetuous Eloquence he hurried away all before him.[13]

After Otis's nearly five-hour speech, young Adams felt that he was ready then and there "to take Arms against Writs of Assistants." He believed that he had just witnessed "the first scene of the first Act of

---

[11] Ibid.
[12] Ibid.
[13] Letter from John Adams to William Tudor, Sr., 29 March 1817

opposition to the Arbitrary claims of Great Britain. . . and that the Child Independence was born."[14]

Although Otis's words would have little effect on the practice of general searches for several more years, his sacrifice, as John T. Morse described, would be "the first log of the pile which afterward made the great blaze of the Revolution."[15]

THE CIDER BILL OF 1763

Meanwhile, back in England, Parliament continued to look for ways to pay off its war debt. Lord Bute, who served as prime minister, proposed a bill that would place a tax of four shillings on every hogshead (barrel) of cider produced. This bill was met with instant protests and riots, especially among the cider-producing areas in the West. It was not just the tax that upset the people, but the manner in which this tax would be enforced. Because this tax would be directly attached to their property, or the fruits of their labors, it would require tax collectors to search personal property to know if a person was paying their fair share. They felt this bill was a direct violation of their right to be secure in their houses and property.

Merchants knew this would lead to more general searches and resistance grew so intense that Lord Bute stepped down as prime minister. However, George Grenville took his place and forced the bill through in February 1764. As expected, many general or warrantless searches ensued and the pressure against Parliament continued to mount until the following year, when Parliament gave in and rescinded the tax.

ENTICK V. CARRINGTON

Parliament's proposals to tax the people's property through the Cider Bill and other such measures caused some free-spirited Englishmen to write papers denouncing these measures and verbally attacking members of Parliament. One of these weekly papers,

---

[14] Ibid.
[15] John T. Morse, Jr., *American Statesmen: John Adams*, 1884

entitled *The Monitor: Or British Freeholder*, was being written and distributed by an unknown author, and was considered by some to be seditious.

Lord Halifax, who had recently been appointed as secretary of state for the Northern Department, ordered a search of John Entick's house, suspecting him of having written the papers. The king's chief messenger and three others, sent under Lord Halifax's order, broke into Entick's home to find supporting evidence of their suspicion. They spent several hours ransacking his home, breaking locks and doors and stealing many pamphlets and charts.

Entick sued the messengers for trespassing, and the case went before Lord Camden, the Chief Justice of the Common Pleas. Camden determined that Halifax had no right under statute or under precedent to issue a warrant and ruled in Entick's favor. In his statement, Camden quoted John Locke, who believed that

> *[The] great end, for which men entered into society, was to secure their property. . .*
>
> *By the laws of England, every invasion of private property, be it ever so minute, is a trespass. No man can set his foot upon my ground without my licence, but he is liable to an action, though the damage be nothing; which is proved by every declaration in trespass, where the defendant is called upon to answer for bruising the grass and even treading upon the soil. If he admits the fact, he is bound to show by way of justification, that some positive law has empowered or excused him.*[16]

Camden's ruling was significant in English legal theory and would prove over time to influence the language and interpretation of the Fourth Amendment.

---

[16] *Entick v. Carrington*, 1765

It was during this time that William Pitt gave one of his best-known speeches before Parliament, which once again played off the notion that a man's home is his castle.

> *The poorest man may, in his cottage, bid defiance to all the forces of the Crown. It may be frail; its roof may shake; the wind may blow through it; the storm may enter; the rain may enter; but the King of England may not enter; all his force dares not cross the threshold of the ruined tenement.*[17]

BOYD V. UNITED STATES (1886)

To more clearly illustrate the original spirit and meaning of the Fourth Amendment, we will now jump forward to *Boyd v. United States*, a court case from the late 1800s dealing with this amendment. The case originated in a New York district court in July 1884 and concerned twenty-nine cases of glass that had been imported into the country and seized by the collector as forfeited to the United States. The reason for the seizure was that the imported glass was subject to the payment of duties.

> *On the trial of the cause, it became important to show the quantity and value of the glass contained in [the] cases... To do this, the district attorney offered in evidence an order made by the District Judge... requiring [claimants] to produce the invoice of the twenty-nine cases. The claimants, in obedience to the notice, but objecting to its validity and to the constitutionality of the law, produced the invoice, and when it was offered in evidence by the district attorney, they objected to its reception on the ground that, in a suit for forfeiture, no evidence can be compelled from the claimants themselves, and also that the statute, so far as*

---

[17] William Pitt, speech in the House of Lords, in opposition to Excise Bill on perry and cider, 1763

it compels production of evidence to be used against the claimants, is unconstitutional and void.[18]

The claimants appealed to the Supreme Court, feeling that their Fourth Amendment rights were being violated. The court sided with the claimants, basing much of their decision on the writings and legal precedents established prior to the adoption of the Bill of Rights.

The court quoted extensively from Lord Camden's case, *Entick v. Carrington,* considering it as one of "the landmarks of English liberty. . . welcomed and applauded by the lovers of liberty in the colonies, as well as in the mother country."[19]

The court believed that the propositions expressed by Camden "were in the minds of those who framed the Fourth Amendment to the Constitution, and were considered as sufficiently explanatory of what was meant by unreasonable searches and seizures."[20]

The Supreme Court ruled that:

> *It does not require actual entry upon premises and search for and seizure of papers to constitute an unreasonable search and seizure within the meaning of the Fourth Amendment; a compulsory production of a party's private books and papers to be used against himself or his property in a criminal or penal proceeding, or for a forfeiture, is within the spirit and meaning of the Amendment.*[21]

They then expressed their final opinion by drawing an intimate connection between the Fourth and Fifth amendments.

> *[These two amendments]. . . throw great light on each other. For the "unreasonable searches and seizures" condemned in the Fourth Amendment are almost always*

---

[18] United States Supreme Court, *Boyd v. United States*, 1 February 1886
[19] Ibid.
[20] Ibid.
[21] Ibid.

made for the purpose of compelling a man to give evidence against himself, which, in criminal cases, is condemned in the Fifth Amendment. . . . And we have been unable to perceive that the seizure of a man's private books and papers to be used in evidence against him is substantially different from compelling him to be a witness against himself.

[We] are further of opinion that a compulsory production of the private books and papers of the owner of goods sought to be forfeited in such a suit is compelling him to be a witness against himself within the meaning of the Fifth Amendment to the Constitution, and is the equivalent of a search and seizure—and an unreasonable search and seizure—within the meaning of the Fourth Amendment.[22]

In other words, the 1886 case of *Boyd v. United States* held that:

- A compulsory production of a person's private papers (i.e., by subpoena) was an unreasonable search and seizure within the meaning of the Fourth Amendment and was therefore forbidden.

- That, in substance, such compulsory seizures of private papers compelled the defendant to be a witness against himself in violation of the Fifth Amendment.

- That, because it was a violation of the Fifth Amendment, it was also an unreasonable search and seizure under the Fourth Amendment.

"LEGAL" VIOLATIONS OF THE FOURTH AMENDMENT

As previously illustrated in the Cider Bill, a direct tax on property, including income, will almost always lead to general searches. This is due to the fact that once a tax has been levied on private property, tax collectors must have the ability to determine if a person is paying

---

[22] Ibid.

their fair share of the tax. This can only be done by requiring individuals to divulge personal information that should be protected under the Fourth Amendment. The Founders understood the danger of a direct tax in relation to the privacy of the people and actually put a prohibition against this type of tax directly in the Constitution.

> *No Capitation, or other direct, Tax shall be laid, unless in Proportion to the Census or Enumeration herein before directed to be taken.*[23]

However, the passage of the Sixteenth Amendment in 1913 eliminated that protection, which allows direct taxes to be levied on private property including houses, land, personal income, etc. The extent to which the Internal Revenue Service is invading the privacy of citizens to make certain each is paying their fair share should be a matter of great concern throughout the entire country. However, the major fault is with the law rather than the IRS. The collection of direct taxes, such as income taxes, is impossible without virtually wiping out the guarantees set forth in the Fourth Amendment.

> *It is not the breaking of [our] doors, and the rummaging of [our] drawers, that constitutes the essence of the offense; but it is the invasion of [our] indefeasible right of personal security, personal liberty, and private property. . .*[24]

CONCLUSION

The Fourth Amendment has earned its place in the Bill of Rights as a critical protection of life, liberty, property, and the pursuit of happiness. But what if a warrant is obtained and incriminating evidence brings criminal charges? The Fifth Amendment handles the next phase should a citizen face that scary prospect. The authors of the Bill of Rights carried the protection of life, liberty, and property through every phase of an individual's existence in society. The amendments bring us from freedom of thought to expression,

---

[23] United States Constitution, Article 1, Section 9, Clause 4, 1787
[24] United States Supreme Court, *Boyd v. United States*, 1 February 1886

from self-preservation to consent, and from protection of rights before an accusation to the protection of rights after an accusation. The pattern continues from one amendment to another until all individual rights are protected.

Fifth Amendment

"NO PERSON SHALL BE HELD TO ANSWER FOR A CAPITAL, OR OTHERWISE INFAMOUS CRIME, UNLESS ON A PRESENTMENT OR INDICTMENT OF A GRAND JURY, EXCEPT IN CASES ARISING IN THE LAND OR NAVAL FORCES, OR IN THE MILITIA, WHEN IN ACTUAL SERVICE IN TIME OF WAR OR PUBLIC DANGER; NOR SHALL ANY PERSON BE SUBJECT FOR THE SAME OFFENSE TO BE TWICE PUT IN JEOPARDY OF LIFE OR LIMB; NOR SHALL BE COMPELLED IN ANY CRIMINAL CASE TO BE A WITNESS AGAINST HIMSELF, NOR BE DEPRIVED OF LIFE, LIBERTY, OR PROPERTY, WITHOUT DUE PROCESS OF LAW; NOR SHALL PRIVATE PROPERTY BE TAKEN FOR PUBLIC USE, WITHOUT JUST COMPENSATION."

The Fifth Amendment has five parts divided into two major sections, each of which reiterates certain rights relating to life, liberty, and property:

Policies for Due Process of Criminal Charges

1. Grand jury: A federal criminal charge must first be presented to a grand jury.

2. Double jeopardy: No person can be tried twice for the same offense (placed in double jeopardy).

3. Witness against oneself: No person may be required to testify against themselves.

Right of Property

4. Due process: No person may be deprived of life, liberty, or property, without due process of law.

5. Takings clause: No private property shall be taken for public use without just compensation.

The fundamental concept underlying the Fifth Amendment is the right to life, liberty, property, and the pursuit of happiness. The first three parts of the amendment, however, do not state those rights directly, or any rights derived from them. Instead, they outline three proven due process policies. These policies are best practices for criminal charges while still protecting fundamental rights.

In addition to best practices for criminal charges, the fourth and fifth parts of the Fifth Amendment protect the unalienable right of life, liberty, and a special emphasis on property. We will now examine these five parts in more detail.

POLICIES FOR DUE PROCESS OF CRIMINAL CHARGES

"NO PERSON SHALL BE HELD TO ANSWER FOR A CAPITAL, OR OTHERWISE INFAMOUS CRIME, UNLESS ON A PRESENTMENT OR INDICTMENT OF A GRAND JURY, EXCEPT IN CASES ARISING IN THE LAND OR NAVAL FORCES, OR IN THE MILITIA, WHEN IN ACTUAL SERVICE IN TIME OF WAR OR PUBLIC DANGER; NOR SHALL ANY PERSON BE SUBJECT FOR THE SAME OFFENSE TO BE TWICE PUT IN JEOPARDY OF LIFE OR LIMB; NOR SHALL BE COMPELLED IN ANY CRIMINAL CASE TO BE A WITNESS AGAINST HIMSELF. . ."

1. THE GRAND JURY

"NO PERSON SHALL BE HELD TO ANSWER FOR A CAPITAL, OR OTHERWISE INFAMOUS CRIME, UNLESS ON A PRESENTMENT OR INDICTMENT OF A GRAND JURY, EXCEPT IN CASES ARISING IN THE LAND OR NAVAL FORCES, OR IN THE MILITIA, WHEN IN ACTUAL SERVICE IN TIME OF WAR OR PUBLIC DANGER. . ."

This provision gives the people the right not to be required to answer for a capital crime unless the case has been heard by a grand jury and formal charges have been issued, either in the form of a presentment or an indictment.

A capital crime is one punishable by death. An infamous crime is one punishable by death or imprisonment.

The grand jury protects the accused from the reckless accusations of malevolent individuals who know they can greatly damage the reputation of an individual simply by making a charge against someone. It forces the prosecutor to screen the facts through the grand jury. The formality of a grand jury hearing also compels the prosecutor to pinpoint the charges and demonstrate that he has witnesses and tangible evidence sufficiently conclusive to warrant a trial.

A grand jury consists of twelve to twenty-three persons called by the sheriff of the county, or by the United States marshal, to hear witnesses respecting any subject that may properly be brought before them as a violation of the law. If they believe a person is guilty, they return a "true bill," or indictment, which is a formal charge indicating that the grand jury had "reasonable cause" to believe that the person had committed the offense as charged. If the grand jury does not believe there is adequate evidence against the accused, they return a "no bill."

A "presentment" by a grand jury is a formal declaration against the offender based on an investigation by grand jury members. An "indictment" is a formal declaration that the jury has heard charges brought by the prosecuting attorney and believes there is reasonable cause that the person should stand trial for the allegations against him.

It is unclear to what society the credit for the first jury is attributed. Some historians say the Greeks and the Romans, with their accusatory councils. Others say it was the Anglo-Saxons that first used the practice. Still others say it was completely foreign to the Anglo-Saxons until the Normans brought it to the island of Britain after the Battle of Hastings in 1066.

Regardless of the origin, the jury was of extreme importance to the Founders. During his bill of rights proposal speech to Congress on August 22, 1789, James Madison said the protection of trial by jury was "the most valuable amendment on the whole list."

There are many comments about trial by jury and its importance to the preservation of liberty among the words of the Founders. Considering their strong opinion of the jury, it is interesting that the Founders spent little time on the fundamental reasons why the jury system is so brilliant. There is no "we hold these truths to be self-evident. . ." moment for the jury. However, its importance in their minds is indisputable. Every state constitution written in the revolutionary period preserved trial by jury. It was the first right discussed and codified in the Constitution by the convention of 1787. But what was its origin and why did the Founders look upon it as a palladium of liberty? In a letter to Thomas Paine in 1789, Thomas Jefferson said of the jury:

> *I consider [the jury] as the only anchor, ever yet imagined by man, by which a government can be held to the principles of its constitution.*[1]

And in a letter to Adamantios Coray in 1823, Jefferson wrote:

> *Trial by jury, the best of all safeguards for the person, the property, and the fame of every individual.*[2]

After all the praise, there is no mention of unalienable, fundamental, natural rights as the core of trial by jury. James Madison says why:

> *Trial by jury cannot be considered as a natural right, but a right resulting from the social compact which regulates the action of the community, but is as essential to secure the liberty of the people as any one of the pre-existent rights of nature.*[3]

Trial by jury was, as Jefferson put it, "imagined by man." It is conceived by people and proven to be a best practice for settling civil disputes and determining innocence or guilt in criminal trials. Although trial by jury was man-made, the Founders understood one unmistakable fact—when it existed, the rights of the individual were better protected, and when it was suspended, tyranny appeared in its ugliest forms.

The best practice of trial by jury took hundreds of years of evolution and refinement to establish the modern-day jury. That evolution began with the grand jury.

---

[1] Letter from Thomas Jefferson to Thomas Paine, 11 July 1789
[2] Letter from Thomas Jefferson to Adamantios Coray, 31 October 1823
[3] James Madison, House of Representatives, 8 Jun 1789

As mentioned above, the first society to use the jury is unknown. It seems likely that many early civilizations discovered that it was much safer to stand before a group of peers to be accused or convicted of a crime than to be accused and convicted by a king or other tyrant. It seems equally obvious that a dispute between two citizens would be best resolved by a group of local individuals who knew the ins and outs of the dispute. By all appearances, it looks as though juries were discovered by many societies independent of each other as a best practice for discovering the truth.

The exact origin of the trial by jury may not be clear, but it is clear that the current jury system in the United States evolved from the English history and use of the mechanism. The first English juries were more akin to grand juries rather than petty or trial juries.

Henry II recognized that keeping the peace among his subjects produced better results in terms of taxes, the ability to raise armies, etc. So he set out to keep the peace—to keep his throne.

In 1164, Henry II established ordinances known as the Constitutions of Clarendon. At the time the clergy were not subject to civil law and therefore could not be accused or convicted in civil court. Rather, they were tried in an ecclesiastical court where they could literally get away with murder, because execution was not a legal punishment in church court. Removal from the priesthood was typically the most extreme punishment.

Along with civil immunity for the clergy, land disputes arose in which the church would claim to own the property of laymen. Since the clergy could not be brought to civil court, property disputes would go unresolved. The Constitutions of Clarendon sought to resolve the matter. The church was restricted to powers of excommunication and forbidden to act against laymen on secret information or accusation. The church still had control over church property, but if there was a dispute with a layman, it had to be resolved by a secular jury.

Among the various provisions in the ordinances in the Constitutions of Clarendon, there were two instances where "twelve lawful men" were to be called. First, to present an accusation if they felt there were enough facts to do so. Second, to settle property disputes between the church and laymen.

> *6. [The] sheriff . . . shall cause twelve lawful men of the neighbourhood or town to swear in the presence of the bishop that they will make manifest the truth in this matter, according to their conscience. . .*

> *9. If a quarrel arise between a clerk and a layman or between a layman and a clerk concerning any tenement which the clerk wishes to attach to the church property but the layman to a lay fee: by the inquest of twelve lawful men, through the judgment of the chief Justice of the king, it shall be determined, in the presence of the Justice himself. . .[4]*

Two years later, in 1166, Henry II established the ordinances known as the Assize of Clarendon. An assize is a sitting or session of judges. It is a court of justice. The Assize of Clarendon further codified grand juries to resolve property disputes and criminal cases—again, with twelve lawful men.

> *1. In the first place the aforesaid king Henry, by thee counsel of all his barons, for the preservation of peace and the observing of justice, has decreed that an inquest shall be made throughout the separate counties, and throughout the separate hundreds,[5] through twelve of the more lawful men of the hundred, and through four of the more lawful men of each township, upon oath that they will speak the truth: whether in their hundred or in their township there be any man who, since the lord king has been king, has been charged or published as being a robber or murderer or thief; or any one who is a harbourer of robbers or murderers or thieves. And the*

---

[4] Constitutions of Clarendon, 1164

[5] A "hundred" was a political subdivision of a county usually consisting of one hundred families.

Justices shall make this inquest by themselves, and the sheriffs by themselves.

2. And he who shall be found through the oath of the aforesaid persons to have been charged or published as being a robber, or murderer, or thief, or a receiver of them, since the lord king has been king, shall be taken and shall go to the ordeal of water, and shall swear that he was not a robber or murderer or thief or receiver of them since the lord king has been king, to the extent of five shillings as far as he knows.[6]

The ordinances go on to detail on the process by which the court shall convene and the punishments brought upon the convicted in criminal cases. The punishment for crimes was usually banishment or a declaration that the guilty was no longer under the protection of the common law. They were declared outside the law—literally, an "outlaw." If the twelve, or four, lawful men presented an accusation, the accused would face ordeal by water, which will be covered in the Sixth Amendment regarding the trial jury.

Regarding property disputes, the king would commission the sheriff to recruit twelve men from the area in which the dispute arose. The idea was that those individuals would be intimately acquainted with the various properties, traditions, inheritances, etc. in the area. That knowledge, or the understanding of those facts, would allow the twelve to come to a truthful conclusion. Spreading that decision among twelve individuals would provide a representative cross section of the community.

These first juries were charged with the duty to gather the facts to either accuse someone of a crime or to settle a property dispute. In either case, they were to investigate the facts themselves and return their findings to the magistrate. This was a significant interruption to the lives of the jurors. Eventually jurors were asked to attend court

---

[6] Assize of Clarendon, 1166

to consider facts presented to them rather than discovering the facts on their own.

The king and other government officials would often stack the jury and strongly encourage the members of that jury to side with them against their adversaries. It was when the juries began to go against the will of the king that the people discovered that juries were a great benefit to the preservation of individual liberty.

In 1681 a grand jury refused to indict Anthony Ashley Cooper, 1st Earl of Shaftesbury, for treason. Charles II pressed the issue, but Cooper was nonetheless not indicted. This enhanced the people's respect for the institution of the jury. They saw it as a shield from tyrannical oppression and vindictive actions from the state.

Those first fact-finding juries evolved into today's grand jury. A United States grand jury is made up of 16–23 individuals. They are called to jury duty for months at a time. A few days a month, they are asked to review the evidence in a case and determine if the accused should be indicted. Their role is to guide the prosecutor in determining if there is enough evidence to indict. They also provide protection to the rights and liberties of individuals from overzealous prosecutors.

Today the grand jury has proven to be a brilliant guard against state abuse, but the evolution and history of the institution revealed some significant weaknesses that had to be worked out. The evolution of the trial jury provided necessary fixes to the grand jury system, but that will be covered in the Sixth Amendment.

2. DOUBLE JEOPARDY

"... NOR SHALL ANY PERSON BE SUBJECT FOR THE SAME OFFENSE TO BE TWICE PUT IN JEOPARDY OF LIFE OR LIMB..."

Double jeopardy means that no person can be tried twice for the same offense. This gives each individual the right to be permanently free of any further prosecution once they have been processed through the trial procedure. This allows the accused to continue their life without perpetual harassment.

A person is considered to have been put in jeopardy when brought before a court of competent jurisdiction upon an indictment or information in adequate form, and a jury empaneled. If the jury finds that it does not have sufficient evidence to convict, the trial cannot be postponed while the prosecutor seeks to discover additional evidence. Since the trial must then proceed to verdict, the defense can move for a directed verdict of not guilty, where the prosecution has not established the basic elements of the crime as charged.

A person is not put in jeopardy when a jury fails to agree and the jury has been discharged by the court for that reason. The accused can therefore be tried again with a new jury. The same is true where a person is convicted but the case is reversed because of some technicality by a higher court. Once more, they may be tried for the same crime but before a different jury.

This provision was inserted in the Constitution to prevent Americans from being prosecuted several times for the same crime, as had happened in England. An English prosecuting attorney who could not get a conviction on existing evidence would have the prisoner reindicted after they had accumulated more evidence.

3. WITNESS AGAINST ONESELF

"... NOR SHALL BE COMPELLED IN ANY CRIMINAL CASE TO BE A WITNESS AGAINST HIMSELF..."

This provision guarantees every American the right not to be a witness against themselves unless they voluntarily decide to do so. A defendant cannot be required to testify either directly or indirectly. In other words, they cannot be compelled to testify against themselves orally, nor can their papers or books be made to speak against them. This ties into the Fourth Amendment provision that a person is secure in their "papers and effects."

Of course, a person may waive the privilege and, if the statute of limitations bars prosecution for the crime, they can be compelled to answer, since they cannot be prosecuted for what they disclose. It has also been held that they cannot claim protection under the Fifth

Amendment if they have been pardoned, for that prevents prosecution of the crime in question.

Compulsory self-incrimination, like that of the Inquisition, existed for four hundred years after the Magna Carta. It was even employed among the early American colonists. Mrs. Anne Hutchinson of Massachusetts was tried for heresy in 1673 by Governor John Winthrop without the governor being aware of any privilege against self-incrimination.

Historically, when a person has been compelled to witness against themselves, the act of compelling often led to coercing, then to punishing, then torturing, and finally killing. Historically, the accused would experience "trial by ordeal" in which they would be punished or killed regardless of their plea. The punishment would be less cruel, or more "bearable," than if they refused to confess. The plea of guilty or not guilty did not prevent the punishment, it only changed its severity.

It was this kind of treatment that led to the Eighth Amendment's "cruel and unusual punishment" prohibition. It is a natural tendency to administer cruel and unusual punishments as a method to elicit a confession. This practice is prevented before it starts by the Fifth Amendment's prohibition of compelling a person to testify against themself.

RIGHT OF PROPERTY

"... NOR BE DEPRIVED OF LIFE, LIBERTY, OR PROPERTY WITHOUT DUE PROCESS OF LAW; NOR SHALL PRIVATE PROPERTY BE TAKEN FOR PUBLIC USE, WITHOUT JUST COMPENSATION."

KEY QUOTES FROM THE FOUNDING ERA

Government is instituted to protect property of every sort; as well that which lies in the various rights of individuals, as that which the term particularly expresses. This being the end of government, that alone is a just government which impartially secures to every man whatever is his own.[7]   —*James Madison*

A wise and frugal government, which shall leave men free to regulate their own pursuits of industry and improvement, and shall not take from the mouth of labor the bread it has earned—this is the sum of good government.[8]   —*Thomas Jefferson*

The moment the idea is admitted into society that property is not as sacred as the Laws of God, and that there is not a force of law and public justice to protect it, anarchy and tyranny commence.[9]

—*John Adams*

4. DUE PROCESS: PROTECTING LIFE, LIBERTY, AND PROPERTY

"... NOR BE DEPRIVED OF LIFE, LIBERTY, OR PROPERTY WITHOUT DUE PROCESS OF LAW..."

This provision guarantees that no person shall be deprived of life, liberty, or property without a legal system specifically designed to protect those rights. This same provision is included in the Fourteenth Amendment, to protect United States citizens from a loss of their rights through actions by any of the states. "Due process of law" is another descriptive name for legal, judicial, and governmental fair play in dealing with its citizens.

The due process provision applies not only to the courts but to the legislative and executive branches of the federal government as well. None of these can confiscate property or deprive a person of their life or liberty without due process of law.

"Due process" has been broadly interpreted so that it does not necessarily require a trial in a court. When a person has had a full hearing before the Secretary of the Interior on some question

---

[7] James Madison, "Property," *National Gazette*, 29 March 1792
[8] Thomas Jefferson, First Inaugural Address, 4 March 1801
[9] John Adams, *Defense of the Constitutions of Government of the United States*, 1787

concerning public lands, it is held that the decision of the secretary may be final, and that the complainant cannot be heard in court. The same would be true with other quasi-judicial hearing boards such as the Federal Communications Commission, the Interstate Commerce Commission, and so forth. Of course, most decisions of these boards are subject to appeal, but not all.

Administrative law in the form of quasi-judicial hearing has introduced a multitude of procedures which could expose Americans to serious loss of rights thanks to a lack of separation of powers. It is argued that "due process of law" includes the process established by the federalist structure of the Constitution, which includes a clear separation of legislative, executive, and judicial powers, along with the protections of certain checks and balances.

Administrative law hearings consist of executive departments legislating administrative rules, executing those rules through enforcement, and adjudicating those rules in administrative hearings—all of which occur without the involvement of the legislative and judicial branches. A person who is subject to these administrative law procedures is therefore deprived of their "due process" as guaranteed by the separation of powers process established by the Constitution.

5. TAKINGS CLAUSE: PROTECTING PRIVATE PROPERTY

"... NOR SHALL PRIVATE PROPERTY BE TAKEN FOR PUBLIC USE, WITHOUT JUST COMPENSATION."

Property is the fruit, or result, of what each person has done with their life and liberty. To take property without just compensation is the same as taking life and liberty, because life and liberty were spent to obtain that property. The practice of using life and liberty to obtain property is exercising the right to pursue happiness. It is for this reason that this provision of the Fifth Amendment is critical to maintaining liberty.

The "no private property shall be taken for public use without just compensation" provision gives every citizen the right to be protected from the exercise of eminent domain against their property unless given just compensation for the same.

This type of provision appeared in early Roman law and was also incorporated in the Magna Carta. Ancient kings and emperors, who considered the lives and property of their people to be subject to their whims, often exercised their sovereign powers to expropriate or confiscate the land of their subjects. This provision was inserted into the Constitution to protect American citizens from this type of abuse.

Property is one of our primary unalienable rights and the protection of property is the primary purpose for establishing government in society. The French statesman Frederic Bastiat put it succinctly:

> *Life, liberty, and property do not exist because men have made laws. On the contrary, it was the fact that life, liberty, and property existed beforehand that caused men to make laws in the first place.*[10]

Property is key to liberty, as John Adams said:

> *Property must be secured or liberty cannot exist.*[11]

The Fifth Amendment secures property by limiting the ability of government officials from taking your property without recognizing who it belongs to and its value. Due to the weight of its importance, property was detailed in the General Principles section in Part 1— what it is, why it is essential to liberty, and why it is unalienable. A review of property in Part 1 may prove helpful while contemplating this provision in the Fifth Amendment.

The protection of property in the Fifth Amendment by limiting the ability of government officials to take a person's property without just compensation is referred to as the "takings clause." A government "taking" can consist of taking property to build a road or other public use. But it can also be considered a taking if the

---

[10] Frederic Bastiat, *The Law*, 1850
[11] John Adams, *Defense of the Constitutions of Government of the United States*, 1787

actions of the government result in the loss of value of property, whether it be real estate, intellectual property, or any other thing of value that you possess.

In 1923, a minimum wage law which required an employer to pay a certain wage, regardless of the earning ability of the employee, was held to be unconstitutional under this provision, since it took private property for the public welfare in violation of this clause. It was reversed in 1937 by the Supreme Court under the influence of New Deal policies.

In 2020, many states commanded businesses to close in an attempt to slow the spread of the Covid-19 virus. Whether governments had the authority, or if there was a need to do so, could be argued. Right or wrong, this was a "taking" of the property that businesses expected, and needed, to earn. The Payroll Protection Program and other payments to businesses were "just compensation" for the taking of property. Because the actions, right or wrong, were done in the name of the public good, it was incumbent upon the public, through government systems, to compensate those businesses.

In addition to "just compensation," the taking of property can only be used for "public use." In the 1990s there was a trend to take property from one private party through eminent domain and transfer the ownership of that property to another private individual. This occurred in Mesa, Arizona in the early 2000s when the city decided to take the property owned by Bailey's Brake Shop, a moderately rundown business on the corner of a busy intersection. The city intended to condemn the shop and transfer the property to a local hardware store that was looking for a more desirable location.

The city of Mesa justified the taking as public use by making the case that the new hardware store would be more attractive than the thirty-year-old brake shop, and would likely bring in more sales tax revenue. The city argued that both reasons were better for the public, and therefore the taking was for public use. On October 1, 2003, the Arizona Court of Appeals unanimously struck down the City of Mesa's use of eminent domain. Judge John C. Gemmill wrote:

The constitutional requirement of "public use" is only satisfied when the public benefits and characteristics of the intended use substantially predominate over the private nature of that use.[12]

Even though the Bailey Brake Shop case was argued as a violation of the Arizona Constitution, not the U.S. Constitution, it became a landmark case in helping to prevent similar misuses of eminent domain (taking) in Arizona and throughout the entire country.

CONCLUSION

The Fifth Amendment has protected the rights of countless citizens from overzealous and biased prosecutors and government officials who, by human nature, would seek to punish the accused at all costs. History is full of horror stories of indefinite incarcerations, torture and bribes to elicit confessions, property taken at whim, and countless other abuses. Similar stories still occur from time to time, but, when compared to earlier eras, these practices have been largely eradicated thanks to the protection of the people's right to due process and private property.

---

[12] John C. Gemmill, *Bailey v. Myers*, 1 October 2003

THE BILL OF RIGHTS

Sixth Amendment

"IN ALL CRIMINAL PROSECUTIONS, THE ACCUSED SHALL ENJOY THE RIGHT TO A SPEEDY AND PUBLIC TRIAL, BY AN IMPARTIAL JURY OF THE STATE AND DISTRICT WHEREIN THE CRIME SHALL HAVE BEEN COMMITTED, WHICH DISTRICT SHALL HAVE BEEN PREVIOUSLY ASCERTAINED BY LAW, AND TO BE INFORMED OF THE NATURE AND CAUSE OF THE ACCUSATION; TO BE CONFRONTED WITH THE WITNESSES AGAINST HIM; TO HAVE COMPULSORY PROCESS FOR OBTAINING WITNESSES IN HIS FAVOR, AND TO HAVE THE ASSISTANCE OF COUNSEL FOR HIS DEFENSE."

Just like the other amendments, the fundamental concept underlying the Sixth Amendment is the right to life, liberty, property, and the pursuit of happiness. This amendment, however, does not state those rights directly or any rights derived from them. Instead, it outlines proven policies. The Fifth Amendment covers policies for criminal charges; the Sixth Amendment covers policies for criminal prosecutions while still protecting those fundamental rights. There are six policies specified in the Sixth Amendment:

1. The right to a speedy and public trial.

2. The right to an impartial jury within the state and district where the crime was committed.

3. The right to be informed of the nature and cause of the accusation.

4. The right to be confronted with witnesses against the accused.

5. The right to subpoena witnesses in favor of the accused.

6. The right to have the assistance of counsel.

POLICIES FOR DUE PROCESS OF CRIMINAL PROSECUTIONS

Policies 3, 4, & 5 are protections designed to allow the accused to develop an aggressive defense. The loss of rights is to be taken very seriously; therefore, it is important that the accused be given every opportunity to prove their innocence. John Adams argued "better the guilty should escape punishment, than the innocent suffer."[1]

The Sixth Amendment states that once a person has been indicted for a federal crime, they have certain specific rights. We will now examine these six rights in more detail.

1. THE RIGHT TO A SPEEDY AND PUBLIC TRIAL

"IN ALL CRIMINAL PROSECUTIONS, THE ACCUSED SHALL ENJOY THE RIGHT TO A SPEEDY AND PUBLIC TRIAL. . ."

This provision entitles an accused person to the right of a speedy, public trial to avoid the injustices of indefinite incarceration and secret trials. History is fraught with examples of prisoners being held indefinitely without official charges or trial.

A "speedy trial" is one without unreasonable delay. A defendant may not demand a trial until the prosecuting attorney has had a reasonable time to prepare a case. However, the Supreme Court has held that in time of insurrection, a person may be held indefinitely without trial until public peace has been restored. This is done on the ground that martial law permits the governor to order insurrectionists to be killed. Incarceration is a less stringent means of protecting the community.

A public trial is for the benefit of the accused and not the public. Therefore, if publicity will prove to be an injustice to the prisoner, the court may exclude all but a few of the public in the interest of the defendant's rights.

2. THE RIGHT TO AN IMPARTIAL JURY WHERE THE CRIME WAS COMMITTED

"IN ALL CRIMINAL PROSECUTIONS, THE ACCUSED SHALL ENJOY THE RIGHT TO. . . AN IMPARTIAL JURY OF THE STATE AND DISTRICT WHEREIN THE CRIME SHALL HAVE BEEN COMMITTED, WHICH DISTRICT SHALL HAVE BEEN PREVIOUSLY ASCERTAINED BY LAW. . ."

---

[1] Adams' Argument for the Defense: 3–4 December 1770

In the body of the Constitution, Article III, Section 2 provides that "the trial of all crimes, except in cases of impeachment, shall be by jury." This is therefore the second time this guarantee of a constitutional right has been mentioned, which emphasizes the importance of jury trial in the minds of the Founders. That same article and section also states that the trial must be held in the state where the crime took place, whereas this provision narrows it down further to the district in which the crime took place. Thomas Jefferson was a strong proponent of the jury. He said:

> *I consider [trial by jury] as the only anchor ever yet imagined by man, by which government can be held to the principles of its constitution.*[2]

The history and evolution of trial by jury is complicated and unclear. To avoid the tedious minutia of every historic detail, we will simplify its history twofold—a continuation of the history we have already covered in the Fifth Amendment regarding the grand jury, and the evolution of juries to settle property disputes.

Like other medieval kings, Henry II was duty-bound to his coronation oath in which he assumed three primary responsibilities: 1) to protect the church, 2) to preserve the peace, and 3) to administer justice. Henry II believed that settling property disputes was a sure method of keeping the peace. As mentioned in the Fifth Amendment chapter, he established juries made up of locals from the area in which a given dispute arose. When first created, this jury was to bring forth the facts of the dispute, assuming as locals they would have more facts than any other people in the kingdom. These fact-finding juries were similar to accusatory juries that evolved into the grand jury. These juries, however, evolved into a body that would present a verdict rather than a recommended indictment, like civil trial juries of our day.

Meanwhile, back at the King's court, grand juries were showing weaknesses. The court began to use members of the grand jury to assist in convicting as well as indicting. If the king and his

---

[2] Letter from Thomas Jefferson to Thomas Paine, 11 July 1789

magistrates wanted to convict an enemy, they would pressure the grand jury to indict. The king would then compel the same individuals to help him convict. Even if the king had no interest in the outcome of a trial, the grand jury would be more apt to convict and thereby validate their original indictment. In either case, the accused was less likely to be acquitted under this system, even if they were clearly innocent.

Using the same people to serve as grand jury and trial jury members proved to be a poor system. Eventually the accused was given the right to reject a juror if they knew them to be their adversary, if they were too close to the king or prosecution, or they stood to profit from a guilty verdict. At this time, the accused was not yet able to call witnesses on their behalf; only the prosecution could call witnesses, so the ability to reject a juror was a significant advancement for the cause of justice for the innocent.

Luckily, the solution for grand jury weaknesses was already in place. That solution was the civil trial jury for settling property disputes. It came just in time.

Prior to the use of the trial jury, the grand jury would indict, and the accused would then face trial by ordeal. Trial by ordeal was just that—an ordeal. The two main forms of trial by ordeal were trial by water and trial by fire. Both were a supernatural ordeal that were thought to reveal God's verdict by the results.

> *And he who shall be found through the oath of the aforesaid persons to have been charged or published as being a robber, or murderer, or thief, or a receiver of them, since the lord king has been king, shall be taken and shall go to the ordeal of water. . .[3]*

To be tried by water meant to be bound and cast into the water. If the accused sank, he was innocent and would hopefully be retrieved before drowning. It was thought that an innocent person would be

---

[3] Assize of Clarendon, 1166

accepted by the water. The guilty would be rejected by the water, signified by floating.

A red-hot iron bar was the tool of trial by fire. The accused would have to carry the searing bar three paces (about nine feet). If the wound healed cleanly in three days—innocent. If it festered—guilty.

Periodically a third trial was offered, trial by battle or trial by combat. This ordeal was a fight between the accused and their accuser. Trial by fight has an obvious flaw: some people are better at fighting than others. So one side could pay a champion to fight on their behalf, leaving the rich with an advantage. Superstition reasoned that God would be on the innocent's side and justice would prevail.

Looking at trial by ordeal through the modern lens may bring a chuckle and bewilderment as to how they could be so naive in times past. Historically, trial by ordeal was a rare occurrence and more people were found innocent by this method than guilty when it did take place. The outcome of the ordeal was left up to the interpretation of the community. Trial by fire, for example, was not determined by whether the accused was burnt or not, but whether the wound festered. The result was much more nuanced than burnt or not burnt. Trial by water was equally as nuanced. Did the accused sink or float as they likely thrashed about?

For most, guilt was determined by a confession to avoid the ordeal, or innocence determined by the willingness to face the ordeal, because divine intervention would prove your innocence. Trial by ordeal was rarely, if ever, used when there was clear evidence of guilt or innocence. It was most often used to stir a confession or prevent an accusation in the first place, in the case of trial by combat. Only a truly wronged person would accept trial by combat, especially if their adversary was twice their size.

What eventually killed trial by ordeal was the clergy, who decided to stop endorsing the practice. To have faith in God's intervention, the clergy had to sanction and bless the event. Eventually they began to recognize the practice as tempting God. Forcing His hand to perform a miracle by their command was a blasphemous act.

Trial by jury became a better, more effective tool of justice than trial by ordeal. In fact, it became so effective that the king and his magistrates became frustrated when juries began to acquit the accused contrary to their desires. For some time, the government would punish jurors if they produced an "incorrect" verdict. This seems contradictory, in that the purpose of the jury was to determine guilt or innocence. If the magistrates could declare an incorrect verdict from the jury, couldn't they render a verdict on their own without a jury? The practice of punishing the jury was an indication that the ruling class desired to use the courts as a tool of politics rather than a tool of justice. Stubborn juries reduced that injustice considerably. The trial of William Penn is a great example of the benefit of the jury system.

In 1670, it was illegal to openly preach any religion other than the Anglican faith. The Conventicle Act had been recently passed. It criminalized gatherings of worship of more than five people, except for services of the Church of England (Anglican).

William Penn and William Mead, both Quakers, were arrested for disturbing the king's peace as they held a worship service with others of their faith. Penn and Mead were tried before twelve judges and twelve jurors. The jury determined as a matter of fact that the Quakers had met, but they refused to convict them of anything other than "speaking in the street." The jury refused to include language that indicated that they had committed a crime. The court was furious and punished the jury until they would return a verdict that the court would accept—which they did not.

After an entertaining back-and-forth between the judges and Penn and Mead regarding the charges, them refusing to take off their hats, their ability to speak at liberty, etc., the jury was dismissed and returned with a verdict. The court record presents it as thus:

Clerk: *Are you agreed upon your verdict?*

Jury: Yes.

Clerk: Look upon the prisoners at the bar; how say you? Is William Penn Guilty of the matter whereof he stands indicted in manner and form, or Not Guilty?

Foreman: Guilty of speaking in Grace-church street.

Court: Is that all?

Foreman: That is all I have in commission.

Recorder: You had as good say nothing.

Mayor: Was it not an unlawful assembly? You mean he was speaking to a tumult of people there?

Foreman: My Lord, This is all I had in commission.

Observer: Here some of the jury seemed to buckle to the questions of the Court: upon which, Bushel, Hammond, and some others, opposed themselves, and said, they allowed of no such word as an unlawful assembly in their Verdict; at which the Recorder, Mayor, Robinson and Bloodworth took great occasion to vilify them with most opprobrious language; and this verdict not serving their turns, the Recorder expressed himself thus:

Recorder: The law of England will not allow you to part till you have given in your Verdict.

Jury: We have given in our Verdict, and we can give in no other.

Recorder: Gentlemen, you have not given in your Verdict, and you had its good say nothing; therefore go and consider it once more, that we may make an end of this troublesome business.

Observer: *The Court adjourned for half an hour, which being expired, the Court returns, and the Jury not long after.*

Clerk: *Are you agreed of your Verdict?*

Jury: *Yes.*

Clerk: *What say you? Look upon the prisoners: Is William Penn Guilty in manner and form, as he stands indicted, or Not Guilty?*

Foreman: *Here is our Verdict; holding forth a piece of paper to the clerk of the peace, which follows.*

"We the jurors, hereafter named, do find William Penn to be Guilty of speaking or preaching to an assembly, met together in Gracechurch-street, the 14th of August last, 1670, And that William Mead is Not Guilty of the said Indictment."

Thomas Veer, Edward Bushel, John Hammond, Henry Henley, Charles Milson, Gregory Walklet, John Baily, William Lever, Henry Michel, John Brightman, James Damask, Wil. Plumsted.

Observer: *This both Mayor and Recorder resented at so high a rate, that they exceeded the bounds of all reason and civility.*

Mayor: *What, will you be led by such a silly fellow as Bushel? an impudent canting fellow? I warrant you, you shall come no more upon juries in haste: You are a foreman indeed, addressing himself to the foreman, I thought you, had understood your place better.*

Recorder: *Gentlemen, you shall not be dismissed till we have a verdict that the court will accept; and you shall be locked up, without meat, drink, fire, and tobacco; you shall not think thus to abuse the* court; we will have a verdict, by the help of God, or you shall starve for it.

Penn: My jury, who are my judges, ought not to be thus menaced; their verdict should be free, and not compelled; the bench ought to wait upon them, but not forestall them. I do desire that justice may be done me, and that the arbitrary resolves of the bench may not be made the measure of my jury's verdict.

Observer: The court being ready to break up, and willing to huddle the prisoners to their goal, and the jury to their chamber.

One of the jury-men pleaded indisposition of body, and therefore desired to be dismissed.

Mayor: You are as strong as any of them; starve them; and hold your principles.

Recorder: Gentlemen, You must be contented with your hard fate, let your patience overcome it; for the court is resolved to have a verdict, and that before you can be dismissed.

Jury: We are agreed, we are agreed, we are agreed.

Observer: The court swore several persons, to keep the Jury all night without meat, drink, fire, or any other accommodation; they had not so much as a chamber pot, though desired.

The court adjourns till 7 of the clock next morning (being the 4th instant, vulgarly called Sunday, at which time the prisoners were brought to the bar: The court sat, and the Jury called to bring in their verdict.

Clerk: Are you agreed upon your verdict?

Jury: *Yes.*

Clerk: *What say you? Look upon the prisoners at the bar; is William Penn guilty of the matter whereof he stands indicted, in manner and form as aforesaid, or Not Guilty?*

Foreman: *William Penn is Guilty of speaking in Gracechurch-Street.*

Mayor: *To an unlawful assembly?*

Bushel: *No, my lord, we give no other verdict than what we gave last night; we have no other verdict to give.*

Mayor: *You are a factious fellow, I'll take a course with you.*

Bloodworth: *I knew Mr. Bushel would not yield.*

Bushel: *Sir Thomas, I have done according to my conscience.*

Mayor: *That conscience of yours would cut my throat.*

Bushel: *No, my lord, it never shall.*

Mayor: *But I will cut yours so soon as I can.*

Recorder: *It cannot be a verdict. . . it could not be a verdict.*

Penn: *If Not Guilty be not a verdict, then you make of the jury and Magna Carta but a mere nose of wax.*

Mead: *How is Not Guilty no verdict?*

Recorder: *No, it is no Verdict.*

Penn.   *I affirm, that the consent of a jury is a Verdict in law; and if William Mead be Not Guilty, it consequently follows, that I am clear, since you have indicted us of a conspiracy, and I could not possibly conspire alone,*

Observer: *The Jury went up again, having received a fresh charge from the Bench, if possible to extort an unjust Verdict.*

Clerk: *What say you? Is William Penn Guilty of the matter whereof he stands indicted, in manner and form aforesaid, or Not Guilty?*

Foreman: *Guilty of speaking in Gracechurch-street.*

Recorder: *What is this to the purpose? I say, I will have a verdict. And speaking to Bushel, said, You are a factious fellow; I will set a mark upon you; and whilst I have any thing to do in the city, I will have an eye upon you.*

Mayor: *Have you no more wit than to be led by such a pitiful fellow? I will cut his nose.*

Penn: *It is intolerable that my jury should he thus menaced: Is this according to the fundamental laws? Are not they my proper judges by the Great Charter of England? What hope is there of ever having justice done, when juries are threatened, and their verdicts rejected? I am concerned to speak, and grieved to see such arbitrary proceedings. Did not the lieutenant of the Tower render one of them worse than a felon? And do you not plainly seem to condemn such for factious fellows, who answer not your ends? Unhappy are those juries, who are threatened to be fined, and starved, and ruined, if they give not in Verdicts contrary to their consciences.*

Recorder: *Till now I never understood the reason of the policy and prudence of the Spaniards, in suffering the inquisition among them: And certainly it will never be well with us, till something like unto the Spanish inquisition be in England.*

Observer:	*The jury being required to go together to find another Verdict, and steadfastly refusing it (saying they could give no other Verdict than what was already given) the Recorder in great passion was running off the bench, with these words in his mouth, "I protest I will sit here no longer to hear these things;" at which the Mayor calling, Stay, stay.*

Recorder:	*Gentlemen, we shall not be at this trade always with you: you will find the next sessions of parliament there will be a law made, that those that will not conform shall not have the protection of the law. Mr. Lee, draw up another Verdict, that they may bring it in special.*

Lee:	*I cannot tell how to do it.*

Jury:	*We ought not to be returned, having all agreed, and set our hands to the Verdict.*

Recorder:	*Your Verdict is nothing, you play upon the Court; I say you shall go together, and bring in another Verdict, or you shall starve; and I will have you carted about the city, as in Edward 3rd's time.*

Foreman:	*We have given in our Verdict, and all agreed to it ; and if we give in another, it will be a force upon us to save our lives.*

Observer:	*The prisoners were remanded to Newgate, where they remained till next morning, and then were brought unto the Court, which being sat, they proceeded as followeth.*

Clerk: Look upon the prisoners. What say you? Is William Penn Guilty of the matter whereof he stands indicted, in manner and form, &c. or Not Guilty?

Foreman: Here is our Verdict in writing, and our hands subscribed.

Observer: The clerk took the Paper, but was stopped by the Recorder from reading of it; and he commanded to ask for a positive Verdict.

Foreman. That is our Verdict; we have subscribed to it.

Clerk: How say you? is William Penn Guilty, &c. or Not Guilty.

Foreman: Not Guilty.

Clerk: How say you? is William Mead Guilty, &c. or Not Guilty?

Foreman: Not Guilty.

Clerk: Then hearken to your Verdict; you say that William Penn is Not Guilty in manner and form as he stands indicted; you say that William Mead is Not Guilty in manner and form as he stands indicted, and so you say all?

Jury: Yes, we do so.

Observer: The Bench being unsatisfied with the Verdict, commanded that every person should distinctly answer to their names, and give in their Verdict, which they unanimously did in saying, Not Guilty, to the great satisfaction of the assembly.

Recorder: I am sorry, gentlemen, you have followed your own judgments and opinions, rather than the good and wholesome advice which was given you; God keep my life out of your hands, but for

> *this[2] the Court fines you 40 marks a man; and imprisonment till paid. At which Penn stept up towards the bench, and said:*

Penn: *I demand my liberty, being freed by the Jury.*

Mayor: *No, you are in for your fines.*

Penn: *Fines, for what?*

Mayor: *For contempt of the Court.*

Penn: *I ask, if it be according to the fundamental laws of England, that any Englishman should be fined or amerced, but by the judgment of his peers or jury; since it expressly contradicts the 14th and 29th chapters of the Great Charter of England, which say, "No freeman ought to be amerced but by the oath of good and lawful men of the vicinage."*

Recorder: *Take him away, take him away, take him out of the Court.*

Penn: *I can never urge the fundamental laws of England, but you cry, Take him away, take him away. But it is no wonder, since the Spanish Inquisition hath so great a place in the Recorder's heart. God Almighty, who is just, will judge you all for these things.*

Observ.   *They hauled the prisoners into the Bale-dock, and from thence sent them to Newgate, for non-payment of their fines; and so were their Jury.[4]*

The jurors in the Penn/Mead case, often referred to as the Bushel case after outspoken juror Edward Bushel, were sent to jail without food, water, and tobacco. Eventually they were all fined and sent

---

[4] The Trial of William Penn and William Mead held at the Old Baily in London, September 1670

back to jail for failing to pay the fines. Bushel petitioned a judge under the right of habeas corpus. Initially the petition was denied, but the judge eventually granted it and the jurors were released from jail.

The Bushel case resulted in the abandonment of the practice of punishing jurors for "incorrect" verdicts. Thanks to the jury's twelve stubborn men, juries became a powerful and effective tool for preserving the individual liberty of an oppressive ruling class.

Over sixty years after the William Penn trial, in 1734, another jury rebuffed pressure from the court and returned a not guilty verdict in the John Peter Zenger trial discussed in the First Amendment chapter. That not guilty verdict ushered in a new era for the freedom of speech and the press. Time and time again the jury has proven essential in the security of liberty.

3. THE RIGHT TO BE INFORMED OF THE NATURE AND CAUSE OF THE ACCUSATION

"IN ALL CRIMINAL PROSECUTIONS, THE ACCUSED SHALL ENJOY THE RIGHT . . . TO BE INFORMED OF THE NATURE AND CAUSE OF THE ACCUSATION. . ."

A person is considered to be informed of the charge against them by having a copy of the grand jury's indictment presented to them. They are then given a reasonable time to prepare their defense. The same thing happens when a federal prisoner has been arrested and is brought before a judicial officer for their "preliminary hearing." At that time the charge is read against them, and they are invited to plead "guilty" or "not guilty."

Historically, oppressive governments have made it difficult for the accused to defend themselves by not informing them of the nature of the accusation. The right to defend oneself must be accompanied by the right to know what to defend oneself against. This provision guarantees that right.

At the beginning of the trial discussed above, William Penn refused to plead guilty or not guilty until presented with the indictment. He eventually pled not guilty after the court assured him that he would be given liberty to plead his case before the court, even if he pled contrary to the court's desire—not guilty:

Recorder: *What say you, William Penn and William Mead, are you Guilty, as you stand indicted, in manner and form, as aforesaid, or Not Guilty?*

Penn: *It is impossible that we should be able to remember the Indictment verbatim, and therefore we desire a copy of it, as is customary on the like occasions.*

Recorder: *You must first plead to the indictment, before you can have a copy of it.*

Penn: *I am unacquainted with the formality of the law, and therefore before I shall answer directly, I request two things of the court. 1. That no advantage may be taken against me, nor I deprived of any benefit, which I might otherwise have received. 2. That you will promise me a fair hearing, and liberty of making my defense.*

Court: *No advantage shall be taken against you; you shall have liberty; you shall be heard.*

Penn: *Then I plead Not Guilty in manner and form.*[5]

4. THE RIGHT TO BE CONFRONTED WITH WITNESSES AGAINST THE ACCUSED

"IN ALL CRIMINAL PROSECUTIONS, THE ACCUSED SHALL ENJOY THE RIGHT . . . TO BE CONFRONTED WITH THE WITNESSES AGAINST HIM. . ."

Under the English system of law there was an odious practice of having witnesses make out depositions (written testimonies) which were read to the accused at the time of their trial. This deprived the defendant of the opportunity to confront their witnesses and cross-

---

[5] Ibid.

examine them. It was based on a mere deposition that Sir Walter Raleigh was convicted of treason and beheaded.

In the old Star Chamber court of England, witnesses stood behind a door and testified through a tiny hole without being seen. The Founders were well acquainted with practices such as these when they included this protective provision in the Constitution.

The one exception to the admission of a deposition or written accusation is a declaration by a dying witness, which may be read against the accused on the ground that the solemnity of the circumstances tends to make the testimony credible.

5. THE RIGHT TO SUBPOENA WITNESSES IN FAVOR OF THE ACCUSED

"IN ALL CRIMINAL PROSECUTIONS, THE ACCUSED SHALL ENJOY THE RIGHT. . . TO HAVE COMPULSORY PROCESS FOR OBTAINING WITNESSES IN HIS FAVOR. . ."

Historically, even as the jury system was evolving, only the king, his representatives, or the prosecution were allowed to call witnesses. The accused was not given this privilege. This is one reason why the ability for the accused to challenge a juror began to evolve. If a juror was a known adversary of the accused, the accused could petition to remove that potential juror. If the accused could not call witnesses, at least they could avoid having a jury biased against them as well.

This provision not only gives the accused the right to call witnesses on their behalf, but they can also compel those witnesses to appear in court, whether they want to appear or not. The Constitution allows the defendant to use the good offices of the court and the enforcement machinery of a U.S. Marshal's office to compel witnesses to participate in the trial in their defense.

Subpoena power is particularly important in criminal cases, since there is often a great reluctance on others' part to become involved in such cases. Even when they have important knowledge concerning the facts of the case, they seldom feel duty-bound to come forward without a subpoena from the court.

6. THE RIGHT TO HAVE ASSISTANCE OF COUNSEL

"IN ALL CRIMINAL PROSECUTIONS, THE ACCUSED SHALL ENJOY THE RIGHT . . . TO HAVE THE ASSISTANCE OF COUNSEL FOR HIS DEFENSE."

After the Boston Massacre it was difficult to find an attorney willing to represent the British soldiers that killed the five Bostonians. John Adams stepped up to the task. He was a strong proponent of legal representation for all. He felt it more important to protect the innocent, if they are innocent, than to punish the guilty. In 1770, during the trial of those British soldiers, he said:

> *It is more important that innocence be protected than it is that guilt be punished, for guilt and crimes are so frequent in this world that they cannot all be punished.*
>
> *But if innocence itself is brought to the bar and condemned, perhaps to die, then the citizen will say, "whether I do good or whether I do evil is immaterial, for innocence itself is no protection," and if such an idea as that were to take hold in the mind of the citizen that would be the end of security whatsoever.*[6]

In the end, John Adams was successful in arguing the innocence of those soldiers on the basis of self-defense and they were acquitted. An American attorney, making sure that the loathed British soldiers were represented, sent a message to the world that anyone could get a fair trial in the American justice system.

---

[6] John Adams, Argument for the Defense, defending the British soldiers who shot and killed Boston citizens in what became known as the Boston Massacre, 3–4 December 1770

Seventh Amendment

"IN SUITS AT COMMON LAW, WHERE THE VALUE IN CONTROVERSY SHALL EXCEED TWENTY DOLLARS, THE RIGHT OF TRIAL BY JURY SHALL BE PRESERVED, AND NO FACT TRIED BY A JURY, SHALL BE OTHERWISE RE-EXAMINED IN ANY COURT OF THE UNITED STATES, THAN ACCORDING TO THE RULES OF THE COMMON LAW."

Just like the Fifth and Sixth Amendments, the fundamental concept underlying the Seventh Amendment is the right to life, liberty, property, and the pursuit of happiness. And as before, the amendment is not stating those rights directly or any rights derived from them. Instead, this amendment is outlining proven policies. The Fifth Amendment covers policies for criminal charges, the Sixth Amendment covers policies for criminal prosecutions, and the Seventh Amendment covers policies for civil suits (common law), while still protecting those fundamental rights. There are two policies specified:

1. In Suits of Common Law, the Right of Trial by Jury Shall be Preserved

2. No Fact Tried by a Jury Shall be Otherwise Reexamined in Any Court

POLICIES FOR DUE PROCESS OF CIVIL SUITS

1. IN SUITS OF COMMON LAW, THE RIGHT OF TRIAL BY JURY SHALL BE PRESERVED

"IN SUITS AT COMMON LAW. . . THE RIGHT OF TRIAL BY JURY SHALL BE PRESERVED. . ."

The first provision gives a defendant in a civil case the right to have a jury, just as in criminal cases (provided, of course, that the suit involves a sum of $20 or more).

The Founders had originally provided for a jury trial in criminal cases but had not included civil cases for two reasons:

1. Civil procedures were so varied in the states that it was not considered justifiable to impose the jury system on those that were using judges to decide both civil and equity cases.

2. It was felt that judges would be more competent to assess damages and liabilities in damage suits and contract cases than a jury.

The states felt differently—hence, the creation of the Seventh Amendment.

In the case of a mistrial, the court may order a hearing before another jury, or a new trial can be ordered by an appellate court if there was an error of law committed by the trial court.

See the Fifth and Sixth Amendments for a history and explanation of the jury.

2. NO FACT TRIED BY A JURY SHALL BE OTHERWISE REEXAMINED IN ANY COURT

"IN SUITS AT COMMON LAW... NO FACT TRIED BY A JURY, SHALL BE OTHERWISE RE-EXAMINED IN ANY COURT OF THE UNITED STATES, THAN ACCORDING TO THE RULES OF THE COMMON LAW."

This gives the jury the right to have its facts "as found" remain unmolested during the appeal process. This also means that no judge in a trial court can substitute their opinion of the facts for that of the jury, nor can an appellate court set aside the jury's findings and make a final order on its own.

The second provision of the Seventh Amendment brings up an interesting doctrine that continues to be the subject of legal and political debate: jury nullification—the ability of the jury to effectively nullify a law by bringing forth a not guilty verdict. The jury might do this because they disagree with a law, or its application, not because they actually believe the accused to be innocent.

Here we will not declare the validity of jury nullification but will explain the logic behind it. The greatest legal minds in the country may use every historical, legal, and case precedent to declare the nonexistence of jury nullification. But, the fact remains, even if the doctrine is not officially codified in law, a jury can effectively nullify a law by returning an irreversible not guilty verdict whether the doctrine's adversaries like it or not. Even if those adversaries think jury nullification illegal, the verdict stands.

The jury's primary responsibility is to consider the facts of the case. They are then encouraged to yield the law to the judge. Respect should be given the judge on the law due to their expertise in the study. The jury can, however, depart from considering the facts only and can consider the law as well if they so choose. Interestingly, jurors are no longer given those instructions. Instead, they are only told to consider the facts. They are led to believe that it is not within their power to consider the law. Below are some enlightening quotes on the subject.

Thomas Jefferson explains the importance of trial by jury in a letter to Abbé Arnoux. He emphasizes that the jury's duty is to judge the facts, but he admits it is within the right of the jury to judge the law as well.

> *[On] the subject of juries. With respect to the value of this institution I must make a general observation. We think in America that it is necessary to introduce the people into every department of government as far as they are capable of exercising it; and that this is the only way to ensure a long-continued and honest administration of it's powers. 1. They are not qualified to exercise themselves the EXECUTIVE department: but they are qualified to name the person who shall exercise it. With us therefore they chuse this officer every 4. years. 2. They are not qualified to LEGISLATE. With us therefore they only chuse the legislators. 3. They are not qualified to JUDGE questions of law; but they are very capable of judging questions of fact. In the form of JURIES therefore they determine all matters of fact, leaving to the permanent judges to decide the law*

resulting from those facts. But we all know that permanent judges acquire an Esprit de corps [pride, fellowship, and common loyalty by the members of a specific group], that being known they are liable to be tempted by bribery, that they are misled by favor, by relationship, by a spirit of party, by a devotion to the Executive or Legislative; that it is better to leave a cause to the decision of cross and pile [coin toss], than to that of a judge biassed to one side; and that the opinion of 12 honest jurymen gives still a better hope of right, than cross and pile does. It is left therefore to the juries, if they think the permanent judges are under any biass whatever in any cause, to take upon themselves to judge the law as well as the fact. They never exercise this power but when they suspect partiality in the judges, and by the exercise of this power they have been the firmest bulwarks of English liberty.[7]

Giving instructions to one of his juries, the first chief justice of the Supreme Court, John Jay, stated that they had the right to judge both the facts and the law. He did ask them to consider the court's opinion of the law because that was their expertise, but he clearly informed them that it was within their rights to judge the law.

It may not be amiss, here, gentlemen, to remind you of the good old rule that on questions of fact, it is the province of the jury, on questions of law it is the province of the court, to decide. But it must be observed, that by the same law, which recognizes this reasonable distribution of jurisdiction you have, nevertheless, a right to take upon yourselves to judge of both, and to determine the law as well as the fact in controversy. On this, and on every other occasion, however, we have no doubt, you will pay that respect which is due to the opinion of the court: for as, on the one hand, it is presumed, that juries are the best judges of facts; it is, on

---

[7] Letter from Thomas Jefferson to Abbé Arnoux, 19 July 1789

the other hand, presumable, that the court are the best judges of law. But still, both objects are lawfully within your power of decision.[8]

To judge the facts means to listen to testimony and look at the evidence presented. Did the accused commit the crime or not? That is considering the facts.

To judge the law means to determine if the law that the person is accused of breaking applies to the particular case. Should this particular law be applied to this particular case to this particular person, in this particular time? The jury can choose to acquit the person for any reason. A judge can overturn a guilty verdict if it is clear that an injustice to the accused has occurred, but a judge cannot overturn or vacate a not guilty verdict.

In the First Amendment chapter, the trial of John Peter Zenger was presented as an example of the early emergence of Americans' passion for free speech and a free press. But that trial also gives us a fine example of jury nullification.

If you'll recall, the case was a libel suit against Zenger, a newspaper publisher. The court refused to allow his attorney, Andrew Hamilton, to argue that the articles published were not libel because they were true. Hamilton shifted his argument to liberty. He catered to the sense of jurors.

> *And I make no doubt but your upright conduct this day will not only entitle you to the love and esteem of your fellow citizens, but every man who prefers freedom to a life of slavery will bless and honor you as men who have baffled the attempt of tyranny, and by an impartial and uncorrupt verdict have laid a noble foundation for securing to ourselves, our posterity, and our neighbors, that to which nature and the laws of our country have given us a right to liberty of both exposing and opposing*

---

[8] John Jay, *Georgia v. Brailsford*, 1794

> *arbitrary power (in these parts of the world at least) by speaking and writing truth.*[9]

Hamilton's words were designed to stir the souls of the jury. But he was not solely relying on their passion for liberty. He was not asking them to rebel against their civic duty as jurors. Rather, he asked them to fulfill their duty of judging not only the facts, but the law too. In doing so, he was encouraging them to practice jury nullification.

After Hamilton hinted to the fact that the jury could interpret the law, the judge interjected.

> *No, Mr. Hamilton, the jury may find that Zenger printed and published those papers, and leave it to the Court to judge whether they are libelous. You know this is very common. It is in the nature of a special verdict, where the jury leave the matter of the law to the court.*[10]

After which Hamilton corrected the judge:

> *I know, may it please Your Honor, the jury may do so. But I do likewise know that they may do otherwise. I know that they have the right beyond all dispute to determine both the law and the fact; and where they do not doubt of the law, they ought to do so. Leaving it to judgment of the court whether the words are libelous or not in effect renders juries useless (to say no worse) in many cases. But this I shall have occasion to speak to by and by.*[11]

Hamilton agreed that if the jury has "not doubt of the law," that is, if they agree with the law, they should leave the law "to the judgement of the court." But if they have doubt in the law, or the application of it, the jury has "the right beyond all dispute to determine. . . the law."

---

[9] *A Brief Narrative of the Case and Trial of John Peter Zenger*, by John Peter Zenger, 1736
[10] Ibid.
[11] Ibid.

Hamilton was so successful in convincing the jury that it was their prerogative to judge the law that it left the judge somewhat speechless.

> *Gentlemen of the Jury: The great pains Mr. Hamilton has taken to show how little regard juries are to pay to the opinion of judges. . . is done no doubt with a design that you should take but very little notice of what I might say upon this occasion. I shall therefore only observe to you that as the facts or words in the information are confessed, the only thing that can come in question before you is whether the words as set forth in the information make a libel. And that is a matter of law, no doubt, and which you may leave to the Court.[12]*

After a short deliberation the jury returned a not guilty verdict. They nullified libel law as it existed then, which clearly stated that words could be considered libel even if they were true. The jury judged the law, found it wanting, and nullified it with their verdict. That action of jury nullification "was the germ of American freedom, the morning star of that liberty which subsequently revolutionized America."[13]

CONCLUSION

From protecting rights through the warrant requirement through indictment and conviction, amendments four through seven address every potential for abuse along the way. But what of conviction? What protects the individual from excessive or cruel punishments? The Eighth Amendment does.

---

[12] Ibid.

[13] "Dr. John W. Francis tells us, in his description of the city of New York, that the late Gouverneur Morris told him that, 'The trial of Zenger in . .'" William Dunlap, *History of the New Netherlands, Province of New York, and State of New York*, 1839

Eighth Amendment

"EXCESSIVE BAIL SHALL NOT BE REQUIRED, NOR EXCESSIVE FINES IMPOSED, NOR CRUEL AND UNUSUAL PUNISHMENTS INFLICTED."

The Fifth, Sixth, and Seventh Amendments outline proven policies in relation to criminal charges, criminal prosecutions, and civil suits. The Eighth Amendment covers policies in relation to the reasonable treatment of accused or convicted persons. This protects the fundamental rights of life, liberty, property, and the pursuit of happiness. There are three policies specified.

POLICIES FOR DUE PROCESS OF CRIMINAL PROSECUTIONS

1. IN CRIMINAL CASES, EXCESSIVE BAIL SHALL NOT BE REQUIRED.

Excessive bail requires a prisoner to put up a bond which is so high that he cannot possibly provide it and thereby regain his freedom pending the date of the trial. Of course, a heavy bail, or refusal to grant bail to a person who has committed a serious crime or is otherwise dangerous to the community, may be considered reasonable and necessary.

2. IN CRIMINAL CASES, EXCESSIVE FINES SHALL NOT BE IMPOSED.

Excessive fines are described in the Magna Carta as those penalties which constitute a forfeiture or deprive a man of his ability to earn a living or pursue his calling and business. That document further provided that the penalty for each crime should be according to the seriousness of the offense.

3. IN CRIMINAL CASES, CRUEL AND UNUSUAL PUNISHMENT SHALL NOT BE INFLICTED.

At the time of the adoption of the Constitution, the British penalty for high treason, as recorded by William Blackstone, was to:

> *. . . be drawn to the gallows, and not be carried or walk.*
> *That he be hanged by the neck, and then cut down alive.*
> *That his entrails be taken out, and burned, while he is yet*
> *alive. That his head be cut off. That his body be divided*
> *into four parts. That his head and quarters be at the*
> *king's disposal.[1]*

English law also provided for cutting off ears, flogging, cutting off hands, castrating, standing in the pillory, slitting of the nose, and branding on the cheek. There were also certain situations for which there was "perpetual imprisonment."

The policies listed above can be summarized as a prohibition of excessive, cruel, and unusual punishments. Historically, excess was the first concern, and early laws reflected that. Once excess was considered a violation of rights, it eventually became obvious cruelty was abhorrent to a civil society. It might be difficult to imagine excessive punishments as worse than cruel punishments. In the past, a quick punishment, like death, was considered less excessive than life in prison. Even an excessive fine that would destroy not only oneself but their family for generations, was considered an excess worse than a cruel punishment.

HISTORY OF THE EIGHTH AMENDMENT

Like trial by jury and other provisions in the Bill of Rights, the Eighth Amendment was derived directly from English law and practice. The English Bill of Rights of 1689 provided:

> *That excessive bail ought not to be required, nor*
> *excessive fines imposed, nor cruel and unusual*
> *punishments inflicted;[2]*

The similarity between the English Bill of Rights and the Eighth Amendment is unmistakable. The wording survived one hundred years because it is sound policy.

---

[1] William Blackstone, *Commentaries on the Laws of England*, 1765
[2] English Bill of Rights, 1689

A concern arose in some of the state ratifying conventions that nothing in the proposed Constitution prevented the use of torture or other cruel methods of punishing criminals. Abraham Holmes from Massachusetts argued that Congress was given authority to determine:

> *. . . what kind of punishments shall be inflicted on persons convicted of crimes. They are nowhere restrained from inventing the most cruel and unheard-of punishments, and annexing them to crimes; and there is no constitutional check on them, but that racks and gibbets may be amongst the most mild instruments of their discipline.*[3]

George Mason contended that a prohibition against torture was not necessary because the proposed Fifth Amendment "expressly provided that no man can give evidence against himself [and that] in those countries where torture is used, evidence was extorted from the criminal himself."[4]

George Mason was not arguing against the prohibition of excessive, cruel, and unusual punishments. He only questioned the necessity of prohibiting them in the national constitution. Prohibiting unreasonable punishments had long been codified in the colonies. The Massachusetts Body of Liberties of 1641 is an example of these early prohibitions.

> *18. No mans person shall be restrained or imprisoned by any Authority what so ever, before the law hath sentenced him thereto, If he can put in sufficient securitie, bayle, or mainprise, for his appearance, and good behaviour in the meane time, unlesse it be in Crimes Capitall, and Contempts in open Court, and in such cases where some expresse act of Court doth allow it.*

---

[3] Abraham Holmes, Massachusetts ratifying convention, 30 Jan 1788
[4] George Mason, Debate in Virginia ratifying convention, 16 June 1788

43. No man shall be beaten with above 40 stripes, nor shall any true gentleman, nor any man equall to a gentleman be punished with whipping, unless his crime be very shamefull, and his course of life vitious and profligate.

45. No man shall be forced by Torture to confesse any Crime against himselfe nor any other unlesse it be in some Capitall case where he is first fullie convicted by cleare and suffitient evidence to be guilty, After which if the cause be of that nature, That it is very apparent there be other conspiratours, or confederates with him, Then he may be tortured, yet not with such Tortures as be Barbarous and inhumane.

46. For bodilie punishments we allow amongst us none that are inhumane Barbarous or cruell.[5]

The Eighth Amendment was passed with little fanfare and argument. "It was agreed to by a considerable majority"[6] according to the Congressional record of 1789. In contrast, excessive, cruel, and unusual punishments have a history too gruesome to dwell upon and detail here, but once the prohibition was put into practice, there were not many who desired their return. However, there were some that felt that strong punishments might still be necessary. Samuel Livermore made that argument during the House debate:

The clause seems to express a great deal of humanity, on which account I have no objection to it; but as it seems to have no meaning in it, I do not think it necessary. What is meant by the terms excessive bail? Who are to be the judges? What is understood by excessive fines? It lies with the court to determine. No cruel and unusual punishment is to be inflicted; it is sometimes necessary to hang a man, villains often deserve whipping, and perhaps having their ears cut off; but are we in future to

---

[5] Massachusetts Body of Liberties, 1641
[6] Annals of Congress, 19 August 1789

be prevented from inflicting these punishments because they are cruel? If a more lenient mode of correcting vice and deterring others from the commission of it could be invented, it would be very prudent in the Legislature to adopt it; but until we have some security that this will be done, we ought not to be restrained from making necessary laws by any declaration of this kind.[7]

PENALTIES SHOULD BE PROPORTIONATE TO THE OFFENCE

It is a natural tendency that when someone violates the law, others immediately feel justified in condemning the accused and demanding that justice be done. However, when the tables are turned, the accused who was once the accuser pleads for mercy. In society, it is difficult to find the balance between justice and mercy. Everyone finds themselves on both sides of this balance at one time or another and to one degree or another. With a vast array of personalities, abilities, opportunities and emotions, the law can be a very rigid tool against human fallibility. This was the genius of the jury system that allowed the guilty to be tried by twelve impartial persons of differing backgrounds and experiences.

Emotions on the side of the victim can easily get tied up in a verdict that is harsher than the crime itself. How far can, or should, punishments go? How does society find the balance between excessive punishment and too little punishment? In the "Eye for an Eye" segment in the General Principles section, the question of when a person can justly lose their unalienable rights is answered. That same concept can apply to punishments.

In ancient Israel, when a person stole a sheep, they had to return two sheep—one for the one they stole and the other as the penalty. The penalty was to lose the very thing that they were willing to take from the victim—in this case a sheep. One sheep was considered restitution or compensatory. The intent was to compensate the

---

[7] Samuel Livermore, House of Representatives, Amendments to the Constitution, 17 August 1789

victim for actual losses—to restore them back whole. The second sheep was considered punitive: additional punishment for the harm caused. However, the punishment should be equal in proportion to the crime. The crime was the stealing of one sheep, so the punishment should be to lose one sheep. To take from the perpetrator more than two sheep would go beyond what the victim lost in both the sheep and their rights, making of the perpetrator a new victim.

If we, as individuals or collectively, do not have the right to take a person's sheep arbitrarily, we do not have the right to arbitrarily take the sheep of a perpetrator beyond compensatory and punitive damages. Where does the authority come from to pile on punishments more than that which is in proportion to the crime? If we do not have the rights to do so as individuals or collectively, we do not have the right to delegate what we do not have to our agent, the government. We may be able to take an eye for an eye, but no authority exists to take an arm or a leg too.

New Hampshire codified the idea of proportioned punishments in their Bill of Rights of 1783:

> *XVIII. All penalties ought to be proportioned to the nature of the offence. No wise legislature will affix the same punishment to the crimes of theft, forgery and the like, which they do to those of murder and treason; where the same undistinguishing severity is exerted against all offences; the people are led to forget the real distinction in the crimes themselves, and to commit the most flagrant with as little compunction as they do those of the lightest dye: For the same reason a multitude of sanguinary laws is both impolitic and unjust. The true design of all punishments being to reform, not to exterminate, mankind.*

XXXIII. No magistrate or court of law shall demand excessive bail or sureties, impose excessive fines, or inflict cruel or unusual punishments.[8]

Thomas Jefferson supported the same idea of proportionate punishment by providing some specific examples:

Punishments I know are necessary, and I would provide them, strict and inflexible, but proportioned to the crime. Death might be inflicted for murder. . . Rape, buggery &c. punish by castration. All other crimes by working on high roads, rivers, gallies &c. a certain time proportioned to the offence . . . Laws thus proportionate and mild should never be dispensed with.[9]

To be clear, proportionate punishment differs from punishments that look identical to the crime. An eye for an eye is not to be taken literally. It does little good for society to have two half-blind people trying to make their way in life. If someone causes injury to another, it is not expected that they would have the same injury inflicted upon them. Rather, they would pay restitution to the victim for actual losses. This may include medical costs and lost wages. Their punitive damages would also be a financial obligation to the victim for a reasonable amount. Historically, "an eye for an eye" has been taken literally and has resulted in cruel and unusual punishments; hence the need for the Eighth Amendment.

REPEAT OFFENDERS

What is society to do if a perpetrator is not deterred by proportionate restitution and punitive punishment? Establishing a punishment for the intent to deter the crime should be secondary to paying restitution and punitive damages to the victim. However, if a person consistently commits the same or similar crimes, the law should provide a way to deter the offender from future crimes. In ancient Israel, if a person was in the business of stealing sheep, they had to

---

[8] New Hampshire Bill of Rights, 1783
[9] Letter from Thomas Jefferson to Edmund Pendleton, 26 August 1776

pay back four sheep rather than the standard two. This was to take the profit out of stealing sheep. How do we know if someone is in the business of stealing sheep? Repeating the offence is a good indicator.

Today, many criminal codes include additional punishments for repeat offences. This may provide an additional deterrent, but is it justified based on natural law principles? The case has been made that there is no authority to punish an offender more than the crime they committed against another. So where does the authority come to establish a greater punishment for a repeat offender?

It can be reasonably assumed that if someone is in the crime business, as indicated by repeat offences, that they have committed other crimes that they have not been caught committing. Extra punishments can be partially justified in response to those crimes—partially justified because society does not have the right to punish someone based on an assumption. However, society can consider themselves as a collective victim because the offender has demonstrated their intent to make everyone a victim if left free to do so, as demonstrated by their repeated offences. With the higher potential of victimhood, citizens have the right to defend themselves by increasing the punishment for the repeat offender.

CAPITAL PUNISHMENT

Past societies have provided capital punishment as a means to punish numerous crimes, not just murder or treason. Some of those societies did so as a strong deterrent. History has shown that people may be deterred initially, but eventually it often resulted in a more hardened society and violent crimes increased in the end. Knowledge of that history led the Founders to limit capital punishment to murder and treason alone. They felt all other crimes should be dealt with mildly and in proportion to the crime.

Some societies, like ancient Israel, provided capital punishment to punish numerous crimes as well, but the sentence of death was rarely carried out. More often, the offender would be banished from their community. They were threatened with death if they returned.

The concept of an eye for an eye, or the taking away from the offender what they were willing to take from the victim, is a justification for capital punishment for murder and treason. Some Founders, like Jefferson and Madison, questioned the validity of capital punishment at all. They went along with it reluctantly, but only for the want of a better solution.

Thomas Jefferson attempted to reduce the number of crimes punishable by the death penalty when he revised Virginia's criminal code. When those attempts failed, James Madison said, "our old bloody code is by this event fully restored."[10]

While Madison did not have a problem with capital punishment for murder, he did welcome the debate over its overall existence.

> *I should not regret a fair and full trial of the entire abolition of capital punishments, by any State willing to make it.[11]*

After capital punishment was limited to murder and treason, there came a reasoned debate as to its validity at all. A lesser-known founder, Benjamin Rush, did not think capital punishment was a valid punishment for any crime. Here is his argument:

> *I. Every man possesses an absolute power over his own liberty and property, but not over his own life. When he becomes a member of political society, he commits the disposal of his liberty and property to his fellow citizens; but as he has no right to dispose of his life, he cannot commit the power over it to any body of men. To take away life, therefore, for any crime, is a violation of the first political compact.*

> *II. The punishment of murder by death, is contrary to reason, and to the order and happiness of society.*

---

[10] Letter from James Madison to Thomas Jefferson, 15 February 1787
[11] Letter from James Madison to G. F. H. Crockett, 6 November 1823

1. It lessens the horror of taking away human life, and thereby tends to multiply murders. . .

5. The punishment of murder by death, has been proved to be contrary to the order and happiness of society by the experiments of some of the wisest legislators in Europe. . .

III. The punishment of murder by death, is contrary to divine revelation. A religion which commands us to forgive and even to do good to our enemies, can never authorise the punishment of murder by death. "Vengeance is mine," said the Lord; "I will repay." It is to no purpose to say here, that this vengeance is taken out of the hands of an individual, and directed against the criminal by the hand of government. It is equally an usurpation of the prerogative of heaven, whether it be inflicted by a single person, or by a whole community.

I cannot take leave of this subject without remarking that capital punishments are the natural offspring of monarchical governments. Kings believe that they possess their crowns by a divine right: no wonder, therefore, they assume the divine power of taking away human life. Kings consider their subjects as their property: no wonder, therefore, they shed their blood with as little emotion as men shed the blood of their sheep or cattle. But the principles of republican governments speak a very different language. They teach us the absurdity of the divine origin of kingly power. They approximate the extreme ranks of men to each other. They restore man to his God—to society—and to himself. They revive and establish the relations of fellow-citizen, friend, and brother. They appreciate human life, and increase public and private obligations to preserve it. They consider human sacrifices as no less offensive to the sovereignty of the people, than they are to the majesty of heaven. They view the attributes of government, like the attributes of the Deity, as infinitely more honoured by destroying evil by means of merciful than by exterminating punishments. The United States have adopted these peaceful and benevolent forms of government. It becomes them therefore to adopt their mild and benevolent principles. An execution in a republic is like a human sacrifice in religion. It is an offering to monarchy, and to that malignant being, who has been styled a murderer from the beginning, and who delights equally in murder, whether it be perpetrated by the cold, but vindictive arm of the law, or by the angry hand of private revenge.[12]

---

[12] Benjamin Rush, *On Punishing Murder by Death*, 1792

THE BILL OF RIGHTS

Ninth Amendment

"THE ENUMERATION IN THE CONSTITUTION, OF CERTAIN RIGHTS, SHALL NOT BE CONSTRUED TO DENY OR DISPARAGE OTHERS RETAINED BY THE PEOPLE."

KEY QUOTE FROM THE FOUNDING ERA

It has been objected also against a bill of rights, that, by enumerating particular exceptions to the grant of power, it would disparage those rights which were not placed in that enumeration; and it might follow by implication, that those rights which were not singled out, were intended to be assigned into the hands of the General Government, and were consequently insecure. This is one of the most plausible arguments I have ever heard urged against the admission of a bill of rights into this system; but, I conceive, that it may be guarded against. I have attempted it, as gentlemen may see by turning to the last clause of the fourth resolution [the Ninth Amendment].[1] —James Madison

The most common modern interpretation of the Ninth Amendment is that because it is impossible to list all of our rights, we must state that we have other rights not listed that we are still going to retain. While that is an accurate interpretation, it falls short of a much more aggressive protection of rights provided by this misunderstood amendment.

The history and original intent of the Ninth Amendment has been largely lost. A more accurate history and interpretation has begun to emerge, thanks to a few legal scholars in recent decades. The near-disappearance of the Ninth Amendment is primarily due to two things: mistakenly assigning Ninth Amendment historical references to the Tenth Amendment and some confusion in the original numbering of the Amendments.

---

[1] Speech to Congress by James Madison, Annals of Congress, 1789

MISTAKE NUMBER ONE: ARE WE TALKING ABOUT THE NINTH OR TENTH AMENDMENT?

At first glance the Ninth and Tenth Amendments seem to be redundant. They both state that things not mentioned in the Constitution are to be left to the people. There are, however, a few key differences in the wording that has caused some historical confusion. The Ninth uses the words *enumeration*, *rights*, and *retained*. The Tenth uses the words *delegated*, *powers*, and *reserved*.

Enumeration means to list things as if counting—to name one by one. This conjures the image of a clean list of rights, as in the Bill of Rights. *Delegated*, on the other hand, is to give instruction or grant authority. Delegated powers may or may not be in the form of a list.

The use of the word *rights* is usually interpreted as *unalienable* rights, as stated in the Declaration of Independence or those listed in the Bill of Rights. Powers are most often looked at as powers delegated for the purposes of administering the government, sometimes for the purpose of protecting rights.

To retain is to keep something that has always been yours. To reserve is to hold something back from one thing to be used in another, to be used in a future time rather than now, or to not give to one in order to reserve it for another.

The usage of these different words has led many to believe that the Ninth Amendment is about a list of rights retained, and the Tenth about delegated power reserved. Any historical quote about delegated power reserved is therefore attributed to the Tenth, and if it is about a list of retained rights it goes to the Ninth.

IT'S NOT ABOUT THE BILL OF RIGHTS

The use of the word *enumeration* may lead one to assume the listing of rights is referring to the Bill of Rights. After all, the Bill of Rights is an enumeration of rights, but a closer reading of the amendment, and a consideration of the timeline of events, reveal what enumeration the amendment is referring to: the text says "the enumeration in the Constitution." The amendment is referring to items enumerated in the Constitution itself, not the Bill of Rights. The Bill of Rights did not yet exist when the Ninth Amendment was suggested, considered, drafted, and ratified. Now that the Bill of Rights is part of the Constitution, the Ninth Amendment includes that enumeration too, but the original intent considered the content of the Constitution only.

There are no clear lists of rights in the original body of the Constitution. To what enumerated rights is the Ninth Amendment referring? Rights, in the amendment, are those rights explicitly named in the Constitution, like the rights of habeas corpus and trial by jury. Those are about the extent of specifically named rights. All other rights in the Constitution are not protected by naming the right, but by limiting the government's ability to trample a right. It is the very essence and purpose of the idea of delegated powers. The purpose is to limit government's powers in order to protect rights.

POWER AND RIGHTS ARE DIFFERENT SIDES OF THE SAME COIN

In a letter to George Washington, James Madison expressed the view that the protection of rights was the same as the limitation of powers:

> *If a line can be drawn between the powers granted and the rights retained, it would seem to be the same thing whether the latter be secured by declaring that they shall not be abridged, or that the former shall not be extended.*[2]

In essence, Madison was stating that limited power and the protection of rights are different sides of the same coin. The purpose of the Constitution is to limit power in order to protect rights. Conversely, the protection of rights comes by limiting power.

---

[2] Letter from James Madison to George Washington, 5 December 1789

Simply put, LIMITED POWER = PROTECTED RIGHTS and PROTECTING RIGHTS = LIMITING POWER.

Using Madison's view, dozens of rights leap from the text of the Constitution. The protection of intellectual property by establishing patents and copyrights.[3] The right to access a free market economy by regulating interstate commerce,[4] punishing piracy,[5] etc. The right of self-preservation by establishing armies and navies.[6] The right to communicate through post offices and post roads.[7] The right to vote.[8] The right to be taxed equally.[9] Equal protection under the law. The right to establish, alter, and abolish our own form of government.[10] And the list goes on and on. Protecting rights can be found indirectly as well. For example, vesting legislative authority in Congress[11] alone protects hundreds of rights—every right ever abused by tyrants.

The Constitution enumerates many rights when looked at from the perspective of what rights it is protecting through the delegation of limited powers.

In *Federalist* No. 84 Alexander Hamilton expressed a similar view, that the Constitution itself was a bill of rights by protecting rights:

> *[The] Constitution is itself, in every rational sense, and to every useful purpose, A BILL OF RIGHTS.[12]*

MISTAKE NUMBER TWO: THE NUMBERING CHANGED

When James Madison tackled the job of drafting the Bill of Rights, he gathered almost two hundred suggestions from the states and narrowed them down to nineteen. After Congress edited, deleted,

---

[3] U.S. Constitution Article I, Section 8
[4] Ibid.
[5] Ibid.
[6] U.S. Constitution Article I, Section 8 & Article II, Section 2
[7] U.S. Constitution Article I, Section 8
[8] U.S. Constitution Article I, Section 2
[9] U.S. Constitution Article I, Section 9
[10] U.S. Constitution, Preamble
[11] U.S. Constitution Article I, Section 1
[12] Alexander Hamilton, *Federalist* No. 84, 1788

added, and consolidated, they passed twelve and sent them to the states for ratification. They were numbered one through twelve. The first and second were regarding apportionment of representatives in the House and Congressional pay raises.[13] The remaining ten are the amendments we know today as one through ten. Therefore, what we know as the First Amendment was originally the third. Our Second Amendment was originally the fourth, and so on.

Even after amendments three through twelve were ratified, they were still numbered three through twelve for quite some time in anticipation of the ratification of one and two. When it became clear that they would not be ratified anytime soon, amendments three through twelve were renumbered to their current sequence. Interestingly enough, the original Second Amendment was ratified two hundred years later, becoming the Twenty-Seventh Amendment.

Due to the original numbering, the many references to the Eleventh and Twelfth amendments during the ratification debates, and for some time after, were referring to our current Ninth and Tenth amendments. This confusion has led many people in our day to overlook significant quotes about those amendments during the various ratification proceedings in the states. Losing these quotes has meant losing the context for the Ninth Amendment.

It is difficult to track the evolution of hundreds of suggestions from the states through the mind of James Madison, into the turbulent debates in Congress, to the state ratification proceedings. Along with the changing numbers associated with the amendments, this difficulty has left modern interpreters to get the Ninth Amendment half right. In fact, tracking the evolution of the Ninth Amendment has proven so difficult for some scholars that they have concluded that it was likely derived from Madison's mind alone and not suggested by the states. As observed by the author Kurt Lash:

> *Common account makes James Madison the source of*
> *the Ninth Amendment. It implies that the Ninth was not*

---

[13] Twenty-Seventh Amendment

proposed by the states, but that its principles originally were deployed against state calls for a Bill of Rights. No wonder, then, that so many scholars ignore the importance of the states in the adoption of the Ninth Amendment: Apparently, the states had little, if any, role.

This account, however, is critically incomplete. As originally drafted by James Madison, the Ninth Amendment expressly adopted language and principles demanded by several states as a condition to their ratifying the Constitution.[14]

Most surprisingly, Supreme Court Justice Arthur Goldberg was ignorant of or completely ignored the history of the Ninth Amendment's evolution from the states to Congress to the Select Committee and back to the states. According to Goldberg:

The Amendment is almost entirely the work of James Madison. It was introduced in Congress by him and passed the House and Senate with little or no debate and virtually no change in language.[15]

The Ninth Amendment was among the suggestions from several states. It was not from the mind of James Madison. He simply refined the verbiage. Confusion between the Ninth and Tenth Amendments and the numbering of the amendments makes it difficult to track its elusive purpose.

OUT OF ONE IS TWO

Madison's original proposal for the wording of the Ninth Amendment makes it much easier to see the two purposes it serves:

The exceptions here or elsewhere in the constitution, made in favor of particular rights, shall not be so construed as to diminish the just importance of other rights retained by the people; or as to enlarge the powers

---

[14] Kurt T. Lash, *The Lost Original Meaning of the Ninth Amendment*, 2004
[15] Arthur Goldberg, *Griswold v. Connecticut*, 1965

delegated by the constitution; but either as actual limitations of such powers, or as inserted merely for greater caution.[16]

We'll unpack Madison's proposal in more detail later. For now, we will look at the two purposes. First, Madison's proposal recognizes other rights that are not specifically listed or protected that should not be diminished simply because they are not in the document. Those unenumerated rights still exist and the people retain them. Secondly, those rights or the protection of rights listed in the form of delegated powers shall not be enlarged or expanded. Those delegated powers are listed not because they are protecting more important rights than those retained, but they are inserted for greater caution. In essence, delegated powers are listed for the explicit purpose of preventing them from being enlarged.

In short, the Ninth Amendment declares, first, that unenumerated rights are retained by the people, and second, that delegated powers cannot be expanded by misinterpretation. Sadly, brevity made the Ninth Amendment much less clear.

THE SELECT COMMITTEE

While considering the newly proposed amendments that would become the Bill of Rights, Congress appointed the Select Committee on July 21, 1789, for the purposes of selecting and fine-tuning the proposed amendments. In an attempt to streamline some of the amendments, the committee reduced Madison's language. They knew the evolution of the subject, so the simpler language may have seemed clear to them at the time. The clouds of history have rolled in and, to subsequent generations, the language is shrouded.

Thanks to some clever scholars of recent years, the language is beginning to clear up again. The enumeration of rights in the Constitution are referring to delegated powers as well as those specifically listed. "Not be construed" prevents the misinterpretation

---

[16] James Madison proposal to Congress, 8 June 1789

or enlargement of those powers for the purpose of denying or disparaging unenumerated rights.

What's worse, the Select Committee did not change the language of the Tenth Amendment, probably because Madison's original was already short and to the point. As a result, scholars have mistakenly assumed that because the committee removed the reference to "powers," they must have purposely assigned rights to the Ninth and powers to the Tenth even though there is no evidence to suggest that. This is not a logical conclusion in that there was not an enumeration of rights in the Constitution when the committee met, but there was protection of rights by the limitation of powers, which Madison clarified as one and the same.

So much for brevity!

During the Virginia ratifying convention, Patrick Henry indicated that we should not be so concerned about brevity when it comes to protecting our rights.

> *A bill of rights may be summed up in a few words. What do they tell us?—That our rights are reserved. Why not say so? Is it because it will consume too much paper?*[17]

Perhaps it would have served us better had the Select Committee not sacrificed clarity for brevity. Madison's original proposal for the Ninth Amendment clearly stated its purpose—unenumerated rights are retained by the people, and delegated powers shall not be construed.

UNENUMERATED RIGHTS ARE RETAINED BY THE PEOPLE

The Ninth Amendment states that the Constitution and the Bill of Rights do not strictly list or define all rights of the people. Rather, the people retain all rights and powers not specifically delegated to the government. Any rights not listed are still retained by the people.

---

[17] Patrick Henry, Virginia Ratification Convention, 12 June 1788

Under their theory of limited government, the Founders wanted it understood that they were not forfeiting anything. Their constitutional rights included not only the ones they had mentioned but all other rights besides. They wanted to make it clear that delegating powers was done for the purpose of protecting rights. In the delegation they were not forfeiting the powers they delegated. Delegation is done, not to give away, but to protect rights and powers.

Article 2 in the Articles of Confederation had a clause to make it clear that the states, and by extension the people, were retaining rights not specifically delegated to the national government.

> *Each state retains its sovereignty, freedom, and independence, and every power, jurisdiction, and right, which is not by this Confederation expressly delegated to the United States, in Congress assembled.*[18]

Because the new Constitution did not have such a clause, many wanted a bill of rights to be added to the document with language that would protect rights not listed. During the North Carolina ratifying convention, Samuel Spencer said:

> *I endeavored to show that, as the government was not to operate against states, but against individuals, the rights of individuals ought to be properly secured. In order to constitute this security, it appears to me there ought to be such a clause in the Constitution as there was in the Confederation, expressly declaring, that every power, jurisdiction, and right, which are not given up by it, remain in the states. Such a clause would render a bill of rights unnecessary. But as there is no such clause, I contend that there should be a bill of rights, ascertaining and securing the great rights of the states and people.*[19]

---

[18] Articles of Confederation, Article 2, 1777
[19] Samuel Spencer, North Carolina ratifying convention, 29 July 1788

AREN'T UNALIENABLE RIGHTS ALWAYS RETAINED?

Archibald Maclaine argued that we did not need a bill of rights because the people already retained unalienable rights because those rights were. . . UNALIENABLE.

> *There is no people on earth so well acquainted with the nature of government as the people of America generally are. We know now that it is agreed upon by most writers, and men of judgment and reflection, that all power is in the people, and immediately derived from them. The gentleman surely must know that, if there be certain rights which never can, nor ought to, be given up, these rights cannot be said to be given away, merely because we have omitted to say that we have not given them up. Can any security arise from declaring that we have a right to what belongs to us? Where is the necessity of such a declaration? If we have this inherent, this unalienable, this indefeasible title to those rights, if they are not given up, are they not retained?[20]*

Unfortunately, the fact that some rights are unalienable is not a sufficient guard against those that would seek to take or abuse those rights. The Ninth Amendment comes after the Founders' historical understanding of "a long train of abuses and usurpations"[21] by governments throughout history. People have unalienable natural rights that are "assumed by the powers of the earth"[22] at birth. A person cannot be alienated from those rights without dire societal consequences. Regardless of natural prohibitions, oppressive abuses have been the plague of humankind. No matter how unalienable a right, there is always someone, or a group of people, who think they can take that right from others.

---

[20] Archibald Maclaine, North Carolina ratifying convention July 29, 1788
[21] Declaration of Independence, 4 July 1776
[22] Ibid.

INCLUDING, BUT NOT LIMITED TO

In *Federalist* No. 84, Alexander Hamilton had argued that a bill of rights was unnecessary because, as mentioned previously, the Constitution was a bill of rights. As such, the Constitution protected our rights.

Hamilton took the issue further by suggesting that a bill of rights could be dangerous because it would list rights that the Constitution did not delegate. It is a point of law, and holds true in contract law too, that if anything is left off an enumeration of items it was done on purpose and that thing is forfeited. This explains why a contract may use a phrase like "including, but not limited to." This legal doctrine was a concern among some of the Founders. During the congressional debates on the Bill of Rights, James Jackson of Georgia said:

> *There is a maxim in law, and it will apply to [any] bill of rights, that when you enumerate exceptions, the exceptions operate to the exclusion of all circumstances that are omitted; consequently, unless you except every right from the grant of power, those omitted are inferred to be resigned to the discretion of the government.*[23]

To some, this was not a logical argument. They did not think it necessary to declare the retention of rights that are the people's rights in the first place and that there was no authority granted to the national government in relation to those rights. In the Virginia ratifying convention George Nicholas said:

> *If they part with any of it, is it necessary to declare that they retain the rest? Liken it to any similar case. If I have one thousand acres of land, and I grant five hundred acres of it, must I declare that I retain the other five hundred? Do I grant the whole thousand acres, when I grant five hundred, unless I declare that the five hundred I do not give belong to me still? It is so in this case. After*

---

[23] James Jackson, Congressional Register, First Congress, 8 June 1789

granting some powers, the rest must remain with the people.[24]

There was a fear that if we listed our rights and left some out, government officials would consider those omitted rights forfeited. But how can all rights be listed, especially if there are many rights that have yet to be discovered or clearly defined?

IT IS NOT POSSIBLE TO LIST ALL RIGHTS

The rights that have been discovered are still undergoing refinement in social experimentation, making it impossible to list all rights. Thomas Jefferson, arguably one of the greatest minds on the subject of unalienable rights, recognized how limited the Founders' understanding of rights and self-government were.

> *[We] appealed to those [rights] of nature, and found them engraved in our hearts. . . we had never been permitted to exercise self-government. When forced to assume it, we were Novices in it's [sic] science. It's principles and forms had entered little into our former education. We established however some, altho' not all it's important principles.*[25]

As "novices," we cannot know the potentially infinite number of unalienable rights. Nor can we know or list vested rights that have yet to be established in future laws and constitutions. James Wilson expressed the absurdity of the suggestion that the Constitutional Convention of 1787 could have produced a comprehensive list of rights.

> *I consider that there are very few who understand the whole of these rights. All the political writers, from Grotius and Puffendorf down to Vattel, have treated on this subject; but in no one of those books, nor in the aggregate of them all, can you find a complete*

---

[24] George Nicholas, Virginia ratifying convention, 12 June 1788
[25] Letter from Thomas Jefferson to John Cartwright, 5 June 1824

enumeration of rights appertaining to the people as men and as citizens.

Enumerate all the rights of men! I am sure, sir, that no gentleman in the late Convention would have attempted such a thing.[26]

In the North Carolina ratifying convention, James Iredell extended the rhetorical challenge to list rights to illustrate his point.

. . . and it would be impossible to enumerate every one. Let anyone make what collection or enumeration of rights he pleases, I will immediately mention twenty or thirty more rights not contained in it.[27]

Patrick Henry of Virginia brings us back to the original problem: we can't list all rights, but leaving some out may be viewed as a forfeiture of rights.

Other essential rights—what are they? The world will say that you intend to give them up. When you go into an enumeration of your rights, and stop that enumeration, the inevitable conclusion is, that what is omitted is intended to be surrendered.[28]

UNENUMERATED RIGHTS MUST BE PROTECTED

The conclusion of the argument was to provide an amendment to the Constitution that would clearly state that any rights not enumerated were not forfeit but were retained by the people. In addition, any powers not specifically delegated to protect a right was not a forfeiture of that right. In fact, because the Constitution is a delegatory document, if a power was not delegated to protect a right, that in and of itself was a protection by not granting the power.

The Ninth Amendment, like its companion the Tenth, is a sort of catchall amendment. They are designed to make it clear that if the

---

[26] James Wilson, Pennsylvania ratifying convention, 4 December 1787
[27] James Iredell, North Carolina ratifying convention, 29 July 1788
[28] Patrick Henry, Virginia Ratification Convention, 24 June 1788

Constitution is silent on any power or right, that power or right is retained by the people—period.

But what of a power that is granted or a right that is listed? Can those powers and rights interfere with unenumerated rights? The second purpose of the Ninth Amendment will answer that important question. We'll get to that in a moment. First, what are our unenumerated rights, sometimes referred to as "Ninth Amendment rights"?

"NINTH AMENDMENT RIGHTS"

For a time, little attention was paid to the Ninth Amendment. Until the mid-1960s it had become all but forgotten and lost. In that transformative decade, the Supreme Court seemed to rediscover the Ninth Amendment. They began making rulings to protect "Ninth Amendment rights." That is, they began to enumerate unenumerated rights. While some of these unenumerated rights, the right to privacy, for example, may undoubtedly exist, there is no power delegated to the national government in the Constitution for the administration of those rights. As such, the courts have established powers in the name of protecting those unenumerated rights. Omitting them from the purview of the national government was a protection in and of itself. There is no power delegated to Congress to distribute new "protective" powers to the national government. Add the courts' newfound delegated powers to the interpretation of the Fourteenth Amendment that the restrictions to the national government also apply to the states and local government, and the result is an expansion of national power—not to mention the violation of the separation of powers in the form of judicial legislation.

There is no such thing as a Ninth Amendment right. The Ninth Amendment was specifically designed to keep those rights in the hands of the people and *not* place them under the purview of the national government, yet the actions of the courts place those unenumerated rights directly under the national government.

Ironically, the Ninth Amendment is being used to violate the Ninth Amendment.

In all fairness to the courts, it is a difficult task to protect unenumerated rights without construing powers and other rights in the attempt. Lucky, the Ninth Amendment addresses how to read and interpret the Constitution to help with such matters. . . well, kind of. Thanks to the Select Committee, that instruction is not so clear. Laurence Tribe observed:

> *It is a common error, but an error nonetheless, to talk of "ninth amendment rights." The ninth amendment is not a source of rights as such; it is simply a rule about how to read the Constitution.*[29]

DELEGATED POWERS SHALL NOT BE CONSTRUED

"Shall not be construed" is the key phrase to the second purpose of the Ninth Amendment: the avoidance of an expansion of powers and rights enumerated in the Constitution to the extent that they "deny or disparage" other unenumerated rights retained by the people. This was a concern expressed by the states during the ratification process of the Constitution.

Now it's time to unpack Madison's original proposal for the Ninth Amendment:

> *The exceptions here or elsewhere in the constitution, made in favor of particular rights, shall not be so construed as to diminish the just importance of other rights retained by the people; or as to enlarge the powers delegated by the constitution; but either as actual limitations of such powers, or as inserted merely for greater caution.*[30]

---

[29] Laurence H. Tribe, *American Constitutional Law*, 1988
[30] James Madison proposal to Congress, 8 June 1789

This language was not from Madison's mind alone. Concern about the expansion of power by reinterpreting powers delegated in the Constitution was a concern among the states.

NINTH AMENDMENT SUGGESTIONS FROM THE STATES

Contrary to some modern opinions, the original proposal to Congress for the Ninth Amendment did not spring solely from the mind of Madison. The states' recommendations were the true genesis of the amendment. The states were concerned that the national government would construe certain clauses of the Constitution into expanded powers not originally intended by the authors of the document. Upon condition of ratification, the states expressed their concerns and suggested amendments "merely for greater caution."[31]

New York's notice of ratification of the Constitution was accompanied by language intended to clarify the state's understanding of what they had just agreed to in ratifying the Constitution:

> *... every Power, Jurisdiction and right, which is not by the said Constitution clearly delegated to the Congress of the United States, or the departments of the Government thereof, remains to the People of the several States, or to their respective State Governments to whom they may have granted the same; And that those Clauses in the said Constitution, which declare, that Congress shall not have or exercise certain Powers, do not imply that Congress is entitled to any Powers not given by the said Constitution; but such Clauses are to be construed either as exceptions to certain specified Powers, or as inserted merely for greater Caution.[32]*

---

[31] Bill of Rights, Preamble, 1789
[32] Ratification of the Constitution by the State of New York; 26 July 1788

Concerns about delegated powers that are construed to abuse other rights and powers retained by the people echo back and forth between Madison's proposal and New York's clarification statement. Rhode Island sent Congress the same language, word for word. Other states did more than send their understanding of the powers delegated in the Constitution. They sent specific suggestions for amendments on the subject. North Carolina proposed:

1. That each state in the union shall, respectively, retain every power, jurisdiction and right, which is not by this constitution delegated to the Congress of the United States, or to the departments of the Federal Government. . .

18. That those clauses which declare that Congress shall not exercise certain powers, be not interpreted in any manner whatsoever to extend the powers of Congress; but that they be construed either as making exceptions to the specified powers where this shall be the case, or otherwise, as inserted merely for greater caution.

Pennsylvania detailed their proposal to include a provision to limit the executive and judicial branches. Like North Carolina, they wanted to be sure Congress did not take their existing delegated powers and expand them beyond protecting only those rights expressly protected. It would be bad enough if Congress expanded their powers, but they wanted to be sure the executive and judicial branches did not misconstrue the Constitution and Bill of Rights to expand powers either.

That Congress shall not exercise any powers whatever, but such as are expressly given to that body by the Constitution of the United States: nor shall any authority, power, or jurisdiction, be assumed or exercised by the executive or judiciary departments of the Union, under color or pretence of construction or fiction; but all the rights of sovereignty, which are not by the said Constitution expressly and plainly vested in the

> *Congress, shall be deemed to remain with, and shall be exercised by, the several states in the Union, according to their respective constitutions; and that every reserve of the rights of individuals, made by the several constitutions of the states in the Union, to the citizens and inhabitants of each state respectively, shall remain inviolate, except so far as they are expressly and manifestly yielded or narrowed by the national Constitution.[33]*

In the Virginia ratifying convention, the delegates appointed a committee to draft the amendment suggestions to forward to Congress on condition of ratification. The committee included James Madison. They proposed:

> *First, That each State in the Union shall respectively retain every power, jurisdiction and right which is not by this Constitution delegated to the Congress of the United States or to the departments of the Federal Government. . .*

> *Seventeenth, That those clauses which declare that Congress shall not exercise certain powers be not interpreted in any manner whatsoever to extend the powers of Congress. But that they may be construed either as making exceptions to the specified powers where this shall be the case, or otherwise as inserted merely for greater caution.[34]*

Based on Madison's original proposal for the Ninth Amendment and suggestions on the same subject from the states, it is clear that the Ninth Amendment is more about limiting the expansion of power than it is about protecting rights not listed.

---

[33] Proceedings of the meeting at Harrisburg, in Pennsylvania, 3 September 1788
[34] Virginia ratification convention, 27 June 1788

MERELY FOR GREATER CAUTION

You will recall from Part 1 that it was argued that a bill of rights was needed to further clarify limits placed on the national government. Alexander Hamilton and others argued that a bill of rights was not necessary because the Constitution is a delegatory document—the national government cannot do what the Constitution does not specifically say it can do. A bill of rights could actually be harmful, they argued, because listing specific rights that the national government is prohibited in acting on could result in disparaging any rights that were not listed.

This argument was quickly rebutted by one simple point. The Constitution already included specific prohibitions of certain actions regarding specific rights. "Habeas Corpus shall not be suspended," "No Bill of Attainder or ex post facto Law shall be passed," "No Capitation. . .," "No tax. . .," "No Preference. . .," "No Money. . .," "No Title of Nobility. . .," etc. are examples of prohibitions in the Constitution as written during the Convention and ratified by the states. If a bill of rights was to cause problems because of prohibitions, those prohibitions already in the document must be problematic too.

This explains the suggestion from the states that language be included in a bill of rights that clearly says that prohibitions in the Constitution should not be construed to mean that if a prohibition does not exist then the national government must be able to do that thing. Those prohibitions were not inserted to be a comprehensive list of prohibitions, but rather were "inserted merely for greater Caution" regarding items of greater import. The New York ratifying convention expressed this in their letter to Congress.

> *And that those Clauses in the said Constitution, which declare, that Congress shall not have or exercise certain Powers, do not imply that Congress is entitled to any Powers not given by the said Constitution; but such Clauses are to be construed either as exceptions to*

certain specified Powers, or as inserted merely for greater Caution.[35]

Basically, there were two layers to the delegatory nature of the Constitution. First, if the document specifically prohibits an action, the national government cannot do that thing. Secondly, if the Constitution does not specifically delegate the authority of a specific action, the national government cannot do that thing either. The states wanted to add a third layer, emphasizing that the national government cannot construe delegated powers or prohibitions to disparage other rights not enumerated in the constitution. That is the primary purpose of the Ninth Amendment.

THE BANK BILL

One might conclude that the Select Committee changed the wording of Madison's original proposal for the Ninth Amendment not for brevity's sake, but because they wanted to limit the amendment to rights rather than include powers and the prohibition of the expansion of those powers. There are some key words, however, that were retained in the Select Committee's language that indicate that the expansion of powers concern was still being addressed. "Shall not be construed" directly prohibits the reinterpretation of the Constitution in a way that expands power that would "deny or disparage" rights that are not specifically mentioned or protected by limited powers.

Not only were those important words retained, but in a 1791 speech, Madison also uses the Ninth Amendment in a way that confirms its purpose of limiting the expansion of powers as a way of protecting unenumerated rights. The speech was given to Congress on 2 February 1791 in opposition to the Bank Bill, a proposal to establish a national bank.

---

[35] Ratification of the Constitution by the State of New York; 26 July 1788

Putting the Bank Bill speech in chronological context:

- The Select Committee recommended the language for the Ninth Amendment on July 28, 1789;

- The House passed it on August 24, 1789;

- The Senate passed it on September 7, 1789;

- It was sent to the states for ratification on October 2, 1789;

- New Jersey is the first state to ratify on November 20, 1789;

- Madison gave his Bank Bill speech on February 2, 1791 (nine of the required eleven states had ratified by this time);

- The eleventh state, Virginia, ratified it on December 15, 1791.

The chronological context is important to show that the current language of the Ninth Amendment had been established eighteen months prior to the Bank Bill speech. It had passed in both houses and been sent to the states sixteen months earlier, and ratified by nine states fourteen months before. The language was well known and accepted by the time Madison gave his speech. Although the Ninth Amendment had yet to be officially ratified, Madison referred to it as if it was a foregone conclusion that it would be part of the Constitution. This is important to note because it indicates, based on its use in the speech, that the amendment was still designed to limit the expansion of powers even in its shortened form.

In his Bank Bill speech, Madison contends that the Constitution does not grant the national government power to establish a national bank. Alexander Hamilton and others argued that the Constitution granted power to pay the debts of the United States and to establish laws "necessary and proper" for fulfilling that grant of power. Madison explained that such an interpretation and action would "construe" the power to pay the debts in an unconstitutional manner, and would be an expansion of power to an extent as to "disparage" other rights retained by the people. He used the Ninth Amendment to defend his position.

> *The explanatory amendments proposed by Congress themselves, at least, would be good authority with them; all these renunciations of power proceeded on a rule of construction, excluding the latitude now contended for. These explanations were the more to be respected, as they had not only been proposed by Congress, but ratified by nearly three-fourths of the states. He read several of the articles proposed, remarking particularly on the 11th. and 12th. the former, as guarding against a latitude of interpretation—the latter, as excluding every source of power not within the constitution itself.*[36]

Madison calls the Ninth and Tenth Amendments the "explanatory amendments" as an indication that they explain how to interpret the Constitution. He then establishes credibility by pointing out that they were passed by Congress and ratified by "nearly three-fourths of the states," almost the requisite number to make them official amendments. Lastly, he defines the Ninth Amendment "as guarding against a latitude of interpretation" and the Tenth "as excluding every source of power not within the constitution itself." The quote above references the Eleventh and Twelfth Amendments; remember, those are the ninth and tenth in their original numeration.

In his notes for the speech Madison jotted "disparage other rights— or constructively enlarge,"[37] indicating that expanding powers is the same as disparaging rights. Remember, limiting powers is the same as protecting rights according to Madison. If limiting powers protect rights, expanding powers must abuse rights. To use 1789 language, construing powers must deny or disparage rights.

Madison took the suggestion from the states to include language guarding against expanding powers that would result in abusing rights and crafted his proposal for the Ninth Amendment. He then

---

[36] James Madison, The Bank Bill, Congressional Record, 2 February 1791, emphasis added
[37] James Madison, notes for speech in Congress, 8 June 1789

participated in streamlining its language as he served on the Select Committee. He knew the intent of the amendment as well as, likely better than, anyone. With his intimate knowledge, he used the Ninth Amendment to oppose the Bank Bill by accusing it of an expansion of power to the detriment of retained rights. His use of the amendment so early after its creation should be attributed as the most accurate interpretation of its original intent.

THE FEAR OF "GENERAL WELFARE" AND "NECESSARY AND PROPER"

The Ninth and Tenth Amendments came to be as a result of the states' fear of two phrases in the Constitution, "general welfare" and "necessary and proper." Many felt that those phrases would eventually be interpreted as a "sky's the limit" approach to national government policy.

Like Madison, Thomas Jefferson opposed the Bank Bill. He argued that if "necessary and proper" were given too much latitude, it would result in Congress acting on anything and everything under the sun.

The incorporation of a bank, and other powers assumed by this bill have not, in my opinion, been delegated to the U.S. by the Constitution...

I consider the foundation of the Constitution as laid on this ground that "all powers not delegated to the U.S. by the Constitution, nor prohibited by it to the states, are reserved to the states or to the people" [XIIth. Amendmt.]. To take a single step beyond the boundaries thus specially drawn around the powers of Congress, is to take possession of a boundless feild [sic] of power, no longer susceptible of any definition...

If such a latitude of construction be allowed to [the necessary and proper] phrase as to give any non-enumerated power, it will go to every one, for these is no one which ingenuity may not torture into a convenience, in some way or other, to some one of so long a list of enumerated powers. It would swallow up all the delegated powers, and reduce the whole to one phrase as before observed. Therefore it was that the constitution restrained them to the necessary means, that is to say, to those means without which the grant of the power would be nugatory.[38]

A lengthy discussion ensued in the Virginia ratifying convention about the phrases "general welfare" and "necessary and proper," the latter referred to as the "sweeping clause" at the time. George Mason expressed a desire to add an amendment that would make it clear that power not delegated was reserved to the states and to the people and that powers could not be expanded to abuse rights. George Nicholas argued that "necessary and proper" only applied to specifically enumerated powers and should not be interpreted in such a way to expand powers.

Mr. George Mason: Among the enumerated powers, Congress are to lay and collect taxes, duties, imposts, and excises, and to pay the debts, and to provide for the general welfare and common defence; and by that clause (so often called the sweeping clause) they are to make all laws necessary to execute those laws. Now, suppose oppressions should arise under this government, and any writer should dare to stand forth, and expose to the community at large the abuses of those powers; could not Congress, under the idea of providing for the general welfare, and under their own construction, say that this was destroying the general peace, encouraging sedition, and poisoning the minds of the people? And could they not, in order to provide against this, lay a dangerous restriction on the press? Might they not even bring the trial of this restriction within the ten miles square, when there is no prohibition against it? Might they not thus destroy the trial by jury? Would they not extend their

---

[38] Thomas Jefferson, opinion on the Constitutionality of the Bill for Establishing a National Bank, 15 February 1791

implication? It appears to me that they may and will. And shall the support of our rights depend on the bounty of men whose interest it may be to oppress us? That Congress should have power to provide for the general welfare of the Union, I grant. But I wish a clause in the Constitution, with respect to all powers which are not granted, that they are retained by the states. Otherwise, the power of providing for the general welfare may be perverted to its destruction.

Many gentlemen, whom I respect, take different sides of this question. We wish this amendment to be introduced, to remove our apprehensions. There was a clause in the Confederation reserving to the states respectively every power, jurisdiction, and right, not expressly delegated to the United States. This clause has never been complained of, but approved by all. Why not, then, have a similar clause in this Constitution, in which it is the more indispensably necessary than in the Confederation, because of the great augmentation of power vested in the former? In my humble apprehension, unless there be some such clear and finite expression, this clause now under consideration will go to any thing our rulers may think proper. Unless there be some express declaration that every thing not given is retained, it will be carried to any power Congress may please.

Mr. GEORGE NICHOLAS, in reply to the gentlemen opposed to the clause under debate, went over the same grounds, and developed the same principles, which Mr. Pendleton and Mr. Madison had done. The opposers of the clause, which gave the power of providing for the general welfare, supposed its dangers to result from its connection with, and extension of, the powers granted in the other clauses. He endeavored to show the committee that it only empowered Congress to make such laws as would be necessary to enable them to pay the public debts and provide for the common defence; that this general welfare was united, not to the general power of legislation, but to the particular power of laying and collecting taxes, imposts, and excises, for the purpose of paying the debts and providing for the common defence,—that is, that they could raise as much money as would pay the debts and provide for the common defence, in consequence of this power. The clause which was affectedly called the sweeping clause contained no new grant of power. To illustrate this position, he observed that, if it had been added at the end of every one of the enumerated powers, instead of being inserted at the end of all, it would be obvious to any one that it was no augmentation of power. If, for instance, at the end of the clause granting power to lay and collect taxes, it had been added that they should have power to make necessary and proper laws to lay and collect taxes, who could suspect it to be an addition of power? As it would grant no new power if inserted at the end of each clause, it could not when subjoined to the whole.[39]

WRAPPING UP THE NINTH AMENDMENT

The National Archives has published a fairly comprehensive history of the Bill of Rights. In it they describe the Ninth Amendment in this way:

This amendment to protect the rights of the people addressed a concern that the enumeration or listing of specific rights in the constitution and the other proposed amendments might be misconstrued to imply that only these enumerated rights were protected. Natural law philosophy at the time was based on the belief that the people only surrendered some of their rights to form governments, leaving the total store of retained rights unstated and untouched.[40]

---

[39] Virginia ratifying convention, 12 June 1788

[40] A Project of The National Archives–Center for Legislative Archives, Congress Creates

While their description is correct, like other sources it is only half correct. They continue to portray the Ninth Amendment as only protecting unenumerated rights simply by stating that they exist and that they are retained by the people, but they miss the second and most important purpose—the prohibition on the expansion of powers. They too quote the states' suggestion only in reference to rights. They fail to reference quotes regarding denying or disparaging rights by construing delegated powers in an expanded form.

Uncovering the complete original intent of the Ninth Amendment is an exciting discovery. Perhaps it is time to reinsert the true intent of the Ninth Amendment into the culture, the law, and jurisprudence.

In a nutshell, the Ninth Amendment sets out to make it clear that there are rights that are not enumerated in the Constitution that are retained by the people. It then presents the manner by which those unenumerated rights are to be protected. It is by not expanding powers beyond their delegated bounds. Rights are protected by not construing powers to deny or disparage those rights. Expanding powers results in denying or disparaging rights and conversely, protecting rights is achieved by limiting powers—and that is the purpose of the Ninth Amendment. It's too bad that it states its purpose in such an elusive manner.

The Ninth Amendment is not complete without the Tenth Amendment. These two are close companions. While the Ninth is for "guarding against a latitude of interpretation,"[41] the Tenth excludes "every source of power not within the constitution itself."[42] They both were created from the concern about the "general welfare" and "necessary and proper" phrases in the Constitution. Details about the abuses of those two phrases have been reserved to the following chapter on the Tenth Amendment, but it should be remembered that the Ninth Amendment is an equal partner in

---

the Bill of Rights, Go Inside the First Congress, Part II B Amendments in Process
[41] James Madison, The Bank Bill, Congressional Record, 2 February 1791
[42] Ibid.

guarding against abuses, and an equal victim of abuses caused by the expansion of powers.

The Tenth Amendment

"THE POWERS NOT DELEGATED TO THE UNITED STATES BY THE CONSTITUTION, NOR PROHIBITED BY IT TO THE STATES, ARE RESERVED TO THE STATES RESPECTIVELY, OR TO THE PEOPLE."

KEY QUOTES FROM THE FOUNDING ERA

I ask for no straining of words against the general government, nor yet against the states. I believe the states can best govern our home concerns and the general government our foreign ones. I wish, therefore, to see maintained that wholesome distribution of powers established by the Constitution for the limitation of both; and never to see all offices transferred to Washington.[1]
—Thomas Jefferson

This balance between the national and state governments ought to be dwelt on with peculiar attention, as it is of the utmost importance. It forms a double security to the people. If one encroaches on their rights, they will find a powerful protection in the other. Indeed, they will both be prevented from overpassing their constitutional limits, by certain rivalship which will ever subsist between them.[2]   —Alexander Hamilton

Power being almost always the rival of power, the general government will at all times stand ready to check the usurpations of the state governments, and these will have the same disposition towards the general government. The people, by throwing themselves into either scale, will infallibly make it preponderate. If their rights are invaded by either, they can make use of the

---

[1] Letter from Thomas Jefferson to William Johnson, 12 June 1823

[2] Alexander Hamilton, New York Ratifying Convention (Francis Childs's Version), 21 June 1788

> *other as the instrument of redress.*[3]
>
> —Alexander Hamilton

The lengthy explanation and history of the expansion of powers seems to be the most efficient way to present the purpose and importance of the Tenth Amendment. This amendment is sometimes referred to as the "catchall" amendment because it is designed to catch everything purposefully or unintentionally left out of the Constitution. The Hamiltonian view seeks a list of constitutional prohibitions to limit the actions of the national government. Such a list would need to be almost infinite to cover every subject. That is not reasonably possible, which is why the Constitution establishes a list of specifically delegated powers rather than a list of specifically prohibited powers.

The Tenth Amendment, in essence, is that infinite list of prohibited powers. It states that any power not specifically delegated is prohibited. Hence, it is a "catchall." It catches every subject conceived, compares it to the document, and if the subject is not in the document, it is specifically prohibited.

The Tenth Amendment is perhaps the most wisely crafted amendment in the Constitution. However, it seems to be the most abused amendment as well, which is proof that it is perhaps the most necessary amendment.

History shows the Founders' intent to reserve all powers to the states or the people that were not expressly delegated to the national government. The Founders were so fearful of returning to a dictatorship that they failed to give enough power to Congress in the Articles of Confederation. They listed very few, and defined, powers and then expressly forbade Congress from assuming any further power in these words:

> *Each state retains its sovereignty, freedom, and independence, and every Power, Jurisdiction and right,*

---

[3] Alexander Hamilton, *Federalist* No. 28, 1787

which is not by this confederation expressly delegated to the United States, in Congress assembled.[4]

James Madison expressed this same concept while the States were considering the adoption of the proposed Constitution.

The powers delegated by the proposed Constitution to the Federal Government, are few and defined. Those which are to remain in the State Governments are numerous and indefinite.[5]

They understood that certain powers had to be delegated to the national government, and that in those powers it had to be supreme. They were well aware, though, of the dangers a national government could pose to their individual liberties and the rights of the states. It was this principle of dual sovereignty that they were carefully trying to balance and perpetuate to ensure the healthy independence of the national and state governments. Without this balance, each would deteriorate and eventually one or the other would become totally dominant.

If the national government became dominant, it would mean the end of local self-government and the freedom of the individual. On the other hand, if the states became dominant, the national government would become so weak that the structure of the nation would begin to fractionalize and disintegrate into smaller units. This nearly happened under the Articles of Confederation. The states began treating each other like foreign countries, there were high tariffs and runaway inflation due to trade wars, and it was nearly impossible to collect taxes from the states to pay the expenses of the national government. On more than one occasion, George Washington attributed the near loss of the War of Independence directly to the Articles of Confederation. Only a balanced dual sovereignty could fix the problem.

---

[4] Articles of Confederation, Article 2, 1777
[5] James Madison, *Federalist* No. 45, 1788

THE PRINCIPLE OF DUAL SOVEREIGNTY

Remember our discussion in Part 1 under General Principles about delegated authority, and how power is divided on the local, state, and national levels? The principle of dual sovereignty will be easier to understand with that concept in mind.

Perhaps Franklin Delano Roosevelt explained it as well as anyone when he was governor of New York. In a national radio address on March 2, 1930, he was asked to define the scope and limits of federal power between the national and state governments, explaining where one ends and the other begins. He began by stating that "As a matter of fact and law the governing rights of the States are all of those which have not been surrendered to the National Government by the Constitution or its amendments."[6]

He admitted that Congress had been permitted to legislate in areas where they may or may not have had a legitimate right, such as Prohibition, but that there were other areas which they were strictly forbidden, "such as the conduct of public utilities, of banks, of insurance, of business, of agriculture, of education, of social welfare, and of a dozen other important features [that]. . . Washington must not be encouraged to interfere."

He then referenced the national Constitution as the legal precedent for this logic:

> *The proper relations between the Government of the United States and the governments of the separate States therefore depend entirely, in their legal aspects, on what powers have been voluntarily ceded to the Central Government by the States themselves. What these powers of government are is contained in our national Constitution, either by direct language, by judicial interpretation thereof during many years, or by*

---

[6] All quotations in this section are from Franklin Delano Roosevelt, national radio address, 2 March 1930

implication so plain as to have been recognized by the people generally.

He explained the concept of vertical separation of powers, or "home rule" as he called it. This is the necessary balance of power between all levels of government in our federal system which protects the minority and keeps the majority of governmental power close to the people.

The whole success of our democracy has not been that it is a democracy herein the will of a bare majority of the total inhabitants is imposed upon the minority, but because it has been a dividing of governments into units called States, the rights and interests of the minority has been respected and have always been given a voice in the control of our affairs. This is the principle on which the little State of Rhode Island is given just as large a voice in our national Senate as the great State of New York.

The moment a mear [sic] numerical superiority by either State or voters in this country proceeds to ignore the needs and desires of the minority, and, for their own selfish purposes or advancement, hamper or oppress that minority, or debar them in any way from equal privileges and equal rights—that moment will mark the failure of our constitutional system. For this reason a proper understanding of the fundamental powers of the States is very necessary and important.

These fundamental powers are based on the principle:

. . . that every citizen was entitled to live his own life in his own way so long as his conduct did not injure any of his fellow men. This was to be a new land of promise where a man could worship God in the way he saw fit; where he could rise by industry, by thrift, by intelligence, to the highest places in the Commonwealth, secure from tyranny, secure from injustice—a free agent—the maker or the destroyer of his own destiny. . .

> *On this sure foundation of the protection of the weak against the strong; stone by stone, our entire edifice of Government has been erected. As the individual is protected from possible oppression by his neighbors, so the smallest political unit, the town, is, in theory at least, allowed to manage its own affairs, secure from undue interference by the larger unit of the county which, in turn, is protected from mischievous meddling by the State.*

> *This is what we call the doctrine of "Home Rule," and the whole spirit and intent of the Constitution is to carry this great principle into the relations between the National Government and the Governments of the States.*

Next, Roosevelt explained what must happen to destroy state sovereignty and bring about the central control of nearly all local affairs under one government.

> *Now, to bring about government by oligarchy, masquerading as democracy, it is foundationally essential that practically all authority and control be centralized in our National Government. The individual sovereignty of our States must first be destroyed, except in mere minor matters of legislation.*

He assured the people that, as of the present time, they were "safe from the danger of any such departure from the principles on which this country was founded" but warned that this will only be the case as long as the principle of "home rule" was scrupulously preserved.

> *Thus, it will be seen that this home rule is a most important thing, the most vital thing, if we are to continue along the course on which we have so far progressed with such unprecedented success.*

Governor Roosevelt then proceeded to list the few and defined powers surrendered by the States in the Constitution.

Now, what are the powers delegated to the United States by the Constitution? First of all, the National Government is entrusted with the duty of protecting any and all States from the danger of invasion or conquest by foreign powers by sea or land, and in return the States surrender the right to engage in any private wars on their own. This involves, of course, the creation of the Army and the Navy and the right to enroll citizens of any State in time of need. Next is given the treaty-making power and the sole right of all intercourse with foreign states; the issuing of money and its protection from counterfeiting. The regulation of weights and measures so as to be uniform; the entire control and regulation of commerce with foreign nations and among the several States; the protection of patents and copyrights; the erection of minor Federal tribunals throughout the country and the establishment of post offices are specifically enumerated. The power to collect taxes, duties, and imposts to pay the debts for the common defense and general welfare of the country is also given to the United States Congress as the law-making body of the Nation.

On such a small foundation have we erected the whole enormous fabric of Federal Government which costs us now $3,500,000,000 every year, and if we do not halt this steady process of building commissions and regulatory bodies and special legislation like huge inverted pyramids over every one of the simple, constitutional provisions, we will soon be spending many billions of dollars more.

A VERTICAL SEPARATION OF POWERS

In addition to the horizontal separation of powers on the national level with three branches—legislative, executive and judicial—the Founders also recognized the wisdom of a vertical separation between local, state, and national governments. This vertical separation begins with the people and ends with the national government. It is by dividing and subdividing that allows each function of government to be performed on the level best suited for the task.

Roosevelt uses the imagery of an inverted pyramid to describe the problems that result from the national government becoming too large. This same imagery was used by James Wilson as he illustrated the separation of powers doctrine. The higher the level of government, the more necessary it is to confine that government. James Wilson explains this by illustrating the vertical separation as a pyramid:

> *A free government has often been compared to a pyramid. This allusion is made with peculiar propriety in the system before you; it is laid on the broad basis of the people; its powers gradually rise, while they are confined, in proportion as they ascend, until they end in that most permanent of all forms. When you examine all its parts, they will invariably be found to preserve that essential mark of free governments—a chain of connection with the people. Such, sir, is the nature of this system of government. . .*[7]

Thomas Jefferson explained it this way:

> *The way to have good and safe government is not to trust it all to one; but to divide it among the many, distributing to every one exactly the functions he is competent to. Let the National government be entrusted with the defense of the nation, and its foreign and federal relations; the State governments with the civil rights, laws, police and administration of what concerns the state generally; the Counties with the local concerns of the counties; and each Ward direct the interests within itself. It is by dividing and subdividing these republics from the great National one down through all its subordinations, until*

---

[7] James Wilson, Pennsylvania ratifying convention, 1787

it ends in the administration of every man's farm and affairs by himself; by placing under every one what his own eye may superintend, that all will be done for the best.

It is by this partition of cares, descending in gradation from general to particular that the mass of human affairs may be best managed for the good and prosperity of all.

In this way we shall be as republican as a large society can be, and secure the continuance of purity in our government by the salutary, peaceable, and regular control of the people.[8]

Notice that Jefferson lists four levels of government: National, State, County, and Ward (i.e., cities and towns). He explains that government should not operate as a single jurisdiction ("not to trust it all to one") but it should function in multiple jurisdictions by "divid[ing] it among the many."

As stated previously, the reason many of the states hesitated to adopt the Constitution was the fear that this new and stronger government would deprive the states and the people of their rights. Even though the powers delegated to it were few and defined, experience had shown that government will almost always abuse power. The farther government gets from the people, the more likely abuse will occur.

For vertical separation to work, the various levels of government were designed to be more limited in proportion to the level, or authority granted at that level.

LIMITED GOVERNMENT AT THE NATIONAL LEVEL

To illustrate what James Madison and others meant by the national Government possessing "few and defined" powers, we have listed those powers that are in the Constitution. They are few, which means they can be listed, and they are defined to specific areas of responsibility. Below is a summary of those powers. The reader is

---

[8] Letter from Thomas Jefferson to Joseph C. Cabell, 2 February 1816

encouraged to go directly to the Constitution for an unabridged listing of these powers.

You may notice many areas of responsibility that Congress, the president, and the courts have assumed that are not enumerated in the Constitution. This is important to note in your continued study of the Tenth Amendment.

The Congress, as the law-making branch, is granted more powers than the executive and judicial branches. As such, it is divided into two houses, the House of Representatives and the Senate, to provide additional checks and balances. The powers listed below are derived from the Constitution only.

Congress shall have power to:

- Collect taxes which shall be uniform throughout the states to:

    - Pay debts.

    - Provide for the common defense.

    - Provide for the general welfare of the United States.

- Borrow money on credit of U.S.

- Regulate commerce with foreign nations and among the several states, and with Indian tribes.

- Establish uniform rules of naturalization.

- Establish uniform laws on the subject of bankruptcy.

- Coin money, regulate its value, and of foreign coin, and establish fixed standards of weights and measures.

- Provide for the punishment of counterfeiting.

- Establish post offices and post roads.

- Promote the arts and sciences by granting copyrights and patents.

- Establish courts inferior to the Supreme Court (see also Article III, Section 1).

- Define and punish piracies and felonies committed on the high seas, and offenses against the law of nations.

- Declare war, grant letters of marque and reprisal, and make rules concerning prisoners of war.

- Appropriate money on a two-year term to raise and support armies;

- Provide and maintain a navy.

- Make rules for the government and regulate the land and naval forces.

- Call forth the militia to execute the laws of the union, suppress insurrections, and repel invasions.

- Organize, arm, and discipline the militia.

- Make exclusive legislation over government-owned property.

- Make all laws which shall be necessary and proper for carrying into execution the powers granted to the federal government by the Constitution.

- The power to impeach and try the president and other officials, including federal justices and judges (Article 1, Section 2, Clause 5, and Section 3, Clause 6).

- Determine the number of judges on the Supreme Court.

- To regulate and place limitations on the jurisdiction of inferior courts, and the Supreme Court in cases that it does not have original jurisdiction (Article III, Section 2, Clause 2).

- Declare the punishment of treason (Article III, Section 3, Clause 2).

- To admit new states to the union (Article IV, Section 3).

- To propose amendments to the Constitution (Article V).

- To lay and collect taxes on incomes. . .(Amendment XVI); and

- The House of Representatives has the power to elect a president, should no candidate receive an absolute majority of the electoral votes cast; and the Senate has the power to elect a vice president, should no candidate receive an absolute majority of the electoral votes cast (Amendment XII).

The president shall have power to:

- Be commander-in-chief of the army and navy, and of the militia when called into actual service by Congress.

- Require the opinion on any subject relating to the duties of national department executives (the cabinet).

- Grant reprieves and pardons for offence against the United States, except in cases of impeachment.

- Negotiate and sign treaties provided two-thirds of the senators present concur.

- Nominate, and with the advice and consent of the Senate, appoint ambassadors, public ministers, consuls, judges of the Supreme Court, and other officers.

- Fill up all vacancies during the recess of the Senate.

- Provide Congress with information regarding the State of the Union and recommend necessary and expedient legislation.

- Convene both houses of Congress on extraordinary occasions.

- Adjourn Congress if House and Senate cannot agree on adjournment.

- Receive ambassadors and other public ministers.

- See that all laws be faithfully executed and commission all the officers of the United States.

- Sign legislation into law or to veto bills enacted by Congress, although Congress may override a veto with a two-thirds vote of both houses.

The judicial power shall extend to:

All cases, in law and equity, arising under:

- the Constitution.

- Laws passed by Congress.

- Treaties.

All cases:

- Affecting ambassadors or other officials of foreign governments.

- Relating to the admiralty or maritime problems.

- In which the United States is a party.

- Disputes between two or more states.

- Disputes between citizens of different states.

- Disputes between citizens of the same state over claims or land grants in different states.

Reviewing the specific powers granted to each branch of the national government, it is not difficult to see that much more is being done on a national level than was intended by the "few and defined" powers granted in the Constitution. In fact, every restricted area that Roosevelt mentioned previously, including banks, insurance, agriculture, education, and social welfare, to name a few, is now under the jurisdiction of the national government. Even in its infancy, elected officials in all three branches of government began pulling more power to the national level. It didn't take long before those "few and defined" powers were broadened to encompass much more than the Founders had intended, despite the Tenth Amendment. This gradual usurpation of powers over two centuries has occurred in several ways, resulting in the Tenth Amendment having little, if any, power to restrain the national government. This process began with a broad interpretation of "general welfare" and "necessary and proper."

THE GENERAL WELFARE CLAUSE

The phrase "general welfare" is in two places in the Constitution. The preamble, "promote the general welfare," and Article I, Section 8, "provide for the general welfare." The common view prior to the adoption of the Constitution was that this clause restricted the taxing power to matters which benefited the whole nation and the federal treasury was not to be used for special interest groups, cities, counties, or even individual states. Taxes raised must benefit the entire nation equally.

The term *general welfare* was not exclusive to the Constitution. The Founders had used the phrase previously in their writings and legal documents. For example, general welfare was used in Article III of the Articles of Confederation in this manner:

> *The said states hereby severally enter into a firm league of friendship with each other, for their common defence, the security of their Liberties, and their mutual and general welfare, binding themselves to assist each other, against all force offered to, or attacks made upon them, or any of them, on account of religion, sovereignty, trade, or any other pretence whatever.[9]*

This term is derived from the unequal treatment often imposed by kings or dictators. Under such governments, the most objectionable element was the discriminatory manner in which favors and privileges were extended to the king's pets. Often the most

---

[9] Articles of Confederation, Article 3, 1777

deserving were deliberately snubbed while the less worthy received the king's royal accolades. It was therefore fundamental to a republic that the national government administer its power without prejudice, discrimination, or favoritism. In other words, all of the laws should be for all of the people all of the time.

This concept has its roots in the unalienable right that "all men are created equal." Gravity, for example, treats all people equally. As such, our laws should treat all people equally too. Refer to the "Principles of Natural Law" segment in the General Principles section in Part I for more detail on this concept.

The Founders emphasized the narrow definition that "general welfare" must benefit the entire nation rather than special interests. Initially Alexander Hamilton held this definition, though he later broadened his view when placed in a position of power and became a key player in expanding legislative authority. Of "general welfare," Hamilton originally said:

> *The welfare of the community [of states] is the only legitimate end for which money can be raised from the community. Congress can be considered as only under one restriction, which does not apply to other governments. They cannot rightfully apply the money they raise to any purpose merely or purely local. . . . The constitutional test of a right application must always be, whether it be for a purpose of general or local nature.*[10]

Archibald MacLaine and Edmond Randolph helped clarify its meaning when they said:

> *Congress will not lay a single tax when it is not to the advantage of the people at large.*[11]

> *The rhetoric of the gentleman has highly colored the dangers of giving the general government an indefinite*

---

[10] Alexander Hamilton, final version of an Opinion on the Constitutionality of an Act to Establish a Bank, 23 February 1791
[11] Archibald MacLaine, Constitutional Convention, 1787

power of providing for the general welfare. I contend that no such power is given.[12]

During the ratifying conventions prior to the adoption of the Constitution, Alexander Hamilton persuasively argued the purpose and extent of government. He emphasized the ever-present danger and natural human tendency of people to draw power to themselves when placed in positions of authority.

Why has government been instituted at all? Because the passions of men will not conform to the dictates of reason and justice, without constraint. . . . there is, in the nature of sovereign power, an impatience of control, which disposes those who are invested with the exercise of it, to look with an evil eye upon all external attempts to restrain or direct its operations. . . . This tendency is not difficult to be accounted for. It has its origin in the love of power. Power controlled or abridged is almost always the rival and enemy of that power by which it is controlled or abridged.[13]

THE NEW HAMILTONIAN DOCTRINE

After Hamilton became Secretary of the Treasury, he proved his previous point concerning the natural tendency to abuse power and began arguing that the welfare clause was a general grant of power. He said that Congress could spend tax money or borrow money for any good cause, even ones not included among the enumerated powers. He even went as far as to say that Congress could and should spend tax dollars for local or special welfare, not only general welfare.

Although it was not formally acknowledged, Hamilton's view was prevalent among government officials in all three branches of government almost from the adoption of the Constitution. Hamilton was opposed by Jefferson and Madison, who emphasized the

---

[12] Edmond Randolph, Virginia ratifying convention, 1788
[13] Alexander Hamilton, *Federalist* No. 15, 1 December 1787

original intent of general welfare pertaining to the national government. Its role was to benefit the nation as a whole, not special groups or special regions.

The battle between the Hamiltonian view and the Jefferson-Madison view went on for another century with no official ruling from the Supreme Court. Although Hamilton's definition was not official, further rulings and court decisions continued to be determined based on his view, and more power continued to be drawn to the national level despite the Tenth Amendment.

Finally, in the Butler case of 1936, the Supreme Court gave its endorsement to Hamilton's views on the taxing power. Justice Roberts wrote the opinion to settle, once and for all, whether the Jefferson-Madison interpretation or the Hamilton theory should prevail.

> *Madison asserted [that general welfare] amounted to no more than a reference to the other powers enumerated in the subsequent clauses of the same section; that, as the United States is a government of limited and enumerated powers, the grant of power to tax and spend for the general national welfare must be confined to the enumerated legislative fields committed to Congress. . . . Hamilton, on the other hand, maintained the clause confers a power separate and distinct from those later enumerated, is not restricted in meaning by the grant of them, and Congress consequently has a substantive power to tax and to appropriate, limited only by the requirement that it shall be exercised to provide for the general welfare of the United States. . . . While, therefore, the power to tax is not unlimited, its confines are set in the clause which confers it, and not in those of Section 8 which bestow and define the legislative powers of Congress.*[14]

---

[14] Owen Roberts, *United States v. Butler*, 1936

The concluding sentence seems to contradict itself. The court admits that Section 8 defines the enumerated powers to which the Congress is restricted, but then uses the words "general welfare" to justify legislating in any field even though it is not enumerated.

This decision alone was sufficient to literally destroy the whole concept of limited government, exactly as Jefferson and Madison had predicted. Justice Roberts wanted to be sure that there would be no further ground for argument in favor of the Jefferson-Madison view and therefore stated as a positive judicial mandate that the "general welfare" clause allows Congress "to authorize expenditure of public moneys for public purposes [and] is not limited by the direct grants of legislative power found in the Constitution."[15]

The only concession the court would make was the fact that the Tenth Amendment would prevent the Congress from invading areas reserved to the states.

The modest reservation left by Justice Roberts lasted barely a year when the court overruled itself in the Social Security Act cases. Some of the states were taxing employers a certain amount to provide unemployment insurance for their workers. The federal government imposed a similar tax and provided that any employer who had paid the federal unemployment tax could deduct it from whatever amount might be due the state.

After the reversal of the Supreme Court's ruling the year before in the Butler case, the states soon found the federal government preempting significant areas of state tax jurisdiction on the grounds that the "relief of unemployment was a legitimate object of federal expenditure under the 'general welfare' clause."[16]

The same reasoning was used to justify the government's collection of funds for old-age pensions and formed the basis for a multitude of other "social service" agencies which soon followed.

---

[15] Ibid.

[16] *Steward Machine Co. v. Davis*, 1937

Once general welfare was officially recognized as a general grant of power and not a restriction, Congress expanded their reach beyond their already expanded powers. It opened the floodgates to tax and spend for any reason.

The next landmark case came in 1947 when the Supreme Court sustained the right to make conditional grants-in-aid to states and then withhold federal funds as a means of enforcing its will on a protesting state. In the case of *Oklahoma v. Civil Service Commission*, the state objected to the enforcement of a provision of the Hatch Act whereby its right to receive its share of federal highway funds would be diminished in consequence of its failure to remove from office a member of the State Highway Commission found to have taken an active part in party politics while in office. The court ruled that:

> *While the United States is not concerned with, and has no power to regulate local political activities as such of State officials, it does have power to fix the terms upon which its money allotments to States shall be disbursed.*[17]

In other words, what the Constitution forbade the federal government to do directly, the government would achieve indirectly by making the allocations of funds to the state dependent upon compliance to the federal will. It was precisely this kind of legal coercion which Madison had warned against in case the general welfare clause was considered a grant of power instead of a limitation on the power to tax.

JAMES MADISON ARGUES THE DEFINITION OF GENERAL WELFARE

James Madison defined general welfare, predicted the results if that definition was changed, and illustrated a government that does not limit itself to "few and defined" powers. He made it clear that the Constitution established a limited government tied down to specific powers rather than an unlimited government. That view, he said,

---

[17] *Oklahoma v. Civil Service Commission*, 1947

was an original view held by himself, those who proposed the Constitution, and those who sought to ratify it. He determined that those who sought to define general welfare as an unlimited grant of power did not understand the consequences of that definition.

Madison said that it would make no sense to give Congress unlimited powers and then list specific limited powers at the same time:

> *It would be absurd to say, first, that Congress may do what they please; and then, that they may do this or that particular thing. After giving Congress power to raise money, and apply it to all purposes which they may pronounce necessary to the general welfare, it would be absurd, to. . . convert the government from one limited. . . to the enumerated powers, into a government without any limits at all.*

> *It is to be recollected, that the terms "common defense and general welfare," as here used, are not novel terms first introduced into this constitution. They are terms familiar in their construction, and well known to the people of America. They are repeatedly found in the old articles of confederation, where. . . it was never supposed or pretended that they conveyed any such powers as is now assigned to them. On the Contrary, it was always considered as clear and certain, that the old Congress was limited to the enumerated powers; and that the enumeration limited and explained the general terms. . .* [18]

An unlimited grant of power to Congress through an expanded definition of general welfare would also corrupt the judicial branch, according to Madison. Expanding Congressional power would result in judges ruling on unlimited subjects rather than the "few and defined" cases outlined in Article III of the Constitution. In short,

---

[18] James Madison, United States House of Representatives, debate on bounty payments for cod fisheries, 6 February 1792

unlimited legislative actions would result in unlimited judicial actions. And that wasn't all; Madison went on:

> *If Congress can apply money indefinitely to the general welfare, and are the sole and supreme judges of the general welfare, they may take the care of religion into their own hands; they may establish teachers in every state, county, and parish, and pay them out of the public treasury; they may take into their own hands the education of children, establishing in like manner schools throughout the union; they may assume the provision for the poor; they may undertake the regulation of all roads other than post roads; in short, every thing, from the highest object of state legislation, down to the most minute object of police, would be thrown under the power of Congress; for every object I have mentioned would admit the application of money, and might be called, if Congress pleased, provisions for the general welfare.*[19]

THE "NECESSARY AND PROPER" CLAUSE

In a similar way as "general welfare," the Supreme Court has used the "necessary and proper" clause to break down the concept of limited government.

Chief Justice John Marshall of the Supreme Court used his opinion on two landmark cases to argue that the Constitution was not nearly so limiting as Jefferson and Madison contended it to be. Marshall believed that the "necessary and proper clause" was a grant of power to Congress to do just about anything they wanted so long as the Constitution didn't expressly forbid them from doing it. In *McCulloch v. Maryland* (1819), Chief Justice Marshall delivered his opinion on a case questioning whether Congress possessed the power to "incorporate a bank":

---

[19] Ibid.

This government is acknowledged by all to be one of enumerated powers. The principle, that it can exercise only the powers granted to it, [is] now universally admitted. But the question respecting the extent of the powers actually granted, is perpetually arising, and will probably continue to arise, as long as our system shall exist. . . .

Among the enumerated powers, we do not find that of establishing a bank or creating a corporation. But there is no phrase in the [Constitution] which, like the articles of confederation, [that] excludes incidental or implied powers; and which requires that everything granted shall be expressly and minutely described. Even the 10th amendment, which was framed for the purpose of quieting the excessive jealousies which had been excited, omits the word "expressly," and declares only that the powers "not delegated to the United States, nor prohibited to the States, are reserved to the States or to the people"; thus leaving the question, whether the particular power which may become the subject of contest has been delegated to the one government, or prohibited to the other, to depend on a fair construction of the whole instrument.

Although, among the enumerated powers of government, we do not find the word "bank," or "incorporation," we find the great powers to lay and collect taxes; to borrow money; to regulate commerce; to declare and conduct a war; and to raise and support armies and navies. The sword and the purse, all the external relations, and no inconsiderable portion of the industry of the nation, are entrusted to its government.

To its enumeration of powers is added that of making "all laws which shall be necessary and proper for carrying into execution the foregoing powers, and all other powers vested by this constitution, in the government of the United States, or in any department thereof."

We admit, as all must admit, that the powers of the government are limited, and that its limits are not to be transcended. But we think the sound construction of the constitution must allow to the national legislature that discretion, with respect to the means by which the powers it confers are to be carried into execution, which will enable that body to perform the high duties assigned to it, in the manner most beneficial to the people. Let the end be legitimate, let it be within the scope of the constitution, and all means which are appropriate, which are plainly adapted to that end, which are not prohibited, but consist with the letter and spirit of the constitution, are constitutional. . .[20]

In the 1824 case of *Gibbon v. Ogden,* which could have been easily settled without further blurring the boundaries of federal authority, John Marshall once again broadened legislative authority by his opinion.

This [Constitution] contains an enumeration of powers expressly granted by the people to their government. It has been said that these powers ought to be construed strictly. But why ought they to be so construed? Is there one sentence in the Constitution which gives countenance to this rule? In the last of the enumerated powers, that which grants, expressly, the means for carrying all others into execution, congress authorized "to make all laws which shall be necessary and proper" for the purpose. But this limitation on the means to be used, is not extended to the powers which are conferred; nor is there one sentence in the constitution, which has been pointed out by the gentlemen of the bar, or which we have been able to discern, that prescribes this rule.

---

[20] John Marshall, *McCulloch v. Maryland,* 1819

We do not, therefore, think ourselves justified in adopting it.[21]

THE RESULTS OF REDEFINING "GENERAL WELFARE" AND "NECESSARY AND PROPER"

Looking back from a vantage point of almost two and a half centuries later, James Madison's warning about redefining "general welfare" and "necessary and proper" is almost prophetic. Restating a previous quote:

> *If Congress can apply money indefinitely to the general welfare, and are the sole and supreme judges of the general welfare. . . it would subvert the very foundation, and transmute the very nature of the limited government established by the people of America: and what inferences might be drawn or what consequences ensue from such a step, it is incumbent on us all well to consider.*

Thomas Jefferson summed up his view of the Tenth Amendment in this way:

> *I consider the foundation of the Constitution as laid on this ground that "all powers not delegated to the United States, by the Constitution, nor prohibited by it to the states, are reserved to the states or to the people." To take a single step beyond the boundaries thus specially drawn around the powers of Congress, is to take possession of a boundless field of power, not longer susceptible of any definition.*[22]

The national budget can be used to illustrate the expansion of national powers since the Butler case. In 1936 the national budget was six billion dollars. Some eighty-five years later, and adjusting for inflation, national government spending has increased almost sixty times. The "few and defined" powers granted to the national

---

[21] John Marshall, *Gibbon v. Ogden*, 1824
[22] Thomas Jefferson, opinion on the constitutionality of a national bank, 1791

government have expanded to encompass virtually every subject imaginable.

THE DEBATE RAGES ON

The debate continues to go on between those who want to do anything the Constitution does not strictly prohibit and those who recognize it as the delegatory document the Founders intended. One is an almost infinite list of loosely defined powers, and the other is a "few and defined" list. Just as Chief Justice John Marshall predicted, the debate between the Hamiltonian view of Constitutional authority and the Madison-Jefferson view continues to rage on even today. Hamilton's view has largely won out, dramatically shifting the interpretation of Constitutional authority which has literally flipped the whole concept of delegated authority upside down and reversed it from one of limited powers to one of limitless powers.

Theodore Roosevelt institutionalized this expanded view in the executive branch while recognizing that many of his predecessors had the more restrictive view and doing so would change the office of the presidency forever. He said:

I declined to adopt the view that what was imperatively necessary for the Nation could not be done by the President unless he could find some specific authorization to do it. My belief was that it was not only his right but his duty to do anything that the needs of the Nation demanded unless such action was forbidden by the Constitution or by the laws. Under this interpretation of executive power I did and caused to be done many things not previously done by the President and the heads of the departments. I did not usurp power, but I did greatly broaden the use of executive power. In other words, I acted for the public welfare, I acted for the common well-being of all our people, whenever and in whatever manner was necessary, unless prevented by direct constitutional or legislative prohibition.[23]

On December 19, 1998, the House of Representatives was discussing whether or not to impeach President Bill Clinton. During the debate, Sheila Jackson Lee, a representative from Texas, wanted to censure the president rather than impeach. Some representatives felt that was not possible since the Constitution did not give censuring authority to Congress. Congresswoman Lee offered the following:

> *Very briefly, Mr. Chairman, I'd like to submit into evidence of this proceedings the Constitution of the United States, particularly noting that there is no prohibition on censure noted in the Constitution of the United States.*[24]

To Which Chairman Henry Hyde, a representative from Illinois, replied:

> *Well, certainly, without objection, even though ours is a government of delegated powers. But, nonetheless, your motion is granted.*[25]

The fact that the argument continues to persist is evidence that there is an attempt to redefine a definition that was already known—that the Constitution established a government of specific enumerated powers, not a government of perpetually expanding powers. The national government continues to expand its powers beyond the original scope of the Constitution, which is evidence that the Tenth Amendment is necessary.

---

[23] Theodore Roosevelt, *An Autobiography*, 1913

[24] Sheila Jackson Lee, Congressional Record Volume 144, Number 155, 19 December 1998

[25] Henry Hyde, Congressional Record Volume 144, Number 155, 19 December 1998

Conclusion

The Bill of Rights was not the first of its kind, nor will it be the last. The Magna Carta was a bill of rights of sorts, and the Petition of Right, the English Declaration of Rights, the many state declarations of rights, and bills of rights in state constitutions all preceded the first ten amendments in the United States Constitution.

The principles behind the Bill of Rights have helped elevate human civilization to a level of liberty never before seen in history. The American experiment inspired the spread of written constitutions and declarations of rights throughout the world, which has raised billions out of poverty, chaos, and oppression. However, without understanding the principles behind the Bill of Rights, all nations, including our own, continue to struggle.

In a letter to his wife, Abigail, John Adams expressed the importance of discovering and establishing sophisticated natural law principles in society—what he called the science of government.

> *I could fill Volumes with Descriptions of Temples and Palaces, Paintings, Sculptures, Tapestry, Porcelaine, &c. &c. &c.—if I could have time. But I could not do this without neglecting my duty.—The Science of Government it is my Duty to study, more than all other Sciences: the Art of Legislation and Administration and Negotiation, ought to take Place, indeed to exclude in a manner all other Arts.—I must study Politicks and War that my sons may have liberty to study Mathematicks and Philosophy. My sons ought to study Mathematicks and Philosophy, Geography, natural History, Naval Architecture, navigation, Commerce and Agriculture, in order to give their Children a right to study Painting, Poetry, Musick, Architecture, Statuary, Tapestry and Porcelaine.[1]*

---

[1] Letter from John Adams to Abigail Adams, 1780

Adams studied the science of government—sophisticated natural law—so we could enjoy the arts. Under primitive natural law, few people could relax long enough to study the arts. Most were too busy toiling or defending. One hand on the plow, the other on the sword. One eye on work, the other over their shoulder. They feared wild animals, weather, outlaws, and tyrants. The Bill of Rights ascends humankind above those fears.

Located in the high Arizona desert, near Camp Verde, is a wildlife park called Out of Africa. It is owned and managed by Dean and Prayeri Harrison. In their decades of studying predatory animals and their prey, they have discovered an interesting law of nature. When animals have little fear, when they know they are relatively safe, they have the emotional capacity to love. In that state, their animalistic instincts can be dimmed and their ability to build and maintain relationships increases.

We humans are not so different. If we live a primitive natural law existence of hand-to-mouth survival of the fittest, like animals, we will progress little in life and from generation to generation. But if we elevate to a society that seeks to replace primitive natural law with sophisticated natural law, we, like those fearless animals, can develop relationships that will propel humankind to heights never before imagined. That begins by identifying and implementing sophisticated natural laws—that is what the Bill of Rights represents and accomplishes. Now, what do you intend to do from here? What will you accomplish without fear? What will you create now that you have been given the environment to do and be more?

Alexander Hamilton and others feared a Bill of Rights—for good reason. They feared government would reinterpret and misconstrue the words that represented profound rights. The Ninth Amendment was written to directly address that fear. In the more than two hundred years since its ratification, people, politicians, government employees, judges, and others have made those fears a reality. But the benefits of the Bill of Rights far outweigh the negatives.

There may be imperfections, but the Bill of Rights has created an environment of liberty so effective that we can continue to seek additional methods of protecting and maintaining our enlightened rights. Thomas Jefferson spoke of the environment of liberty they created and how that helped them experiment with different ideas of self-government.

Our revolution commenced on more favorable ground. It presented us an Album on which we were free to write what we pleased. We had no occasion to search into musty records, to hunt up Royal parchments, or to investigate the laws & institutions of a semi-barbarous ancestry. We appealed to those of nature, and found them engraved in our hearts. . . we had never been permitted to exercise self-government. When forced to assume it, we were Novices in it's [sic] science. It's principles and forms had entered little into our former education. We established however some, altho' not all it's important principles. The constitutions of most of our states assert that all power is inherent in the people; that they may exercise it by themselves, in all cases to which they think themselves competent. . . that it is their right and duty to be at all times armed; that they are entitled to freedom of person; freedom of religion; freedom of property; and freedom of the press. . . Virginia, of which I am myself a native and resident, was not only the first of the states, but I believe I may say, the first of the nations of the earth, which assembled it's wise men peaceably together to form a fundamental constitution, to commit it to writing, and place it among their archives, where every one should be free to appeal to it's text. But this act was very imperfect. The other states, as they proceeded successively to the same work, made successive improvements; and several of them, still further corrected by experience, have, by conventions, still further amended their first forms. My own state has gone on so far with it's premiere ebauche; but it is now proposing to call a convention for amendment.[2]

Two hundred years later we have advanced further in our creature comforts. We have freed up more of our time to advance society—to continue where they left off. How are we doing in our own endeavors to expand society through more sophisticated natural law discoveries?

As beneficiaries of the efforts of those before us, it is our duty to continue in their work, not only for us, but for all humankind. Jefferson echoed these sentiments:

> *In the great work which has been affected in America, no individual has a right to take any great share to himself. Our people in a body are wise, because they are under the unrestrained and unperverted operation of their own understandings. . . . A nation composed of such materials, and free in all it's members from distressing wants, furnishes hopeful implements for the interesting experiment of self-government: and we feel that we are acting under obligations not confined to the limits of our own society. It is impossible not to be sensible that we are acting for all mankind: that circumstances denied to others, but indulged to us, have imposed on us the duty of proving what is the degree of freedom and self-government in which a society may venture to leave it's individual members.*[3]

Thanks to James Madison, Thomas Jefferson, John Adams, and others who studied natural law principles in the science of government, we can pursue a more enlightened and creative course. We too should keep the science of government alive in our minds so we can raise humankind to new heights. Thus we may afford to our children and grandchildren the same blessings of liberty that have been afforded to us.

---

[2] Letter from Thomas Jefferson to John Cartwright, 1824
[3] Letter from Thomas Jefferson to Joseph Priestley, 1802